Also by Aljean Harmetz

Production #1060

The Making of
THE
WIZARD OF OZ

With an Introduction by MARGARET HAMILTON
(the Wicked Witch of the West)

Movie Magic and Studio Power

in the Prime of MGM—

and the Miracle of Production #1060

The Making of
THE
WIZARD OF OZ

ALJEAN HARMETZ

New York

Library of Congress Cataloging-in-Publication Data

ISBN: 0-7868-8352-9

FIRST EDITION

10 9 8 7 6 5 4 3

To Richard S. Harmetz

Contents

Production #1060

CONTENTS

"I couldn't lie down in that costume. I couldn't even sit in it. I could only lean against a reclining board. . . ." They were not allowed to eat in the commissary. They tried it once . . . their faces covered with rubber and fur and aluminum paste. . . . If they would eat in their dressing rooms, the studio would pay for lunch.

The infinite details that created the illusion, including . . . the nearly 1,000 costumes designed by Adrian . . . the creation of the Emerald City and 60 other sets by Cedric Gibbons (executed by the 500 carpenters, 150 laborers, and 20 scenic artists of the Construction Department) . . . the curious intricacies of Technicolor

The art of melting a witch and stirring up a tornado

[x]

Acknowledgments	
Production #1060	

I would like to express my gratitude to the following people who worked on *The Wizard of Oz* and who graciously shared their memories with me:

George Bassman	E. Y. Harburg	Sheila O'Brien
Ray Bolger	Henri Jaffa	Marian Parker
Dona Massin Carn	Dolly Kramer	Margaret Pellegrini
George Cukor	Henry Kramer	Hazel Resmondo
Billy Curtis	Noel Langley	Glenn Robinson
Murray Cutter	Grace Lee	Marie Rose
Betty Danko	Mervyn LeRoy	Harold Rosson
Ken Darby	John Lee Mahin	Charles Schram
Randall Duell	Jerry Maren	Billy Scott
Buddy Ebsen	Mary Mayer	John B. Scura
George Gibson	Jack McMaster	Howard Smit
Buddy Gillespie	Hal Millar	Jack Martin Smith
Henry Greutert	Franklin Milton	Carl Spitz
Henry Imus	Harry Monty	Bill Tuttle
Jack Haley	Vera Mordaunt	King Vidor
Margaret Hamilton	Leonard Murphy	Jack Young

I would also like to thank those men and women who broadened my knowledge of MGM or helped me pursue *The Wizard of Oz* from 1938 to 1977:

June Allyson	Douglas Byers	J. J. Cohn
Helene Bowman	Justin Call	Jerry Collins
Jan Brockway	Dick Carroll	Jack Cummings
Robert Buckley	Saul Chaplin	Frank Davis
Sally Burchell	George Chasin	Fred Detmers

[xi]

ACKNOWLEDGMENTS

Don Durgin
Victoria Fleming
S. Douglas Frasier
Reneé Freed
Dennis Galling
John Green
Jack Haley, Jr.
Alfred Hitchcock
Mary Ann Nyberg Knight
Harold Kress
John Lahr
Mildred Lahr
Jennings Lang
Peter Lawford
Edward Lawrence

John Lindon
Martin Lotz
William Ludwig
Rouben Mamoulian
Sara Mankiewicz
Julius Marini
Sam Marx
Robert McDonald
Johnny Mercer
John Money
Carmel Myers
Jack Pentes
Debbie Reynolds
Allan Rivkin
William Rosar

David Rose
Hazel Gibbons Ross
Barbara Saltzman
Gale Sondergaard
Richard Tatro
Norman Taurog
Sue Taurog
Benjamin Thau
Garry Trudeau
Harry Warren
David Weisz
Robert Weitman
Richard M. Wonder
Jerry Wunderlich
Lorey Yzuel

A special note of thanks to Metro-Goldwyn-Mayer, which generously gave me access to records, script files, and photographs, and to the American Film Institute, which—through the Louis B. Mayer Foundation—supplied me with a research grant.

In particular, I would like to thank James Earie, Richard Kahn, Norman Kaphan, and Florence Meeter of MGM; Daniel Melnick and Charles Powell, formerly of MGM; and Jean Poling and James Powers of the AFI. I owe an extra debt to Mr. Powers for reading and correcting the final manuscript.

In addition, my gratitude to:

Dr. Robert Knudson, curator of Special Collections of the University of Southern California, whose help went far beyond allowing me to use materials from that library; to USC librarians Edward Comstock, Sandra Bailey, and James Wagner; and to Nuri Erturk, Photographer, Department of Cinema, USC;

Tom Tarr of Technicolor Corporation for providing me with invaluable reference materials;

Sam Gill, Alice Mitchell, and Bonnie Rothbart of the Margaret Herrick Library of the Academy of Motion Picture Arts and Sciences for answering innumerable questions;

My editor, Vicky Wilson, who came to me with the idea for this book and who gave it the finest of her editorial skills.

ACKNOWLEDGMENTS

There remains the necessity of acknowledging the private kinds of help that enabled me to get through the last three years. To my children Daniel and Elizabeth Harmetz, for surviving; my housekeeper, Maizie Howard; my friend, Zelda Kress; my transcribers, Donald Chase and Deborah Lott. To my son Anthony Harmetz, for his enthusiasm; the International Wizard of Oz Club and at least a dozen of its members, for information; my husband, Richard Harmetz, for reading each draft with a critical eye and helping with the research.

And *The Making of THE WIZARD OF OZ* literally would not have been written without the tolerance and comfort of Robin and Doug Frasier, who allowed me to spend a year and a half in their living room writing it.

—Aljean Harmetz
Los Angeles, *1977*

Illustration Credits

Production #1060

Grateful acknowledgment is given to the following for permission to reproduce illustrations on the pages indicated:

Ray Bolger: page 113
Dona Massin Carn: pages 110 and 138
Cinemabilia collection (New York City): page 128
Victoria Fleming: page 147
A. Arnold (Buddy) Gillespie: page 249
Evie Goldich: page 122
Jack Haley: page 170
Margaret Hamilton: page 125
E. Y. Harburg: page 64
Mrs. Mildred Lahr: page 130
Noel Langley: page 41
John Lee Mahin: page 155
Sara Mankiewicz: page 27
Metro-Goldwyn-Mayer, Inc.: pages 121, 159, 161, 162, 221, 234, 237, 240, 241, 251, 253, 254, 277, and the first page of color photographs following page 202—from the MGM release *The Wizard of Oz* © Loew's Incorporated. Copyright renewed 1966 by Metro-Goldwyn-Mayer, Inc.
Also for pages 2, 5, 15, 28, 30, 33, 44, 49, 53, 55, 56, 79, 86, 88, 91, 94, 96, 106, 117, 142, 144, 157, 160, 190, 200, 210, 213, 214, 215, 216, 217, 219, 220, 223, 224, 231, 236, 245, 256, 257, 259, 260, 271, 275, 282, 283, 284, 286, 287, 289, 293, the color photographs following page 202 (except page 1), and the color photographs following page 266
Barbara Saltzman: pages 18, 63, 69, and 70
Alice Spitz: pages 133 and 134
Technicolor, Inc.: page 228
King Vidor: page 150

In addition, the author would like to thank the following for their help in locating and supplying illustrations and photographs:

Fred Balak
George Bassman
Betty Danko
James Earie
Dore Freeman

Robert Knudson
Mervyn LeRoy
Howard Strickling
Technicolor, Inc.
University of Southern California

[xiv]

Foreword

Some movies never die.

In 1998, the American Film Institute asked film historians, studio heads, screenwriters, directors, movie stars, and movie critics to name the top 100 American films of the twentieth century. All such polls are unscientific. But if they are usually a blend of reason and emotion—solemn analysis and popularity contest—a dozen surveys over the last two decades have come to the same conclusion: MGM's 1939 movie *The Wizard of Oz* has triumphantly survived the test of time.

In the American Film Institute's 1998 poll—taken fifty-nine years after the movie was created—*The Wizard of Oz* placed sixth. We are all, by definition, ignorant of the future, but what engages my imagination so long after the creation of the movie is how unaware they all were—the actors running up and down the stairs of a witch's castle under the hot arc lights, the craftsmen who wired an acre of artifical poppies to the floor of Stage 29 and sewed sequins onto half a dozen pairs of red shoes, even the movie's directors and producer. In an era when each studio made forty movies a year, almost all of the men and women who worked on MGM's Production #1060 between October 1938 and March 1939 considered *The Wizard of Oz* a job, as exciting or tedious as any other job.

Until recently, Hollywood paid little attention to its heritage. Colors faded. Negatives turned to dust. But today there is new money to be earned from old films. Because of cable television, videocassettes, digital videodiscs, and the nostalgia of a younger generation for the artifacts from Hollywood's golden age, Hollywood studios are restoring and preserving vintage old movies.

Warner Bros., which inherited *The Wizard of Oz* four years ago, has spent the last two years and $2 million re-creating the movie's original look, making a digital Dolby sound track, and refurbishing several minutes of the Scarecrow's dance that were cut before the movie's premiere in August 1939. Warner Bros. intended to insert those bits of Ray Bolger's dance into the movie but, in the end, backed away from tampering with a classic.

Reels 1A, 1B, and 5B, the black-and-white Kansas sequences,

have been digitally restored. Since the negative of the Kansas sequences was destroyed in an Eastman House fire decades ago, Phil Feiner of Pacific Title, who restored the film, had to work from a printing fine grain master made off the original negative in the MGM laboratory in 1960. All current films are printed in a liquid solution that heals dirt and scratches. In 1960, that liquid process didn't exist. So, during the spring and summer of 1998, the scratches were taken out of *The Wizard of Oz* by hand on a computer; the time spent to do this was between 15,000 and 20,000 hours.

Restoring the extra bits of the Scarecrow's dance was a different problem. In the 1970s, the Culver City fire department asked MGM to remove its flammable nitrate negatives from the lot. The studio had several two-story buildings crammed with "nitrate trims," the bits and pieces of film that never made it into the final version of a movie. *The Wizard of Oz* had been shot in three-strip Technicolor. All the trims from MGM's three-strip Technicolor movies, including the extra bits of the Scarecrow's dance, were put on single strips of Eastman Kodak CRI color film stock; then the nitrate trims were loaded onto a barge and dumped in the Pacific Ocean. All colored coupler film fades over time and the extra pieces of the Scarecrow's dance have faded. To match the original dance in the movie, color and contrast enhancements had to be painstakingly augmented by computer. Since Ray Bolger was lifted by wires in a sequence where he flew across the cornfield, the wires had to be digitally erased from each frame.

All in all, 44,000 frames of film were cleaned up or enhanced on *The Wizard of Oz*.

In trying to reproduce the original sound of *The Wizard of Oz*, as audiences heard it in theaters in 1939, Ned Price of Warner Bros. was luckier than Phil Feiner who restored the picture. Although the original nitrate sound track was missing, Price could use a second generation audio source in excellent condition that had been printed directly off the original nitrate master in 1963. To get as much audio information as possible, Warner Bros. took a digital snapshot of the soundtrack and then weeded out the clicks and pops, the noise and distortion. To make the new stereo soundtrack sound like the movie audiences have listened to for sixty years was more difficult, because dialogue, music, and sound effects were already mixed together.

The sound team struggled for months before deciding to let the original mono track play up front on screen with stereo added on the sides and back to augment the central soundtrack. The stereo that was introduced was true stereo since it was MGM's practice to create protection recordings from various parts of the scoring stage. When Warner Bros. recombined these various angles, it reproduced the natural stereo separation of the musical score.

With two slight exceptions, nothing was added to the original soundtrack. Perspective was added to the tornado so that when Dorothy was in her bedroom, the roar of the tornado was muffled. And the sound technicians discovered that a thunderclap had preceded the explosion during which the Wicked Witch of the West disappeared from Munchkinland. So the thunderclap was returned to the film.

The restoration of *The Wizard of Oz* was done in preparation for the Warner Bros. re-release of the movie in approximately 2,000 theaters during the 1998 holiday season, on the eve of the movie's sixtieth anniversary.

Some movies never die. From underwear to marshmallows, wall masks to thimbles, cake decorating kits to lithographs and porcelain figurines of a Cowardly Lion, a Tin Woodman, and a small dog, hundreds of different products have accompanied *The Wizard of Oz* into its sixtieth year. We live in a world where almost everything can be bought or sold. And commerce has its place. But, at its heart, the yellow brick road is beyond commerce. I envy the children who have yet to see *The Wizard of Oz* for the first time.

Los Angeles, 1998

Preface to
The Making of THE WIZARD OF OZ
by
ALJEAN HARMETZ

It has been fifty years since *The Wizard of Oz* reached theaters and nearly fifteen years since I took my first frightened steps down the Yellow Brick Road. Like Dorothy, I was looking for the past. But the road onto which I stepped was full of potholes, a jumble of broken and missing bricks. Bert Lahr and Judy Garland were dead. So was director Victor Fleming and the cocky Arthur Freed, who had made *Oz* the forerunner of a new kind of movie musical. Songwriter Harold Arlen was a recluse, penned by his own will in his New York apartment. And most of the written records had been burned or casually thrown away.

I came eventually to see my task as archaeology. But what I was exploring was not just the rubble that remained of the world that had been created at Metro-Goldwyn-Mayer studio in 1938 and 1939. I was digging, also, into my own past. I had grown up just outside the walls of MGM with a famous producer at the studio as my cousin and a mother who worked in the wardrobe department for twenty years. She brought me a copy of *The Wizard of Oz* signed by the members of the cast. Too young to appreciate it as an artifact that would be priceless fifty years later, I read the book to death.

To Judy Garland, MGM was home. To me, the studio was the unattainable. My definition of myself came from working in the fan mail department the summer I was twelve years old, sending wallet-sized pictures of June Allyson, Lana Turner, and Elizabeth Taylor to ten thousand strangers who adored them, and measuring myself against movie stars. Fatherless, fat, and lonely, I saw salvation in being a part of MGM.

Grown up, the mother of three children, my yearning to be a movie star stifled by time, I began to excavate *Oz* when my own daughter was three years old.

During my search, I made one friend—Margaret Hamilton, the kindest of witches. I would pick her up at the Shubert Theatre a few blocks away from my house at midnight, after her performance in

A Little Night Music. We would sit and drink coffee until 3 a.m., the tape recorder on the table between us recording her astonishment that this small part in what she called "a picture for children, an interesting picture and sort of an innovation and somewhat overdone in some tiny places but very pleasant" should have made her famous. Then and in the years that followed, she reminded me of a fractured fairy tale, her clauses bumping up against each other, her sentences spinning from present to past to farther past as though her mind were a chest full of fascinating oddments kept in no particular order. In 1939 she was on the fringes of Oz. By 1980 she had been made the center of that mythical country by grown-ups whom she had frightened year after year on television when they were children. At public appearances and solemn forums about *Oz*, she whispered to me to sit between her and Ray Bolger. She felt that The Boys, as she called Bolger, Lahr, and Jack Haley, had elbowed her out of their way during the making of the movie and that she never got a chance to speak when they were on the same platform. I was to keep Bolger, in particular, from answering all the questions addressed to her as well as his own.

Margaret Hamilton had been raised to be modest—unpretentious, unassuming, decorous—as befitted a midwestern lady born in 1902. Ray Bolger pulled the spotlight toward him, like a moon he had lassoed and permanently attached to his right shoulder. Bolger loved applause and would do his Scarecrow dance in the middle of the living room of his big house in Beverly Hills and wait eagerly for approval. He was sentimental about *Oz*, while Jack Haley saw the Tin Woodman as just another job and Margaret Hamilton puzzled over the celebrity the movie had brought her. Bolger's sentimentality made some of his memories suspect.

Over and over again, one person's memories would bump up against someone else's contradictory recollections. Who brought Judy Garland to the studio to audition, or was she discovered accidentally by L. B. Mayer at a Hollywood nightclub? When two versions seemed equally probable, I used both. But some people's memories were sturdier and their accounts verified by written evidence or the memories of others.

I had expected that the people who had the most important jobs on *The Wizard of Oz* would be the keys to fitting together the pieces of this jigsaw puzzle. One of my earliest interviews, with the movie's producer, Mervyn LeRoy, made me realize that things would be considerably more complicated. A vague little man smoking a long brown cigar, he had kept no records—on paper or in his head. He spoke of working on *The Wizard of Oz* with men who didn't arrive at MGM until a decade later and insisted, for example, that Buddy Ebsen, the first Tin Man, had never worked on the movie at all.

It was from the unimportant people, men and women to whom *Oz* was not just another movie in a career crowded with movies, that the revelations came. When Margaret Hamilton's stunt double Betty Danko came home from the hospital after suffering a nearly fatal accident on the film, she wrote an eight-page account of everything that had happened. Thirty-six years later, I picked up the torn and yellowed papers and took them to a Xerox machine down the street from the Hollywood bungalow Betty Danko's father had bought in 1927 and in which she still lived.

Two men over eighty years old—King Vidor, who directed the Kansas sequence, and Carl Spitz, the German immigrant who had become a Hollywood dog trainer—had almost total recall and clear insights into how things had worked on the set of *The Wizard of Oz*.

MGM had at least kept its script files. I sat on a high iron stool in the basement of the Thalberg Building for weeks, my face and fingers coated with dust, reading through five feet of scripts on *The Wizard of Oz*. There were three or four duplicates of many of the scripts, and memos from the writers to Arthur Freed and his notes back had been absentmindedly tucked between the pages decades earlier.

Occasionally things were rescued from the carelessness with which Hollywood, until recently, treated its history. When a warehouse at MGM was demolished, a young technician saw a stack of matte paintings thrown in the middle of a studio street for the junkman. He filled his station wagon with the black cardboard drawings and took them to the University of Southern California. Among the three dozen crayon pastel drawings he saved were the witch's castle and the Emerald City. A Technicolor consultant, Tom Tarr, saved color test strips from all the early color films, including *The Wizard of Oz,* when Technicolor threw them away. A few years later, when I was nearly finished with the book, someone searching for Christmas decorations in a closet in an MGM prop building found a box of sets stills from *The Wizard of Oz,* photographs of the finished sets before the actors set foot on them.

Other things have surfaced since this book was written, including daily music reports showing the songs recorded by Buddy Ebsen before fate removed him from *The Wizard of Oz.* And recently a controversy developed over whether all of Judy Garland's ruby slippers were made at MGM. The new information is tucked into notes at the back of the book.

As I write this, my three-year-old daughter is seventeen. She was born on L. Frank Baum's birthday, May 15. For me, the most astonishing discovery I made about *Oz* was personal. One of my sons was born on the anniversary of the beginning of production on *The Wizard of Oz,* October 12. My other son was born on the date the picture was finished, March 16. If those three birthdays are coincidence, what long odds there are against it.

Things change. MGM has been gutted, its library of old motion pictures sold to Ted Turner. The studio lot where *The Wizard of Oz* was made belongs to Lorimar, a studio that will soon be swallowed by Warner Bros. But Judy Garland is still safe inside her red shoes, and there's still no place like home.

—*Los Angeles, 1989*

by
MARGARET HAMILTON
(the Wicked Witch of the West)

I opened the package with the keen anticipation and there it was, page upon page, the book I had been waiting and longing for—*The Making of THE WIZARD OF OZ.*

About two years before, during three midnight question-and-answer sessions in Aljean Harmetz's kitchen, I had looked forward to it for my own selfish reasons. The questions she had asked me about my experience as The Wicked Witch of the West made me feel that the book would answer all of the myriad questions I am constantly asked about *Oz.* Here was a source to guarantee "the answer," an accurate, clear, and concise description to draw upon.

A great deal of my mail comes from fans of the *Oz* picture—fans of all ages. The scholarly, the curious, the disbelievers write and ask how? why? when? what for? did you fly? melt? scream? cackle? appear? disappear? produce? sky-write? deal with monkeys? etc., etc., etc. "I can't tell you—I don't know—it's too difficult to write—I haven't the time," were not satisfactory. Back came the demands, "You do too know, you did it—you were in it, you must know—just tell me exactly how it was because I need it, for a paper—a theme—a degree. . . . And if you can't write it; maybe you could come to my school and tell it. You could stay with us. My mother would like that. Or maybe I could come to New York for a day and you could tell it to me," and so on.

As for my awareness of what was going on and where during the making of the film, I was familiar with the hair-styling and makeup room, and the costume-fitting room; I knew the sound stage—dark and shadowy and cavernous, until the cameras took over. But of the astonishing organization that controlled the present and the future of the picture, the constant adjustments of all parts and functions that interplayed like some superb piece of machinery pulling it all together and keeping it progressing in the chosen directions, of all this I knew nothing. But I do now, thanks to Aljean Harmetz. I have read the manuscript, and now at last I know how I flew, how I melted, how I wrote in the sky SURRENDER DOROTHY OR DIE. *The Making of THE WIZARD OF OZ* is written with great understanding, and the author has tied together the many elements that somehow merged at the right time and place. The research alone is a staggering accomplishment—the challenging and comparing of each and every fact by the author, the weaving in and out of all the people who were involved, and finally the distilling of all the elements into an accurate picture of the times that made *Oz* possible. For me it is a well of information. And one of the most fascinating things about it is how differently particular events, especially what happened while certain scenes were being filmed, were interpreted by various people who were involved. Of course, it is a thirty-eight-year-old memory, and in telling my version to the author, I used the qualifying phrase, "at least that is my memory of it."

Reading the book, I have inevitably been moved to probe and recall clearly some experiences of mine which had gradually become clouded. Among them is a clear memory of the first day of actual shooting and, before that, the weeks of working out the necessary details of the movie: contract details, interviews with the press, and discussions with four possible directors.

It was in October of 1938 that we started the preliminary "tests" (they continued into November), and I had been living in La Jolla since my own house in Beverly Hills was rented out. Every day during that time I drove back and forth from La Jolla to Culver City, starting three hours before I was due at the studio and stopping for the day around five or six p.m. to begin the drive back down to La Jolla; I was never quite sure what time I would be home.

It was during those early weeks, as I recall, that we met three directors. Each of us—Ray Bolger, Bert Lahr, Jack Haley and I—worried that we would lose the part after the arrival of each new director, but the interviews, as I recall, were quite pleasant and, for me, astonishingly brief. First came Richard Thorpe, whom I had worked for before and liked. About a week later Mr. Thorpe was gone, and we were introduced to George Cukor, whom I had not met before. He interviewed each of us and we continued to work. After a certain period Mr. Cukor departed, and we met, finally, Mr. Victor Fleming, for whom I had worked in the movie version of *The Farmer Takes a Wife* at Fox Studio, before it became 20th Century-Fox. (I had had the pleasure of playing this part in a company headed by Henry Fonda in his first Broadway hit and eventually his first part in a film.) After Mr. Fleming left to direct *Gone With the Wind*, King Vidor finished directing *Oz*. I cannot remember doing camera work for any of them except Mr. Fleming. I recall my sense of uneasiness and the feeling each time of "Here goes nothing!" But during the previous six years in New York and California in the business, I had "cut my teeth" on the gold ring of the merry-go-round that is theater, and I had learned to trust in a higher power and relax.

There were preliminary decisions to be made about what the Witch would look like: tests in color and in black and white for design, as well as for the degree of black (black tones could be a problem and cameramen could lose their equanimity). Black next to your skin seemed to give rise to a thin line of white on the edge of the black, which did not look like edging but rather like a separation. But with *Oz* the problem was solved—perhaps that was why they chose green makeup for my face, neck, and hands. The problem of the thin white line was only apparent when black was the basic color. However, I never asked about it then. In fact, I was not really aware of the problem until after several attempts, when they told me what they were doing.

I also had to try on various experimental versions of my chin and nose until we found the best fit and shape and shade of green. This was followed by many, many costume fittings and tests with and without costume. Was the Witch's sleeve to have a medieval look? How long should the sleeves be—over the wrist or hand? How long a train on the dress and cape? Once or twice someone said, "Tell us how you feel about it." But during most of these discussions my opinion was not sought. I did say I wanted the dress length to clear the floor by an inch so I would not have to pick up the skirt, or trip coming downstairs; the cape could brush the floor in the back if they wished. There was a question regarding a huge watch that was supposed to hang on my left side, as old-fashioned glasses did. But that was decided against. Other details were considered, and accepted or turned down on the basis of the whole effect. Then there was the Witch's hair—was it to hang down around my neck or be in an enormous knot or a sort of braid? The stills I have of makeup tests show several styles, but the large knot to which the hat could be pinned looked best, as well as affording some balance to the very tall hat. The final decision was to go with the large knot. The shoes were to be high-laced, as I remember, so they would stay on when the Witch went up and down the stairs.

Then came tests of the Witch, in makeup, wearing dress and hat, against the various backgrounds that were to be used in the film. And finally there were the tests—painstaking, time-consuming— with Dorothy, the Scarecrow, and one monkey. I used the test periods to practice moving in the long skirt and cape, using wide, high gestures that would give an added sweep and excitement to the Witch's movements. I learned how to balance the huge hat to keep it from tilting back in the rush of movement. I also got used to the feel of the green makeup as it dried on my face. It never cracked or really felt uncomfortable. The long fingernails were glued to my own. (Once, as I rushed to grab the great iron rings and shut the huge doors to prevent Dorothy from "leaving so soon," they had left no space between the rings and the actual doors, and all ten fingernails popped off in a shower of green. That gave everyone a great laugh.)

The first day of shooting began at 4:45 a.m. I woke full of anticipation and excitement. It was late fall and cool in the early morning light. The house was dark and quiet. I tiptoed about, not wanting to wake my young son or his nurse. After a proper breakfast, I picked up my small lunch box and went stealthily out to the car. The streets were empty as I headed for Culver City and MGM. I was aware of the quickening light, the early morning fog (quite without smog in those days).

At the MGM gate, I was directed to what would be my parking place for the next six months. I walked to the makeup department, reporting at 6:45. We had our own particular chairs and makeup men. (It was Jack Dawn who designed the makeup for each of us.) I climbed into my dentist-like chair and was greeted by my own remarkable makeup man, Jack Young, who was responsible for my daily transformation for the entire picture. From the other chairs came greetings from my fellow actors, who would become such an integral part of my life for the next twenty-three weeks. Because of the fantasy-like nature of the work, the sense of being on a ship and separated from the mainstream of life would become even greater than usual.

Since we arrived at the studio earlier than most actors, we felt that each day we were opening the studio. Makeup took two hours; after that, we were usually driven to the stage far away at the back of the main lot. Unless an actor was working or was going to work, he did not report at 6:45 a.m. Most people think that when the studios made movies the principal actors worked together a great deal of the time. But most of my scenes were with Judy or the monkeys or just myself, and except for the early morning encounters in makeup, I saw almost nothing of the Lion, the Tin Woodman, or Ray Bolger, who, as the Scarecrow, had two scenes with me. In the first, he and Dorothy were coming down the yellow brick road. The Witch suddenly appeared on the roof of a small cottage. There followed the scene in which the Witch asked the Scarecrow if he would like to play ball, whereupon she conjured up a ball of fire and quickly tossed it at him. Another scene, inside the Witch's castle, actually involved no contact, but we were together, all of us, with the Witch at the top of the great, long stairs, screaming at the four below and lowering the chandelier on what she hoped would be Bolger, Lahr, and Haley, but instead turned out to be her soldiers. The final scene—the melting scene—was again with Judy. I remember being very concerned that I had to grab a torch and set fire to Ray. (After an earlier experience when my broom caught fire, it was almost too much for me, but I was assured Bolger's suit was asbestos and there was little danger of its catching fire.) Dorothy would then throw a bucket of water at Bolger that would by chance land on me and I would begin to melt. This was to be the end of the Witch.

At the time the actual shooting finally began, my son, Hamilton, was almost two and a half years old. I had decided I would be very careful in my choice of what he would be exposed to. That decision was based on his sensitivity and an occasional nightmare. At that time, whether little Ham should see *Oz* or not wasn't a problem, since it was not until the movie's opening at Grauman's Chinese Theatre (bleachers, klieg lights, limousines, beautiful ladies in beautiful gowns, and screaming fans) that I had any idea of what had been wrought. When I cringed at a few shots of the Witch, I was all the more convinced my son should not see this movie. (There were a few stills around the house with which Ham practiced early "show and tell" for anyone who would pay attention. He would say "That's my mommy, the Witch.")

Ham had never seen a movie until his classmate Michael Berman (whose daddy was movie producer Pandro S. Berman) invited the entire first grade of Hawthorne Public School in Beverly Hills to his sixth birthday party. A half-hour after I had delivered Ham, Michael's mother called, saying Ham had run out of the room while she was showing *The Wizard of Oz*. I explained that Ham had not seen the movie, but since he didn't seem upset, we agreed to let him remain at the party.

At the suggested time I picked up my son. He climbed into the car all smiles and joy over his loot. He settled back and then—the spell broken—said, "Mom, I saw a movie." I said, "How great, dear; did you like it?" Silence. Then he said, "What did you do with those men?" "What men?" I asked. "You know, Mom, those big, tall men in the sort of fur hats; what did you do with them?" "Oh, well, you know, they're all actors, just as your mom is an actress, and acting is just pretending, so when the end of the day came we all took off our costumes and makeup and came home to our children." Silence. Then he said, "But what did you do with them?" "Nothing, dear, they are not really guards; I am not really a witch, am I?" "No. But what did you *do* with them?" I was a little desperate; then I realized that I had not listened to his question. I was answering something that I had not been asked. "You see, the Witch had cast a spell on the guards," I explained, "and they had no choice; they had to do as she wished until she was melted." (Mrs. Berman had told me that Ham had returned just as the Witch was melting.) "Then her spell was broken and they were all free to do as they wished and I am sure they wished to go home." "Oh," he said with a sigh of evident relief. "I see."

| Production #1060 | 1. |

THE STUDIO, 1938

In the fall of 1937, either Mervyn LeRoy or Arthur Freed persuaded Louis B. Mayer to buy *The Wizard of Oz*. That much, and only that much, is certain.

"Mr. Mayer bought the book for me," said LeRoy, sitting in his trophy-stuffed office, nearly forty years later.

"It was always understood," said Arthur Freed's widow, a year after her husband's death, "that Mr. Mayer purchased the book because Arthur said it would make a great musical."

Arthur Freed and Mervyn LeRoy had first met in 1923 on the set of a silent picture at First National. They had been roughly equal

Metro-Goldwyn-Mayer in the early 1940's. By the late thirties MGM was the largest of the Hollywood studios—120 "stars and featured players" under contract; a movie completed every nine days. In the foreground, the Thalberg building (three wings). To the left, Lots 3, 4, and 5, where Westerns were made. Lot 2 (rear center beyond the studio stages): the New York and Paris streets, the small train depot, the street where Andy Hardy lived.

at that first meeting. LeRoy was on the set as a gag man, Freed to play background music on the organ. Fourteen years later, LeRoy had by far the higher status within the movie industry. At the age of thirty-seven, he was a $6,000-a-week producer at Metro-Goldwyn-Mayer. Freed, then forty-three, was also at MGM, but as a $1,500-a-week songwriter.

The Metro-Goldwyn-Mayer studio at which both Mervyn LeRoy and Arthur Freed worked in 1937 was a factory—the largest and most exclusive of the Hollywood factories. It was part of what insiders affectionately called The Industry, as though no product other than motion pictures was worth making. MGM's quota of one movie a week, fifty-two movies a year, was seldom met. The studio was more likely to produce one movie every nine days, since cans of film are not directly analogous to cans of asparagus. *The Wizard of Oz* would become Production #1060, one of forty-one movies released by Metro-Goldwyn-Mayer in 1939.

The Metro in Metro-Goldwyn-Mayer stood for a corporation formed in 1915 to finance the making of movies. The Goldwyn was Samuel Goldwyn, who had formed his own producing company in 1915 and resigned from it in 1922. The Mayer was Louis B. Mayer, who was brought in to run the amalgamated Metro-Goldwyn in 1924. It was Mayer who gave the order to purchase L. Frank Baum's children's story from Samuel Goldwyn for $75,000. Both MGM's contract brief and the Goldwyn Studio records give the final purchase date as June 3, 1938. But the optioning of the book occurred late in February,* and MGM was not the only studio interested in buying it. On February 19, 1938, *The New York Times* ran a short article on that subject.

With the industry convinced that "Snow White" will be a box-office success, there is a wild search by producers for comparable fantasies. Within the last ten days Samuel Goldwyn has received five offers for L. Frank Baum's "Wizard of Oz," the highest being $75,000. Twentieth Century-Fox is reported anxious to purchase

---

* An MGM inter-office communication from Arthur Freed and presumably directed to Mayer suggests that casting discussions for *The Wizard of Oz* began as early as January 31, prior to the actual purchase of the book.

the book for Shirley Temple, but all offers have been rejected. Goldwyn has owned the property for five years.

Goldwyn had purchased the book almost by accident. Playwright Sidney Howard, urging it on him, had even bought him a copy, an elaborate children's edition. The sequel to that purchase gave Howard a Goldwyn anecdote: he had, he told friends, asked Sam Goldwyn a few weeks later how he had liked the book. "Wonderful," Goldwyn said. Howard then asked if Goldwyn had finished it. "No," Goldwyn said, "I'm on page six." Whether Goldwyn ever finished reading the book or not, he bought it. For $40,000. And he was not unhappy to turn a $35,000 profit five years later.*

Once the book had been purchased, Mayer assigned Mervyn LeRoy to produce the movie—and insisted that LeRoy accept Arthur Freed as his assistant.

"Mr. Mayer bought the book for *me*," Mervyn LeRoy repeated. "I wanted to make a movie out of *The Wizard of Oz* from the time I was a kid. I'm getting sick of hearing about Arthur Freed and *The Wizard of Oz*. Arthur Freed's name isn't on the picture. Mine is. Mr. Mayer asked me to take Arthur as my assistant, and he helped a lot with the music. I never took credit for anything that didn't belong to me. But *I* produced that picture."

At seventy-six, LeRoy is an eager, vague, paunchy little man. For most of his forty-eight-year career in Hollywood, he has had two reputations. He is considered by most people to be "a nice guy, a sweetheart." He reminds others of the Hollywood opportunist Sammy Glick, in Budd Schulberg's novel *What Makes Sammy Run?*

He is, more than anything else, a survivor—proud of his seventy-five movies, prouder that twenty of them played the Radio City Music Hall: "I had more films play the Music Hall than anyone else." From the giant paper clip to the giant desk blotter, everything in his office is engraved.

There are two Academy Awards. Both are special, rather than competitive, awards. The first was given to him in 1945 for his "tolerance short subject," *The House I Live In*. The second, the Irving G.

---

* The thirteen other Oz books written by Baum are owned by Walt Disney Productions, which purchased them in November 1954.

Louis B. Mayer, head of MGM from 1924 to 1951.

Thalberg Memorial Award, was given to him in 1975 for the body of his work as a producer. Despite his seventy-five movies, he was nominated only once as a director, for *Random Harvest* in 1942. Although *The Wizard of Oz* was nominated as Best Picture of 1939, MGM, rather than LeRoy, received the nomination. By the time Arthur Freed won the first of *his* Oscars for Best Picture a decade later, the Academy of Motion Picture Arts and Sciences had changed its rules.

On the walls in the outer office are 130 autographed pictures, including one "To my very loyal friend, Mervyn LeRoy, with all good wishes" from Louis B. Mayer. The framed photographs and the hundreds more that fill his filing cabinets testify to a directing career that started in 1928 and included *Anthony Adverse*, *Little Caesar*, *I Am a Fugitive From a Chain Gang*, *Madame Curie*, *Johnny Eager*, *Mister Roberts*, and *The Bad Seed*, along with *Hot Stuff*, *Broadway Babies*, *Show Girl in Hollywood*, *Quo Vadis*, *Two Seconds*, *Million Dollar Mermaid*, and *Latin Lovers*. He produced and directed his last film, *Moment to Moment*, in 1965, and by 1976 was more a horseman than a moviemaker, spending most of his time as president of Hollywood Park racetrack. Recently, however, he has been trying to finance a film version of James Thurber's *Thirteen Clocks*, perhaps hoping wistfully in his mid-seventies to re-create the success of the children's movie he produced nearly forty years before.

Arthur Freed's equally trophy-stuffed office has been dismantled. It was actually a suite of offices on the second floor of MGM's Thalberg Building, overlooking the mortuary next door so that—for inspiration—the members of the Freed Unit could watch the bodies come and go. They always took a ghoulish pleasure in the fact that great musicals were being created just above the nose, so to speak, of a funeral parlor. Freed's Academy nomination plaques and his awards crisscrossed the walls of his secretary's office. Freed's own office had Rouaults on the walls and orchid plants on every available surface. He was successful at the tricky business of growing orchids and was probably as proud of his plants as he was of his movies. Arthur Freed died on April 12, 1973. According to an account he provided just before his death,* he dropped in at Mayer's house for breakfast one morning and was told to "Find a property and make a picture." Over lunch a few hours later, he authorized agent Frank Orsatti to negotiate with Sam Goldwyn for *The Wizard of Oz*.

Freed's office had a private bathroom with a shower, a point of status that he was quick to display to new members of his unit. But that was later, much later. In 1937 he was housed in the row of shabby music bungalows near the railroad tracks at the end of the

---

*In interviews given to Hugh Fordin for his book *The World of Entertainment*. (Garden City, N.Y.: Doubleday, 1975).

main lot. Freed won an Academy Award for producing the Best Picture of 1951, *An American in Paris*, and another for producing the Best Picture of 1958, *Gigi*. He also produced *Meet Me in St. Louis, On the Town, Cabin in the Sky, Summer Holiday, The Band Wagon*, and *Easter Parade*. But in 1937 Freed had never produced a musical or any other film. He was a writer of song lyrics, half the team of Nacio Herb Brown and Arthur Freed, responsible for "You Are My Lucky Star," "The Wedding of the Painted Doll," and "Singin' in the Rain."

It was no secret at MGM that Arthur Freed wanted to be a producer. "He was a very pushy person," recalls Frank Davis, a junior producer at MGM during the late thirties. "He wanted to be tops in the picture business. He always showed up at every preview of every picture whether he should have been there or not. He had definite opinions. He had courageous opinions. He didn't mind sticking his neck out, and Mayer may have admired that. They were intelligent opinions. They were good opinions. I never cared for Arthur very much, but I recognized his ability."

Freed was enormously ambitious. "A very ruthless, ambitious man," according to Jack Cummings, who was L. B. Mayer's nephew and also a producer of musicals at MGM. About ten years after Freed got his first chance to produce a movie, he came to Cummings and the other producer of MGM musicals, Joe Pasternak, and told them he wanted to be the head of all the musicals. Twenty-eight years later, the sting of that moment had not quite stopped smarting for Cummings. "Arthur said, 'The Boss wants me to be the head of the musicals so everything will be better organized. We've got to get organized around here.' I told him it was fine with me because the day he took over I was leaving the studio. Then I told him the only one of us who needed to be better organized was himself. Which was true. His pictures cost lots and lots of money. Too much money, although in trying for new horizons in musicals you sometimes have to spend the money, and he did make some good pictures. I told Mr. Mayer what my answer to Freed was. He never said a word. But that was the end of it."

Freed was almost maddeningly inarticulate. E. Y. Harburg, who wrote the lyrics for *The Wizard of Oz*, recalls that "Whenever Arthur talked, all you could do was guess at his meaning." "The word was out that he was lecherous," says Mary Ann Nyberg, who became his costume designer in 1949. "But I wanted the job badly. When I walked into his office, I decided that the best thing was to let him make a pass at me in a hurry and quit because gossip moves fast in this town. His first words to me were, 'How do you like sex?' I said, 'I just love it, but there's one terrible thing. I really put my passions into my work. So anyone who fools around with me when I'm working is losing money.' Freed sighed and said, 'Would you like to go to the commissary and have lunch?' He was a sweet man and he never made a pass. But girls used to go through his office every fifteen minutes. If he had that kind of energy, no wonder he had no energy for conversation. The joke was that when the Freed Unit got through with a girl she went to the LeRoy Unit and then to the Pasternak Unit."

If there was one quality that Freed had in great abundance, it was self-confidence. Even so, his belief in himself was probably a fraction lower than LeRoy's. "Mervyn had absolute confidence in himself," says Frank Davis. "He knew he couldn't fail." LeRoy had two other qualities in common with Freed: he also was enormously ambitious, maddeningly inarticulate. "People always used to wonder how Mervyn was ever able to direct a picture," says someone whose career paralleled LeRoy's at MGM. "He'd say, 'Put a little more into it, baby.' But he somehow got his emotions over to his actors. They understood him in some way. And he made some good films." The two men had been friends almost since their first meeting in 1923. When Arthur Freed brought his bride, Reneé, south from San Francisco later that year, the first person to whom he introduced her in Hollywood was Mervyn LeRoy. Before LeRoy's marriage to Doris Warner, he was the Freeds' classic bachelor friend, in and out of the house and most often staying to dinner. The friendship lasted, more or less, for fifty years. And yet, after Arthur Freed's death LeRoy did not call. Freed's widow waited for a word of sympathy that never came.

In the long run, perhaps it hardly matters whether it was LeRoy or Freed who asked L. B. Mayer to buy *The Wizard of Oz*. Once bought, the book became part of the MGM system, ready to be turned into the kind of lush, elaborate, technically proficient film for which MGM was already—and would continue to be—famous. Warner Bros.* films were harsh, grainy, and abrasive, filled with the nervous energy of James Cagney, Bette Davis, Edward G. Robinson. Columbia had director Frank Capra, little money, and heart-warming comedy just on the far edge of sanity. Paramount was "sophisticated," its films full of gleaming black and dazzling white; the image that film historian Arthur Knight still carries of Paramount is "Cary Grant in an evening suit in a boudoir hung with velvet draperies." At 20th Century-Fox, it was Shirley Temple, Alice Faye, Tyrone Power—syrup and sentiment, pleasant but forgettable. MGM did it all more extravagantly, more opulently, often better. Years later, Frank Capra remembered preview audiences anticipating the quality of a film by the symbol preceding it. Columbia's lady with a torch always caused groans, while MGM's lion or Paramount's star-circled mountain brought "anticipatory applause." And publicist Eddie Lawrence and screenwriter William Ludwig spoke of MGM in the exact same seven words: "MGM was the Tiffany of the business."†

MGM's pictures of the early thirties bore the imprint of Irving Thalberg. By 1938, when *The Wizard of Oz* went into production, the stamp was that of L. B. Mayer. When Mayer came to Metro-Goldwyn as vice-president and general manager at a salary of $1,500 a week in 1924, he brought with him Irving Thalberg, a short, frail young man with a heart damaged by rheumatic fever, to whom Mayer always referred as The Little Giant. Thalberg—the model for Monroe Stahr in F. Scott Fitzgerald's *The Last Tycoon*—was the creative force at MGM from 1924 until his death in 1936, although he stopped personally overseeing every single MGM movie in 1933. Mayer had the larger salary and the bigger title. Thalberg had what was commonly called, even then, genius. Even Mervyn LeRoy, who had been Mayer's man, said, "I only met two geniuses in all my years in the business: Irving Thalberg and Walt Disney."

If a preview audience was unresponsive to a finished film, Thal-

* The official spelling.
† From 1930 to 1940, MGM won four Academy Awards for Best Picture, six for Best Actor, six for Best Actress. The runners-up, Columbia and RKO, tied with four awards each to MGM's sixteen.

berg could take it into an editing room and recut it into a success. If a film was good, he could make it superior. In addition, he was courteous, gentle, and worked from 10 a.m. until long after midnight, his capacity for work seemingly based on the curious proposition that if he wasn't bored, there was no reason to get tired. With the passage of time Mayer's antagonism toward his Little Giant was so great that the two men rarely spoke.

Irving Thalberg died in September 1936, and playwright Charles MacArthur once described working at MGM thereafter as "like going to the Automat." From then on MGM belonged to Mayer. It belonged to him for sixteen years, until he was deposed in favor of Dore Schary in 1951. After Thalberg's death, his assistant, Al Lewin, resigned, and some of his favorite writers and directors found more congenial work elsewhere. Here and there a few contracts were not renewed. But Mayer did not attempt wholesale executions in order to rid the studio of all of Thalberg's camp-followers: he needed them to make the successful pictures that the money men in New York expected from MGM.

Thalberg was suitably immortalized by having his name placed on the four-story white administration building Mayer built in 1937. When Mervyn LeRoy came to MGM, he took possession of one of the corner executive suites complete with private conference rooms and private bathroom on the third and most exclusive floor. The center of that floor contained Mayer's private flock, the executives who became powerful as studio administrators after Thalberg. Benny Thau, Eddie Mannix, Sam Katz, and Mayer's assistant Ida Koverman lined the corridor leading to Mayer's labyrinth of secretaries and his secretaries' secretaries.

Adjoining Mayer's office were a rather small sitting room and bathroom. A private elevator in the sitting room led to a rear entrance of the building. The elevator allowed Mayer to make an unobserved exit from his office whenever he found it politically desirable. The private elevator no longer works. Studio president James Aubrey had it disconnected in 1970 because he was afraid someone might use it to gain access to his office.

Mayer's executive dining room on the fourth floor of the Thalberg Building has also—long since—been closed. It was that private dining room to which Mayer invited Ethel Waters, Lena Horne, and the rest of the black cast of *Cabin in the Sky* in 1943 when the studio manager—his brother, Jerry—refused to allow them to sit at tables in the commissary. And the next day the commissary was open to them. Black or white, L. B. Mayer's stars were his stars.

Although the executive gymnasium on the fourth floor still existed in 1976, it no longer contained—as it had in Mayer's day—a resident chiropractor. The fourth floor was being used mainly for storage. Mayer's office, too, was gone. Each succeeding president or vice-president in charge of production to occupy Mayer's office—Dore Schary, Sol Siegel, Robert O'Brien, Bo Polk, James Aubrey—changed it to his whim. Dore Schary built a patio, where he could lie in the sun and read scripts. Bo Polk knocked out walls. James Aubrey paneled the office in green leather and put back the walls Polk had knocked out. Only Frank Rosenfelt stifled the urge to make Mayer's office his own. Since becoming president on October 31, 1973, he has lived in the office exactly as his predecessor, James Aubrey, chose to decorate it.

By 1938, a year and a half after Thalberg died, the emphasis at MGM had already shifted from sophistication to sentimentality. Thalberg had starred Alfred Lunt and Lynn Fontanne in *The Guardsman*; his wife, Norma Shearer, in Eugene O'Neill's *Strange Interlude*; and what seemed like half of MGM's stars in the immensely successful Academy Award–winner *Grand Hotel*. Mayer is said to have considered the Andy Hardy series, in which Mickey Rooney starred between 1937 and 1945, as his masterpiece. That is probably being unfair to Mayer, who had his own considerable strengths as a studio head. But he was—to say the least—less magnanimous and less intellectual than Thalberg. Mayer has been described by film critic Bosley Crowther as a man whose "emotional reflexes were unpredictable to a bewildering and terrifying degree." He cried easily. He also carried a number of grudges to his grave. If someone quit MGM to get more money or a more interesting job elsewhere, Mayer never spoke to him again, although if he fired someone—no matter how angrily—he was usually willing to hire him back within two or three years.

Mayer believed fervently in God, America, and motherhood.

Part of Mayer's antagonism toward people who left MGM for some other studio was his very real belief that his employees were his extended family. The "homemade" apple pie (that most American of desserts, selected by a man who chose to celebrate his birthday on the Fourth of July) and the chicken soup prepared to Mayer's own recipe that were always available in the studio commissary were sincere gestures of concern for the digestive tracts of his employees. The majority of them responded to him with affection. There was an intense loyalty to Mayer and to MGM, especially among the artisans and technicians: men spent their entire careers in the Wardrobe Department or the Property Department or the Makeup Department and, after their retirement, returned each week to get their hair cut at the studio barber shop. June Allyson, who came to MGM in 1942, insists that "He was the father of all of us. When I left the studio in 1956, I felt I was leaving home. I was that sad. And yet I was already married and had two children." "There was a sense of pride at the studio, a sense of community," says William Ludwig, a screenwriter at MGM during the thirties. "There were five major studios—Warner Brothers. Columbia, 20th Century-Fox, Paramount, and MGM—and you supported your own." "There was a sense of enjoyment in making movies then," says ex–story editor Sam Marx, a bit wistfully. "There were no jealousies in the early days," adds John Lee Mahin, another MGM writer. "Whatever we were working on was an MGM picture, and we all wanted MGM pictures to be the best. In the very early days, we used to play softball on Sundays, with Mayer pitching for one team and Thalberg for the other. A truck would come and take everybody to the back lot. And everybody would play—writers, executives, electricians."

That changed, of course. Thalberg had personally supervised every one of MGM's films until a quarrel over money and a partly hypochondriacal crisis over his health caused him to take six months off in 1933. During his absence, Mayer rearranged the system of making films, putting each film in the hands of an individual producer who, for the first time at MGM, was to be given screen credit and who chose stories, actors, and directors from those available at the studio. Mayer's system caused a rivalry that had not been there before. "I was one of twenty-seven or twenty-eight producers," says Frank Davis, "and we only made somewhere around forty pictures a year. We were always supposed to make fifty-two, but we never did. That meant that the producers could barely make one picture a year. Yes, there were jealousies."

Mayer's personal sentimentality is remembered best by his stars, all of whom have more or less the same story to tell. In June Allyson's version: "You never won an argument with Mr. Mayer. If you were winning and he knew you were winning, he would cry and tell you how you were one of the family. And you would put your arm around him and say, 'It's all right, Poppa.' " That sentimentality was reflected in his films. He believed that men should be manly, that women should be respected, and that children should revere their parents. John Lee Mahin tells a sad story of Mayer after he was deposed in 1951 and sat waiting for a triumphant return to MGM that never came. Mahin wrote *Joseph and His Brethren,* which was to be Mayer's opulent debut as an independent producer. "It never saw the light of day because Mayer wouldn't let me have Joseph lose his faith. Not even after he was thrown into a pit, sold into slavery by his brothers, betrayed by Potiphar's wife. 'He must keep the faith of his fathers,' Mayer said. So he was a pretty dull Joseph and the picture was never made."

Although Mayer's influence on MGM pictures was pervasive by 1938, it was never felt, as Thalberg's had been, at the subtle level of scripts and camera angles. "He never made pictures," one of his employees remembers, "he made contracts." He assembled for MGM a stable of stars and character actors that ran to several single-spaced pages. He also acquired half of the best directors in Hollywood and some eighty or ninety writers, including, at one time or another, Charles MacArthur, Ben Hecht, Herman J. Mankiewicz, Conrad Richter, James Hilton, Philip Wylie, Vicki Baum, Ogden Nash, Dorothy Parker, Lillian Hellman, Joseph L. Mankiewicz, Robert E. Sherwood, Robert Benchley, Dashiell Hammett, S. J. Perelman, F. Scott Fitzgerald, Sidney Howard, John O'Hara, and William Faulkner.

"Mayer was a marvelous picker," says Frank Davis, "He picked the right people. That was his great talent." Jack Cummings—who in addition to being Mayer's nephew was the catcher on his softball team—says, "He was intolerant of mediocrity. He looked the world over for people who were bright and up to date." Recalls William Ludwig, "L. B. had a frightening philosophy. Once he said to me, 'I hire what I think is the best and I leave them alone. If they do all right, fine. If not, I fire them.' It was nothing unusual at Metro to put somebody on a project, let him alone for a year, then not like what he did and start all over."

Mervyn LeRoy, an alien director from Warner Bros., was brought to MGM in 1937 by Mayer at $6,000 a week. LeRoy's salary was to be kept a secret—no other producer at MGM was making more than $3,500. But nothing remained secret at MGM for very long. "Hell," says writer Noel Langley, "if you went to the can at MGM in those days, the can was probably wired." LeRoy's guaranteed $300,000 a year was common knowledge more quickly and uncomfortably than either LeRoy or Mayer wished. For Mayer, it meant a string of other producers who wanted their contracts rewritten. For LeRoy, it meant that the other producers were out to get him—at any time and in any way they could.

LeRoy's position was not helped by his youthful appearance. He was then thirty-seven years old, but he looked twenty-seven, a fact of which he remained extremely proud four decades later, still recalling half a dozen pictures early in his career when people refused to believe that "that kid" could be the director. His youthful appearance and slight build recalled Thalberg, who was barely twenty-five years old when he and Mayer joined Metro-Goldwyn in 1924. (Youth has always had a peculiar currency in Hollywood. In the late 1960's—after the success of *Easy Rider*—fifty-eight-year-old studio heads prodigally handed out money and power to any recent film-school graduate or alienated young writer who could prove he was under twenty-eight. Those studio heads would then imitate the hair styles and clothes of their protégés, whose films were, for the most part, financial and artistic failures, leaving the studio executives with nothing but longer hair, love beads, and a wardrobe of faded denims to show for their lavish expenditures.)

Thalberg's importance at such a young age was one of the reasons for the awe in which he was held. LeRoy's youth was part of the cause for the jealousy with which the producers at MGM who were making $3,000 a week less regarded him. Not really young in 1937, LeRoy nevertheless had an air of youthful cockiness when he appeared at MGM, bringing with him Lana Turner, a seventeen-year-old girl he had under personal contract.

LeRoy was the cousin of Hollywood pioneer Jesse Lasky and the son-in-law of one of the Warner brothers, Harry Warner. But one cannot explain away his $6,000-a-week salary by pointing to his Hollywood pedigree, since L. B. Mayer was not prone to be over-generous with the company's money. "When business wasn't going too well during the Depression," says Frank Davis, "Mayer wouldn't

Mervyn LeRoy, producer of The Wizard of Oz. *At thirty-seven, he was hired away from Warner Bros. by Mayer to replace the mercurial Irving Thalberg, who had died of a heart attack the year before.*

shave for a couple of days. Then he would come in and weep and tell us how he had been up night and day arguing with 'the General' —that was Nick Schenck back in New York—about how our people are loyal and we shouldn't cut their salaries. But, sadly, Schenck had decided that everyone was to take a ten-percent pay cut. Mayer was great on those speeches, wonderful!"

LeRoy had been at MGM twice before—in 1931 to direct a faded John Gilbert in *Gentleman's Fate*, and in 1933 to direct Marie Dressler and Wallace Beery in *Tugboat Annie*. He had directed forty pictures but had produced only one when Mayer hired him away from Warner Bros. in the hope that he could replace Thalberg at quarterback. Mayer, having his rival Thalberg removed by an act of God, was not about to turn over signal-calling power to anyone else. But he would not have paid LeRoy $6,000 a week if he had not expected LeRoy to bring to producing the same speed, slickness, craftsmanship, and financial success he had shown at First National and Warner Bros. as a director. Mayer's expectations were soon, to say the least, deferred. During his first year and a half at MGM, LeRoy produced four pictures: *The Wizard of Oz; Dramatic School,* starring Luise Rainer and Paulette Goddard; *Stand Up and Fight,* co-starring Wallace Beery and Robert Taylor; and *At the Circus,* with the Marx Brothers. Then he went to Mayer and asked him for a $2,500-a-week cut in salary so he could return to directing. (The cut in salary gives some indication of the relative status of producers versus directors at MGM in the thirties. At Columbia, directors Frank Capra and Leo McCarey were salvaging a bankrupt studio with *You Can't Take It With You, The Awful Truth, It Happened One Night, Mr. Smith Goes to Washington, Mr. Deeds Goes to Town.* At the more elegant MGM, a director was automatically in the wrong when he quarreled with his producer.) Mayer cut LeRoy's salary and granted his wish. After 1939, LeRoy did not produce again until he both produced and directed the June Allyson–Elizabeth Taylor *Little Women* in 1948.

If LeRoy had been cast by Mayer as a substitute for Thalberg on the MGM team, Arthur Freed had been picked for more subtle purposes. Freed was one of a group of four or five men who were, as one ex-MGM employee phrases it, "slaves to Mayer at night after office hours." As another observer puts it, less delicately, "If Mayer's ass itched, Freed scratched." But there were any number of men at MGM who would have eagerly provided the same service. The forty-three-year-old songwriter offered Mayer more than flattery.

"Mr. Mayer was used to being 'Yessed' to death," says Reneé Freed. "If Arthur found it was just as easy to say 'Yes' as 'No,' he'd say 'Yes.' Otherwise, he'd fight. I think Mr. Mayer admired him for that."

Mayer's circle also included Frank Orsatti, the agent to whom Freed went to negotiate the purchase of *The Wizard of Oz*. (A large number of MGM actors and actresses eventually became Orsatti clients. Judy Garland was only one of a number who were called in and told that their careers would be regarded more favorably if Orsatti represented them.) MGM story editor Sam Marx once asked Mayer, as tactfully as possible, why he chose to spend his evenings with underlings. Mayer's answer was that "the men most readily available to me for running around at night are the other studio heads. Those men, they always want something I've got. When I get home at night, I can't sleep. I keep worrying, did I give my studio away?"

The irony is that in his after-hours playmate Arthur Freed, Mayer would find the producer for whom he was searching in Mervyn LeRoy. The details of costumes, set design, and where to trim $75,000 off the budget that were sour milk to LeRoy were wine to Freed. "All of us would meet in his office," says Mary Ann Nyberg of the days, a decade later, when Freed was the most important and successful producer on the MGM lot, "and Freed would work out the total visual concept for the film. He always knew exactly what he didn't want and quite often he knew exactly what he *did* want."

Even in 1937 Freed had almost unlimited access to his employer, including the privilege of dropping in at Mayer's house for breakfast. He used every opportunity to try to cajole Mayer into allowing him to produce a movie. If—as Freed always insisted—Mayer finally turned him loose and allowed him to start negotiations for *The*

Mervyn LeRoy (left) and Arthur Freed, his assistant (right), relaxing at Mayer's ranch in Perris, California. The two men originally met in 1923 at First National Pictures. LeRoy was a gag man; Freed played background music on the organ (and as a songwriter, he collaborated with Nacio Herb Brown on Broadway Melody *and other films). It was Freed who hired Harold Arlen and E. Y. ("Yip") Harburg to write the words and the music for* Oz.

Wizard of Oz, Freed was shrewd enough to buy a story that would not require the use of Jeanette MacDonald, Eleanor Powell, Joan Crawford, Myrna Loy, Norma Shearer, or any other of MGM's top stars. He saw *The Wizard of Oz* as a vehicle for a fifteen-year-old MGM featured player, Judy Garland. What Freed was not shrewd enough to realize was that *The Wizard of Oz* would have to be an expensive picture. And Mayer was too cautious to place an expensive picture in the hands of a novice producer.

The Wizard of Oz—Production #1060, budgeted at slightly over $2 million—was, from the first, considered an *important* film. It cost more and took longer to make than any other MGM film made that year. Thalberg's personal production of *Mutiny on the Bounty* had taken over three months to film and cost nearly $2 million in 1935. *Captains Courageous*, for which Spencer Tracy won the first of his Academy Awards in 1937, cost $1,645,000. *Idiot's Delight*, starring Clark Gable and Norma Shearer, was being filmed down an MGM street from *The Wizard of Oz* in November and December of 1938; it cost $1,519,000 and had a shooting schedule of eight weeks—both about average for a *big* MGM film. (A small film ranged in cost from $250,000 to $500,000 and was completed in less than a month.) The final cost of *The Wizard of Oz* was $2,777,000. The final shooting schedule—including a week off to change directors—lasted twenty-two weeks.

It took *The Wizard of Oz* over twenty years to earn its money back. During its first release, from August 1939 through September 1942, the film brought MGM $3,017,000—earning $2,052,333 in the United States and $964,000 abroad. Under the studio bookkeeping system, however, which adds the cost of prints, advertising, and distribution to a picture's cost, that meant a net loss of roughly $1 million.

The picture was probably never intended to make money. Despite Walt Disney's successful *Snow White and the Seven Dwarfs* the year before, there was a Hollywood truism that fantasies were failures at the box office. Disney's gamble on a full-length cartoon was daring, and it could have made Mayer daydream of equal success. But Mayer was too shrewd to daydream very often. *The Wizard of Oz* was intended as a prestige picture that would more or less break even. "They didn't think they were going to make any money with the picture," according to the film's lyricist, E. Y. ("Yip") Harburg. "Once a year they did a loser for prestige." MGM always had room for one such picture—people who worked at the studio in the thirties even speak of certain films as "our prestige picture that year." A few years earlier, Thalberg's *The Barretts of Wimpole Street* had been "our prestige picture." In 1939, that mantle was draped around *The Wizard of Oz*. It was hoped that the picture would show up heavily in the Academy Awards. The film did win a special award for Judy Garland and two of the regular awards—Best Song to Harold Arlen and Harburg for "Over the Rainbow" and Best Original Score to MGM Musical Director Herbert Stothart. And it did get its nomination for Best Picture. Beyond that, it had the misfortune to be released the same year as *Gone With the Wind*.

Prestige picture or not, *The Wizard of Oz* was well within the boundaries of the MGM system. It is doubtful whether anybody connected with the film was even trying to make a classic. Men with the bullheadedness and fanaticism of Preston Sturges and Orson Welles could try to subvert the industry. Mayer's son-in-law David O. Selznick could turn the producer into a Medici with the creed that "Any picture worth making is worth being obsessed with." At poverty-stricken Columbia, a producer or director who could promise a profit could even demand a certain autonomy. But *The Wizard of Oz* had ten screenwriters and four directors. W. C. Fields, for whom the part of the Wizard was written, turned it down. Two weeks after the picture started production, one of the other major parts was recast. By the time the film went before the cameras in October 1938, neither Mervyn LeRoy nor Arthur Freed was even fully concentrating on it—LeRoy's two other films, *Dramatic School* and *Stand Up and Fight*, were also in production, and Freed had just been officially given the title of producer by Mayer and was allowed to buy *Babes in Arms* as his first film.

"When I wrote *Finian's Rainbow*," says Yip Harburg, "I knew that the play was an important classic right away because of what it dealt with and because of the response from intellectuals all over the world. That play dealt with the cause of racism and the whole economic illogic of our system. It contained economic and social ideas in fantasy form. Universities were charmed by it immediately. But *The Wizard of Oz* was just for children."

"We didn't know it was a classic," says Tin Woodman Jack Haley. "It was a job. We were getting paid, and it was a lot of weeks of steady work."

"Some of the reviews were very pleasant, but they were not what people in the business call 'money reviews,'" remembers the Wicked Witch, Margaret Hamilton.

It is tempting to imagine that the film was embraced by the critics. In fact, most of the serious critics thought it dreadful. Otis Ferguson, considered one of the best reviewers of the era, wrote in *The New Republic*:

"The Wizard of Oz" was intended to hit the same audience as "Snow White" and won't fail for lack of trying. It has dwarfs, music, Technicolor, freak characters and Judy Garland. It can't be expected to have a sense of humor as well—and as for the light touch of fantasy, it weighs like a pound of fruitcake soaking wet. Children will not object to it, especially as it is a thing of many interesting gadgets; but it will be delightful for children mostly to their mothers, and any kid tall enough to reach up to a ticket window will be found at the Tarzan film down the street. The story of course has some lovely and wild ideas—men of straw and tin, a cowardly lion, a wizard who isn't a very good wizard—but the picture doesn't know what to do with them, except to be painfully literal and elaborate about everything. Cecil B. DeMille. The Seven Thousand Dwarfs by Actual Count.

Nor was Ferguson taken by Judy Garland:

It isn't that this little slip of a miss spoils the fantasy so much as that her thumping, overgrown gambols are characteristic of its treatment here. When she is merry the house shakes, and everybody gets wet when she is forlorn.

And Russel Maloney in *The New Yorker* was hardly more friendly toward the film.

Fantasy is still Walt Disney's undisputed domain. Nobody else can tell a fairy tale with his clarity of imagination, his supple good taste, or his technical ingenuity. This was forcibly borne in on me as I sat cringing before MGM's Technicolor production of "The Wizard of Oz," which displays no trace of imagination, good taste, or ingenuity.

Maloney labeled the film "a stinkeroo," although he found "Bert Lahr, as the Cowardly Lion, funny but out of place."

Of the few respected critics who were completely won by the film, Frank S. Nugent, writing in *The New York Times*, was the most important.

[21]

Not since Disney's "Snow White" has anything quite so fantastic succeeded half so well. A fairybook tale has been told in the fairybook style with witches, goblins, pixies, and other wondrous things drawn in the brightest colors. It is all so well-intentioned, so genial, and so gay that any reviewer who would look down his nose at the fun-making should be spanked and sent off, supperless, to bed.

What is curious is that most of the middlebrow magazines were not overly enthusiastic. *Newsweek* praised the "magnificent sets and costumes" and enjoyed the trick photography. *Scholastic* liked the special effects, but found only Judy Garland believable. In *McCalls*, Pare Lorentz complained that the film was not a fantasy but a Broadway musical comedy, unfortunately equipped with a score by Broadway musical-comedy writers. He described "the evil witch chasing the little girl from Kansas all around the castle—a business that is produced as though the girl were a gangster and the witch and her cohorts a band of G-men." *Time* also thought it "a Broadway spectacle" with a final sequence "as sentimental as 'Little Women.'" Yet the *Time* reviewer was captivated by the fantasy: "As long as 'The Wizard of Oz' sticks to whimsey and magic it floats in the same rare atmosphere of enchantment that distinguished Disney's 'Snow White,' etc. When it descends to earth it collapses like a scarecrow in a cloudburst."

Despite mixed reviews, the film was still being watched thirty-eight years later, and even had become the object of active hero worship. This was the result more of a series of accidents than any grand design. In 1956, CBS tried to lease *Gone With the Wind* from MGM for $1 million. MGM refused. As an afterthought, CBS made a $225,000 offer for *The Wizard of Oz*. MGM agreed and also gave CBS an option to broadcast the film annually. Without the once-a-year repetition on television as a special, the film would not have been seen enough times for a new generation to become aware of it. Nor would it have become an event rather than just another movie.

And without Judy Garland's unique voice and tragic future being tied to "Over the Rainbow"—so that one could never watch the frenzied self-caricature of her last years without being reminded of a time when rainbows were possible for her—the picture would never have taken on the qualities of poignancy, seriousness, and irony.

Distance would do many things to *The Wizard of Oz*. The over-produced quality that was so offensive to critics in 1939 has thirty-eight years later lent a hand to the picture's being seen as significant. Time has given a wistful charm to the painfully literal Kansas in the picture. By now it seems quaint enough (observe the mocking of just such comfy Hollywood farms in the opening scene of Martin Scorsese's 1974 *Alice Doesn't Live Here Any More*) to be all of a piece with the fantasy that followed. Also, now that the burlesque/vaudeville world in which Jack Haley, Ray Bolger, and Bert Lahr learned their trade has vanished, their bravura style seems part of Oz's fantasy world in a way that was impossible in 1939, when almost all adults could still remember vaudeville. In 1976, Jack Haley told an instructive story of reminiscing with old friends a year or two earlier. The sixteen-year-old son of his friends finally entered the conversation with, "Where *is* Vaudeville?"

And, of course, L. Frank Baum's Oz still shines through the film. Somehow—eliminate half the book as they did, turn Dorothy's companions into nervy Broadway stars, turn six-year-old Dorothy herself into an adolescent girl corseted to look twelve—the film's makers only changed and did not destroy Baum's fantasy. A man made of straw, a man of tin, a lion half bully and half coward, and a wizard who is a good man but a very bad wizard remained unique companions on paper or on film seventy-seven years after Baum created them.

The movie made from Baum's book was "an MGM film," with all that those three words implied. From the moment of its purchase, the book was fed into the MGM system. L. B. Mayer, aloof as he was from the day-to-day details of filmmaking, had his finger early in the *Wizard of Oz* pie. He approved the purchase of the book from Goldwyn. He turned down Arthur Freed's pleas that he be allowed

[23]

to produce the movie, but, on Mayer's explicit instructions, Freed was made LeRoy's assistant. LeRoy, on the other hand, wanted not only to produce but also to direct *The Wizard of Oz*. Mayer turned him down flat. He was told that it was "too big a picture for you to do both."

The essentials settled, Mayer figuratively closed the door of his office. He was only peripherally involved in the making of *The Wizard of Oz* for the next eighteen months: he approved the cast and even tried to borrow Shirley Temple from Fox for the role of Dorothy; he stood behind LeRoy when the money man in New York, company president Nicholas M. Schenck, balked at the film's ever rising cost; he helped LeRoy talk Victor Fleming into taking over as director after Richard Thorpe was fired. But he had no creative responsibility for the film—that belonged to LeRoy and Freed. LeRoy was definitely in command; after all, he was the producer. With the title went the responsibility for the thousands of decisions that transformed *The Wizard of Oz* into a completed film. All the while Freed tried to influence those decisions and, in any case, carried them out. Not until a preview in June 1939 did L. B. Mayer judge their work.

Production #1060	2.

THE SCRIPT(S)

by Herman Mankiewicz . . . by Ogden Nash . . . by Noel Langley . . .
by Herbert Fields . . . by Samuel Hoffenstein . . .
by Florence Ryerson . . . by Edgar Allan Woolf . . . by Jack Mintz . . .
by Sid Silvers . . . by John Lee Mahin

A little girl is whirled from her home in Kansas by a cyclone which deposits her in the magic land of Oz. There she meets a number of strange companions who accompany her to the city of the Wizard who rules the land and with his help she returns to Kansas.

    —1938 MGM synopsis of L. Frank Baum's book
      The Wizard of Oz

On February 28, 1938, Herman J. Mankiewicz was assigned to *The Wizard of Oz*. He was the first of ten screenwriters who tried to turn L. Frank Baum's fairy tale into a movie.

Herman Mankiewicz was an acknowledged genius at writing the fast, irreverent comedies of the early thirties. In 1928 he had received credit on seventeen movies. In 1930 he had written or produced seven. By 1938 he had run out of studios from which to be fired. It wasn't so much because he was an alcoholic. Excessive drinking has always been an occupational hazard of screenwriters, the price many of the good ones pay in self-hatred for taking all that easy money. Of the ten writers on *The Wizard of Oz*, two were alcoholics, and a third was trying to drown a rotten marriage in a shot glass. Mankiewicz's trouble was more his compulsive gambling and his penchant for getting bored in the middle of a picture. He wrote *Dinner at Eight* at MGM in 1934. Irving Thalberg threw him off *A Night at the Opera* in 1935 and never used him again. L. B. Mayer hired him back in 1938 and fired him in 1939 after advancing him money to clear up his gambling debts on Mankiewicz's solemn vow never to gamble again and then finding him betting $10,000 in a poker game the next day. The year after that—1940—he wrote *Citizen Kane*, thus winning himself an Academy Award and Hollywood immortality in 1941.

On March 3, three days after he was assigned to *The Wizard of Oz*, Mankiewicz handed in a seventeen-page treatment of what was later known as "the Kansas sequence." Baum had wasted less than one thousand words of his book on Kansas. Dorothy lived in a grey house on a grey prairie with a grey Aunt Em and a grey Uncle Henry and was blown to Oz on page 5. But all the scriptwriters, starting with Mankiewicz, focused almost as much of their attention on Kansas as they did on Oz. They felt it necessary to have an audience relate to Dorothy in a real world before transporting her to a magic one.

On the first page of Mankiewicz's treatment, there is an underlined paragraph:

As discussed, this part of the picture—until the door is flung open after Dorothy has arrived in the land of the Munchkins—will be shot in black and white, but every effort should be made, through tinting, to emphasize the grey nature of the landscape and Dorothy's daily life.

Thus, before a word of the script was written, it had already been decided that only the Oz sequences would be photographed in color,

Herman Mankiewicz. He was the first of ten writers assigned to The Wizard of Oz *and, after one week, turned in a fifty-six-page script treatment, unaware that Ogden Nash and Noel Langley had also been assigned.*

ASSIGNMENT	STARTED	FINISHED	MATERIAL IN FILE	DATE
HOORAY I'M ALIVE	10/7/38	10/17/38	Section of dialogue	10/6/38
The Ghost Man Returns			Section of dialogue	10/7/38
The Bold Seafarer			Section of dialogue	10/8/38
			Section of dialogue	10/8/38
Produced: "THE GHOST COMES HOME"			Incomplete dialogue script	10/11/38
B2878 F1126 Scen.#7402			Section of dialogue	10/12/38
Received no screen credit.			Section of dialogue	10/12/38
			Section of dialogue	10/12/38
CONGO MAISIE	6/15/34	8/9/34	Incomplete script	6/15/34
Congo Landing			Section of dialogue (B.Hyman)	6/18/34
Dolly, Purple Night			Section of dialogue	6/19/34
			Section of dialogue	6/22/34
Produced: "CONGO MAISIE"			Incomplete script	6/26/34
B2342 Prod#1119 Scen#6448			Section of dialogue	6/26/34
Received no screen credit.			Section of dialogue (B. Hyman)	6/26/34
			Section of dialogue	6/27/34
			Section of dialogue (B. Hyman)	6/27/34
IT'S A WONDERFUL WORLD	11/30/38	2/15/39	Section of dialogue	12/12/38
Life Is A Wonderful Thing			Notes & Suggestions	12/22/38
The Lady Protests				
Produced: "IT'S A WONDERFUL WORLD"				
B2308 Prod#1083 Scen#7421				
Screen play by Ben Hecht-Based				
on an original story by Ben				
Hecht & Herman J. Mankiewicz.				
THE WIZARD OF OZ	2/28/38	3/23/38	Incomplete treatment	3/3/38
			Incomplete script	3/7/38
Produced: "THE WIZARD OF OZ"			Section of dialogue	3/9/38
B2285 Prod#1060 Scen#7333			Section of dialogue	3/11/38
Received no screen credit.			Section of dialogue	3/12/38

NAME MANKIEWICZ, HERMAN J. ▼ 1220

*A portion of Mankiewicz's assignment sheet, recording
and dating his contributions to Oz.*

that the film would try to capture in pictures what Baum had captured in words—the grey lifelessness of Kansas contrasting with the visual richness of Oz.

Mervyn LeRoy took credit for that decision. But in 1976 he did not remember discussing it with Herman Mankiewicz. In fact, he did not really recall Mankiewicz's being assigned to *The Wizard of Oz* at all. Considering the status of the screenwriter at MGM in 1938, LeRoy's failure to remember is understandable. (The Screen Writers' Guild had been formed in 1937 against the vicious opposition of Mayer and all the other Hollywood executives, but the Guild was not able to force the Motion Picture Producers Association to sign a contract until 1942; and there was almost no arbitration of credits until 1945.) Writers were assigned in relays, rather as though they were pieces of sandpaper to be used up and replaced. Scripts resembled nothing so much as a seven-layer cake, and it often took an archaeological expedition to discover who was responsible for which layer. Irving Thalberg had not invented the system of teaming up writers as though they were matched pairs in a horse show and bringing in new teams when he felt the old ones were stale. But the success of his pictures made the system seem efficient and reasonable. At MGM the system continued even more rigorously after his death.

Mankiewicz's Dorothy was an unfailingly cheerful and simple soul, enraptured by the possibility of corn on the cob with butter ("I guess it's about the best food there is") and sure that everything about her life was "the most beautiful" in the world.

AUNT EM: Something special for dinner today, darling. Do you want to guess?

DOROTHY: Oh, I don't know. I really don't know.
   (*to Toto*)
Can you help me decide?
   (*Toto shakes his head*)
Uncle Henry, you help me, please. Because if I don't guess, it all comes as a surprise—but I don't get the fun of guessing. But if I *do* guess, I'm apt to guess right—and then I don't get the surprise.

UNCLE HENRY: Maybe you could be surprised that you guessed right.

Since Mankiewicz was considered by writer Nunnally Johnson to be the most brilliant man he ever met, the similarities in attitude between the orphaned Dorothy and her dog Toto and Little Orphan Annie and her dog Sandy were probably intentional tomfoolery on Mankiewicz's part. He went on to invent a lost limousine containing a chauffeur, an obnoxious rich woman, her more obnoxious daughter, and the little girl's Pekingese, Adolphus Ajax Rittenstaufen III. There are five pages of dialogue comparing Adolphus Ajax Rittenstaufen III (who is "too valuable to play) with Toto (who "can count up to eight"). When the limousine departs, the cyclone arrives.

[29]

Four days later, on March 7, Mankiewicz turned in an incomplete fifty-six-page script. The generation of newspapermen-turned-screenwriters to which Mankiewicz belonged wrote scripts at breakneck speed. Mankiewicz was fast, but even faster was Ben Hecht, who won the first Academy Award for a script—Josef von Sternberg's *Underworld*—that he had finished in a week and who, while at MGM working at some project that required even more speed, had demanded a payment in cash of $1,000 a day. It is quite possible that Mankiewicz's peculiar blend of the saccharine and the eccentric was a deliberate attempt to get himself taken off the pic-

Florence Ryerson's assignment sheet. She received final screenplay credit along with her collaborator Edgar Allan Woolf, and Noel Langley. It was Ryerson and Woolf's idea that the Wizard should appear throughout the film in different guises.

ASSIGNMENT	STARTED	FINISHED	MATERIAL IN FILE	DATE
THE WIZARD OF OZ			Miscellaneous pages (Woolf)	7/12/38
(continued 1)			Section of dialogue "	7/13/38
			Suggestions for revising "	7/14/38
			Sections of dialogue "	7/14/38
			Sections of dialogue "	7/15/38
			Sections of dialogue "	7/16/38
			Sections of dialogue "	7/18/38
			Sections of dialogue "	7/21/38
			Suggested new set-up "	7/22/38
			Sections of dialogue "	7/22/38
			Sections of dialogue "	7/23/38
			Sections of dialogue "	7/25/38
			Sections of dialogue "	7/25/38
			Sections of dialogue "	7/27/38
			Sections of dialogue "	7/27/38
			Complete script (Langley,Woolf)	7/28/38
			Complete script (Langley,Woolf)	8/8/38
			Complete OK Script (Langley & Woolf)	10/10/38
JUDY GARLAND STORY (cf)	8/15/36	8/18/36	Notes (Woolf)	8/18/36
Everbody Sing	10/13/36	12/2/36	Incomplete Outline "	10/14/36
	12/9/36	12/10/36	Section of outline "	10/15/36
	12/29/36	3/23/37	Complete story outline "	10/20/36
	5/27/37	7/6/37	Notes "	10/23/36
	7/8/37	8/10/37	Section of treatment "	10/26/36
	11/15/37	11/23/37	Section of treatment "	10/27/36
			Complete outline "	10/28/36
			Section of script "	10/29/36
Produced: "EVERYBODY SING"			Incomplete script "	11/2/36
B2248 Prod#1020 Scen#7027			Section of dialogue "	11/4/36
Original story & screen play			Section of dialogue "	11/5/36
by Florence Ryerson and			Section of dialogue "	11/6/36
Edgar Allan Woolf-Additional			Section of dialogue "	11/9/36
dialogue by James Gruen.			Section of dialogue "	11/10/36
			Section of dialogue "	11/16/36
			Section of dialogue "	11/17/36
			Section of dialogue "	2/5/37
CONTINUED: 1			Section of dialogue "	2/8/37
NAME RYERSON, FLORENCE				▼ 1507

ture. (Once, when Mankiewicz was punished by being assigned to a Rin-Tin-Tin picture, he retaliated by writing a script that ended with a cowardly Rin-Tin-Tin carrying a baby *into* a burning building.) If so, he succeeded. The same day that Mankiewicz turned in his incomplete script, Ogden Nash was assigned to write a treatment for *The Wizard of Oz*. On March 11 a third writer, Noel Langley, was given the same assignment.

Mankiewicz did not know that Ogden Nash and Noel Langley had been set down in his footsteps, nor did Langley know that Mankiewicz had preceded him. It was customary for three, four, or even five writers to be assigned to write for the same film at the same time. One treatment or script would be accepted, the others discarded and their writers sent to write treatments for some other film. "It was part of the affluence of MGM at that time," said William Ludwig, one of only three writers who stayed at MGM long enough to be able to collect a pension. "The people were under contract, so the paper was the cheapest thing. It didn't cost much until the film actually started getting made." If Mankiewicz had known about Nash and Langley, it wouldn't have bothered him. By 1938 he had lived with the system for eleven years. And he once told a friend who was apologizing for having to rewrite one of his scripts to "go ahead and write me out and then find someone to write you out."

Noel Langley was still new enough to both screenwriting and Hollywood to believe in art and fair play. MGM screenwriter Allan Rivkin recalls him as "a tall, austere man, not given to much levity. He didn't sit at the writers' table at lunch and make jokes with the rest of us."

Langley may not have felt that he was welcome at the writers' table. In March 1938, Langley was twenty-six years old, 6′ 5″ tall, and lonely. The loneliness was the result of culture shock. He had been brought to California in July 1936, when some MGM executive had gone to London, seen his two plays on the London stage, and acquired him. In October 1936, after a brief period of acclimatization, he had been assigned to *Maytime* and had written an acceptable script for Nelson Eddy and Jeanette MacDonald in less than four days.

"Alice Duer Miller was ahead of me on *Maytime*, but everybody had taken a whack at it. Ogden Nash had, Dorothy Parker had, Albert Hackett and Frances Goodrich had, and, I believe, Vicki Baum had. I completed the whole script in three and a half days flat, and [Robert Z.] Pop Leonard was directing it by the end of the same week: no changes, no alterations, no midnight conferences. Leonard and producer Hunt Stromberg were happy, but MGM's eighty-eight contract screenwriters weren't. They were sore as hell that I got a script done in three and a half days. They wanted a year of fooling around. When the picture turned out to be a commercial hit, they wanted me out of the town on a rail. I suffered from some nasty infighting. Mayer was told I was a Communist, as cross-eyed as Ben Turpin, and totally untalented." Although Langley was not a Communist, not cross-eyed, and not untalented, he was given no more work that year by Hunt Stromberg. "Stromberg more or less asked me to play golf rather than check in at the office every day."

Between *Maytime* and *The Wizard of Oz*, Langley worked on four scripts without getting a screen credit. In 1938, he was assigned to *Sweethearts, Babes in Arms, Northwest Passage,* and *Listen, Darling,* without receiving screen credit. But, despite his lack of credits, he had hardly been idle. He had put his time to good use by learning to drink. The drinking coincided with his marriage in 1937. "Eleven years of drunken hell," he says now of that union. "If I drank, I was sorry for her, so I just kept drinking." He eventually got a divorce and stopped drinking. In 1938, however, liquor was "probably giving me a great deal of Dutch courage without affecting my work."

On March 22, 1938, Langley turned in a forty-three-page treatment of *The Wizard of Oz*. On March 23, Herman Mankiewicz was officially taken off the film. Ogden Nash stayed assigned to the film until April 16, but he turned in no written material.

Langley's forty-three-page treatment included much of what

In their first draft, the fourth draft of the script, Woolf and Ryerson made the Wicked Witch of the West more menacing than Langley had made her; in their second, they focused on Dorothy's desire to return to Kansas (introducing the theme "There's no place like home").

ASSIGNMENT	STARTED	FINISHED	MATERIAL IN FILE	DATE
THE WIZARD OF OZ	6/4/38	7/27/38	Notes (Ryerson)	6/4/38
			Section of dialogue "	6/6/38
Produced: "THE WIZARD OF OZ"			Section of dialogue "	6/6/38
B2285 Prod#1060 Scen#7333			Notes on Oz Sequence "	6/6/38
Screen play by Noel Langley,			Outline of Kansas sequence "	6/7/38
Florence Ryerson & Edgar			Section of dialogue "	6/8/38
Allan Woolf-Adaptation by			Incomplete script "	6/9/38
Noel Langley-From the book			Incomplete script "	6/10/38
by L. Frank Baum.			Section of dialogue "	6/13/38
			Incomplete script "	6/13/38
			Section of dialogue "	6/15/38
			Section of dialogue "	6/15/38
			Notes on changes "	6/15/38
			Section of dialogue "	6/16/38
			Rough Outline "	6/17/38
			Action Outline of Oz Seq. "	
			Tin Man scene "	6/22/38
			Tin Man scene "	6/23/38
			Section of dialogue "	6/23/38
			Section of dialogue "	6/24/38
			Notes "	6/27/38
			Section of dialogue "	6/27/38
			Section of dialogue "	6/27/38
			Section of dialogue "	6/27/38
			Section of dialogue "	6/28/38
			Section of dialogue "	6/29/38
			Outline of Sequence "	6/30/38
			Complete script "	7/5/38
			Section of dialogue "	7/5/38
			Miscellaneous pages "	7/6/38
			Section of dialogue "	7/8/38
			Brief Outline of end "	7/8/38
			Suggestions for cuts "	7/8/38
			Section of dialogue "	7/11/38
			Section of dialogue "	7/11/38
			Miscellaneous pages "	7/11/38
			Section of dialogue "	7/12/38
			Miscellaneous pages "	7/12/38
			Section of dialogue "	7/13/38
			Suggestions for revising "	7/14/38
			Section of dialogue "	7/14/38
			Section of dialogue "	7/15/38
			Section of dialogue "	7/16/38
			Section of dialogue "	7/18/38
			Section of dialogue "	7/21/38
			Suggested new set-up "	7/22/38
			Section of dialogue "	7/22/38
			Section of dialogue "	7/23/38
			Section of dialogue "	7/25/38
			Section of dialogue "	7/25/38
			Section of dialogue "	7/27/38
			Section of dialogue "	7/27/38
			Complete script (Ryerson,Langley)	7/28/38
			Section of dialogue (Ryerson)	7/30/38
			Complete script (Ryerson,Langley)	8/8/30
			Complete OK Script (Ryerson, & Langley)	10/10/38

NAME WOOLF, EDGAR ALLAN

▼ 1805

would be the framework of the finished film one year later. He had invented the two Kansas farmhands who reappear in Oz as the Scarecrow and the Tin Woodman. (Langley may have been influenced by the 1925 silent version of *The Wizard of Oz*, in which Oliver Hardy played the Tin Woodman. In that dreadful movie, both the Scarecrow and the Tin Woodman were first seen as Kansas farmhands.) He had also invented Miss Gulch, who reappears as the Wicked Witch of the West. Even the striking montage of Miss Gulch riding in mid-air on her bicycle, which gradually turns into the Wicked Witch riding her broomstick, was fully developed.

While defending his treatment at the first script conference, Langley told LeRoy and Freed "that you cannot put fantastic people in strange places in front of an audience unless they have seen them as human beings first. And I quoted a silent picture of Mary Pickford's called *Poor Little Rich Girl*. At that time I had total recall of the silent films I had seen in South Africa during the twenties, when I was an unhappy schoolboy who hid out in the local flea pit rather than slug it out in a world controlled by my Edward Moulton Barrett father. I put several silent-film devices I had liked into *The Wizard of Oz*. The prologue came from *Poor Little Rich Girl*. That film had a nightmare sequence in which all the people who had been the poor little rich girl's servants turned up. The two-faced nurse had two faces. That sort of thing. And the witch in Annette Kellerman's *Queen of the Sea*, a silent version of Hans Christian Andersen's 'Little Mermaid,' had first appeared as a bubble. So I felt we could do worse than allow Glinda the same mode of transport."

Langley's mention of *Poor Little Rich Girl* was met with blank stares. "Arthur Freed said, 'For Christ's sake, what are you talking about?' In those days, everybody was looking down on silent pictures. But, even so, Freed said he wanted to see the film and he had a phone call put through to Mary Pickford and asked her to send a copy of the picture to us. When we watched the film, Mervyn LeRoy died laughing at the old-fashioned acting style. He kept saying how bad the makeup was. His own suggestion for a prologue was simple. He wanted Dorothy to be reading *The Wizard of Oz* in bed. She would fall asleep. Then the book would fall down from its shelf and hit her on the head. And she would dream the picture. But Freed's values were sound and practical. He was a nice, quiet man, and I never saw him in a temper. He understood that it was important to have a prologue where you see the Scarecrow and the Tin Woodman as ordinary people."

Langley's outline, however, was still far from the final shooting script of October 10, 1938. It was peopled with extraneous characters as a result of Langley's attempt to tie Kansas as literally as possible to Oz. For example, the farmhand who becomes the Tin Woodman— and, as the Tin Woodman, petitions the Wizard of Oz for a heart —had stiff joints and was labeled "heartless" by Lizzie Smithers, who worked at the soda fountain. This then required that Lizzie Smithers turn up in Oz. Dorothy's Uncle Henry also turned up in Oz as the son of the Wicked Witch of the West.*

For some reason, Langley did not invent a third farmhand to correspond to the Cowardly Lion. The Lion's Kansas alter ego, Zeke, does not show up until the final shooting script. In Langley's treatment, the Cowardly Lion was strictly an Oz character—handsome Florizel, fiancé of Sylvia, a beautiful girl held prisoner by the Wicked Witch of the West. Florizel had been transformed into a lion by the Witch in order to force the girl to marry her son, Bulbo. It was Florizel, released from his enchantment, who killed the Witch by cutting her broomstick to pieces with his sword in a mid-air duel.

The invention of such standard fairy-tale characters by Langley is ironic, since *The Wizard of Oz*, written in 1899 and published in 1900, was consciously intended by its author to be a new kind of fairy tale—an American fairy tale not dependent on the winged fairies, enchantments, cruelty, and blood-letting of the classical European variety. It was no accident that, the year after *The Wizard of Oz*, Baum wrote a fairy tale about electricity, *The Master Key*.

---

* Langley insists that he never invented the extraneous characters who fill his treatment and the early drafts of his scripts. "Not my scripts, dearie," Langley says of the fading pages with their torn blue covers. The only characters he is willing to recognize as his are those in the final shooting script. He insists that even though the early scripts have his name on them they must have been written by some other writer. But they are the only early scripts bearing Langley's name. They correspond to listings on a master sheet, according to which no other writer turned in material during that time period, nor was any other writer assigned to *The Wizard of Oz* at the times when Langley's scripts are dated. In addition, Langley received sole screen credit for "adaptation," a credit that must have been based on the forty-three-page treatment of March 22.

A Scarecrow who must continually be stuffed with fresh straw, a Tin Man constantly in need of his oil can are inventions that extend the limits and gently mock the conventions of fairy stories at the same moment.

Langley's treatment also did fatal damage to Baum's most original concept. At the time Baum wrote *The Wizard of Oz*, fairy tales came essentially in two forms. There were the magic and often bloody enchantments of the Brothers Grimm, Hans Christian Andersen, and their imitators. There was also a newer tradition, based on Lewis Carroll's *Alice in Wonderland*, of fantasies that took place in a dream. To Baum, Oz was a real country to which a real child named Dorothy had actually gone. But Langley's first treatment made it clear—as did the final movie—that Dorothy's adventures in Oz were only a dream.

What seems most wrong—too clever, too adult—in Langley's treatment are the extra characters and fancy curlicues he added to Baum's plot. Langley's plot follows Baum's plot up to a point. In the book, Dorothy's house falls on the Wicked Witch of the East, killing her. Dorothy sets out for the Emerald City, wearing the Witch's silver shoes, in hopes that the Wizard of Oz will help her get back to Kansas. On the way, she meets a Scarecrow who goes along to ask Oz for a brain, a Tin Woodman who wants Oz to give him a heart, and a Cowardly Lion who wishes to ask Oz for courage. The Wizard promises to provide these things—after the four companions kill the Wicked Witch of the West.

It is at this point that Langley's plot diverges from Baum's plot. One of the greatest pleasures of the book is Dorothy's discovery that the Wizard of Oz is a humbug—after she has fulfilled his command to kill the Witch. In Langley's treatment, the Wizard is uncovered as a humbug before Dorothy ever leaves for the Witch's country, and the Wizard and Lizzie Smithers then accompany Dorothy on her journey.

The rest of Langley's treatment is comic opera. The travelers disguise themselves as a traveling circus. They try to start a revolution against the Witch. True love triumphs in the end. After the Cowardly Lion/Florizel, restored to human shape, has killed the Witch:

Florizel has Sylvia in his arms and we blend in strain of their love song: Lizzie Smithers and the Tin Man have their arms about each other; and then, as Dorothy watches, the whole thing begins to go out of focus and start swirling and swaying and eddying. She tries to cry out to Toto, and then we dissolve right out and through to her lying on the ground calling, "Toto! Toto!" with Aunt Em bending over her weeping, and Hunk, Hickory, and Uncle Henry watching.

Langley's Kansas sequence was, of course, his own invention. It also contained one severe lapse of plot and characterization. Aunt Em was presented as the harsh and cruel woman who forced Dorothy to get rid of her dog. "You have disobeyed your Uncle and myself and broken the school rules; so you have only yourself to blame for your punishment." Miss Gulch, the schoolteacher, played no part in the decision. She merely informed Aunt Em that Toto had bitten another student.

Dorothy's feelings about Aunt Em were that

she never really wanted me here . . . or she wouldn't always be saying how ungrateful I am, after she and Uncle Henry took me out of the asylum: but Hickory, it *really* wasn't very dreadful in the asylum; they didn't used to get angry. Not as often as Aunt Em.

Such a characterization not only made inexplicable Dorothy's ardent desire to live forever on the farm—"This is *home!*"—it also left the reader unsure exactly *who* was the Wicked Witch. By Langley's second script—dated May 4, 1938—Aunt Em, although still harsh, did not initiate the idea of giving Toto away. By his fourth script—dated May 14—her character was drastically softened.

Langley's first script—dated April 5, 1938—was essentially his forty-three-page treatment in script form. But he was already tinkering with the unworkable elements of Florizel/Sylvia/Lizzie Smithers and a comic-magician Wizard.

In the April script, Florizel is Kenelm the Lion Hearted, still betrothed to Sylvia, still turned into a Cowardly Lion by the Witch.

A dragon has been added for him to fight, since in this version, as in Baum's book, it is Dorothy who kills the Witch. In Langley's May 4 script, Kenelm and Sylvia are even more elaborate characters, as though Langley felt he could solve his problems by building up their roles. He did not yet realize that he could not fashion a completely satisfactory script while those characters remained. In this script, Kenelm is a prince, Sylvia a princess, and their betrothal party is broken up by the Wicked Witch rather in the manner of the bad fairy at Sleeping Beauty's christening. And in this version, Kenelm fights a gorilla. (All of Langley's scripts show the Cowardly Lion proving his courage by killing some beast or other. They are thus both more literal and more romantic than the final film, in which Bert Lahr's Cowardly Lion is harmless.) Kenelm and Sylvia are even introduced in Kansas, Sylvia as niece to the tyrannical Mrs. Gulch. Lizzie Smithers has left the soda fountain to become Aunt Em's kitchen help, while Miss Gulch—now *Mrs.* Gulch—has been provided with a nasty child, Walter.

Not all of the changes Langley made in Baum were unnecessary. Baum's Oz contained two good witches (North and South) and two bad witches (East and West). Langley amalgamated the Good Witch of the North and Glinda, the Good Witch of the South, into one character without harm to Baum's plot.

More important, the Wicked Witch of the West was only one of a number of threats Dorothy encountered in the book. In the book, Dorothy was menaced by the Kalidahs, fierce animals with bodies like bears and heads like tigers; a Deadly Poppy Field whose overwhelming scent would put one to sleep forever; a monstrous spider with a body as big as an elephant and legs as long as a tree trunk; fighting trees capable of using their branches as tentacles; and armless creatures who struck out with their Hammerheads to keep anyone from entering their territory.

Langley began what seemed the necessary dramatic process of turning the Wicked Witch of the West into Dorothy's sole adversary. Two generations later, the Broadway musical *The Wiz* successfully returned to the book's episodic line. *The Wiz* introduced Kalidahs and a Deadly Poppy Field that had no connection with the Wicked Witch.

In the book, Dorothy does not meet with the Wicked Witch until she travels to the West to kill her. In Langley's outline—as in the final movie—the Wicked Witch appears on the scene almost as soon as Dorothy's house kills the Wicked Witch of the East. And some of the language in Langley's March treatment is almost identical to that of the shooting script six months later.

Langley, in March:

"Accident!" cries the West Witch. "You kill my dearest friend and severest critic by accident, did you? Well, now I'm going to cause a little accident."

The shooting script:

"Accident, eh? Well, I can cause accidents too, my little pretty . . ."

Langley, referring to the silver shoes:

"You keep right inside them!" says the North Witch to Dorothy. "They're magic, and there's a very useful spell attached to them once you find out what it is."

The shooting script:

"You keep tight inside of them—their magic must be very powerful or *she* wouldn't want them so badly!"

Langley's second script included a Deadly Poppy Field that had been sown by the Wicked Witch. By his "DO NOT MAKE CHANGES" script of May 14, the Witch followed the travelers' journey in her crystal ball and appeared on the roof of the Tin Woodman's cottage to throw a fireball at the Scarecrow.

The primacy of the Witch was dramatically unavoidable, but it coarsened the movie. What is gained in the translation from book to movie is brassy self-confidence. The movie is a familiar nightmare set in Technicolor to a lovely musical score. But its antecedents are as much *Snow White* and *Sleeping Beauty* as they are Baum's *Wizard of Oz*. What is lost is innocence. Internal evidence within the fourteen books that L. Frank Baum wrote about Oz suggests that Dorothy was five or six years old at the time of her first visit. Sixteen-year-old Judy Garland might be carefully corseted and dressed in gingham to appear twelve, but she could never have made believable the simple, uncritical acceptance of the very young child who was Dorothy in the book. Innocence had been given its death blow, of course, by the fact that the Scarecrow, Tin Woodman, and Cowardly Lion were played by three actors trained in burlesque and vaudeville. But it vanished long before then, written out of each successive script as carelessly as the stork picked up the Scarecrow, who was stuck on a pole in the river, and miraculously restored him to his companions. (A scene from the book that was not, could not have been, in the movie.)

Langley was obviously struggling to fashion a script that would retain as much of Baum as possible. In one of his scripts, the Good Witch Glinda protects Dorothy, as she does in Baum, with a kiss. But that would have meant that the Wicked Witch could not menace Dorothy. Although the kiss remained in the next script and in the finished film, it lost its magic meaning. In another of Langley's scripts, the travelers cross Baum's China Country, where not only the people are china but even the earth is a china plate. But that gentle episode, meaningless to the book's central quest, was impossible to reproduce. The Winged Monkeys, who are merely the Witch's servants in the final film, start out in Langley's adaptation—as they do in Baum's book—as servants of the Golden Cap. But Langley chooses to use them, in the best swashbuckling fashion, as a weapon for Dorothy. Summoned by Dorothy, who grabs the Golden Cap, they fight with her and Florizel against the Witch. (" 'You're fighting for us!' shouts Dorothy to the monkeys. 'Fine!' shout the monkeys. 'Get the Witch, boys.' ")

Even the silver shoes—that magical means of transportation—were a problem. They appeared in Langley's March adaptation, but served no magical purpose. They were not used—as they are in Baum's book and the final movie—to enable Dorothy to return to Kansas. He wrote them out of his first script. They were back in his second script as some vague magical object desired by the Wicked Witch. In his final "DO NOT MAKE CHANGES" script of May 14, they had become the ruby slippers. On page 25, shot 114: "The ruby shoes appear on Dorothy's feet, glittering and sparkling in the sun." In that script, the slippers were used, for the first time, to return Dorothy to Kansas, since Glinda had "found out how to use those slippers."

For three months Langley sat in his office on the bottom floor of Hunt Stromberg's bungalow creating his own Oz in ink on long sheets of lined yellow paper. He was being loaned to Mervyn LeRoy, but he was still Stromberg's property. Although he was "low man on Stromberg's tribal totem," his office was habitable enough, befitting a $750-a-week writer. And there were innumerable girls from the stenographic pool who would take his yellow sheets and turn them into properly typed and mimeographed scenes.

He was twenty-six years old, the author of two successful plays and two novels, one of them a children's story, *The Land of Green Ginger*. At the studio, he was considered "a very slick hand." About his most serious problem there was the arches and chandeliers against which he was continually bashing his head. Doorways and offices at MGM did not seem to be suitable for men who were 6′ 5″ tall. (Langley blames the stroke he suffered in 1970 "on all those years of bashing my head against chandeliers and beams.")

Noel Langley, then twenty-six, wrote the first script for Oz *(he wrote four in all). Most of his material remained as the framework of the movie.*

Before two years had passed, he was blacklisted by the same
L. B. Mayer who had employed him. The blacklisting broke his spirit
or, at least, his momentum. He never again was the Wonder Boy
who could write a movie in a weekend. He worked on many movies,
got screen credit on a few. Years later, he even directed one film in
Hollywood, *The Search for Bridey Murphy*, on which—still star-
struck with the silent films of his childhood—he gave jobs to old
silent-film stars registered with the Screen Extras or Screen Actors'
guilds. But his memories were of all the defeats—the producers
who took advantage, the partners who took the money and ran.

Langley's third and last screen credit at MGM was *Florian*,
starring Robert Young and dozens of precisely bred Austrian riding
horses. It was on the set of *Florian* that Langley was condescended
to by L. B. Mayer and could not keep his waspish tongue silent.

It was a stupid thing to say, the wisecrack that got him blacklisted. "Every time Mayer smiles at me, I feel a snake has crawled
over my foot." He did not say it loudly enough for Mayer to hear.
But other people heard. "Old Reggie Owen, who was playing the
Emperor, moved to the other side of the ring. Even the extras moved
away. In two minutes, I was alone on that whole goddamned sound
stage. And that was the end of me." When he couldn't get a job at
any other studio, Langley retaliated by writing a short story for
Town & Country in which he satirized Mayer as Dante Gabriel
Rosettenstein and into which he dumped as many scandalous and
scurrilous things as he could remember or invent about the then current situation of MGM playing footsie with labor racketeers.

Mayer sent for Langley's agent after Mayer had read the short
story. The agent was asked if Noel Langley expected to work in
Hollywood ever again. "After the dastardly fucking you gave him,
what was he going to do except become a professional satirist at
your expense?" asked the agent.

"The bastard, for all his black rage, completely understood
that," says Langley. "He was a very *big* bastard. He was a shark that
killed when it wasn't hungry, but he was a giant compared to the
cigar-store Indians who came after him." Mayer did eventually call
off the blacklist. "But Mary Pickford broke it first. My agent showed
her the *Town & Country* story and she died laughing and said, 'No-

body as funny as that should be blacklisted by this town. Bring him here.' And that took courage."

When Langley went back to MGM in 1942 at $1,000 a week, he "never saw Mayer, never even once."

On June 10, 1938, Langley was removed from *The Wizard of Oz.* He had written one treatment and four scripts. His "DO NOT MAKE CHANGES" script of May 14 was—he assumed—the final script for the picture. He was pleased with it and so were Freed and the film's songwriters, E. Y. Harburg and Harold Arlen.

The "DO NOT MAKE CHANGES" script, dated May 14, was actually a "temporary complete" script; changes were made two or three times a week by Langley at the direction of Freed, LeRoy, and Harburg between May 14 and June 4, when it was made untouchable by the black stamp "DO NOT MAKE CHANGES."

Much of what Langley had written was, of course, in the October 10 final shooting script. He had invented a Cowardly Lion who could scare himself by pulling on his own tail. He had created talking apple trees that could slap the hands of anyone trying to pick their fruit. (Langley may have got the idea for his apple trees from Baum's fighting trees.) Huge chunks of dialogue, including almost all of Dorothy's first scene with the Good Witch in the land of the Munchkins, remained unchanged.

But the script had one devastating central flaw. Dorothy was peripheral to much of the action. The script moves uneasily between the Witch's desire for the ruby slippers and her equally intense desire to conquer the Emerald City. Since the Deadly Poppy Field is missing, Dorothy is occasionally followed by the Witch but is hardly bothered by her until the end of the movie. The Witch seems much more interested in conquering the Emerald City than in doing anything to Dorothy. On page 45, the Witch sends her armies to destroy the Wizard of Oz. She sends "ten thousand men, four thousand wolves, and two hundred winged monkeys." The men are "dressed in Japanese ceremonial armour, the ugly wasp-like death's-head type, which half suggests skeletons." The Witch is attacking the Wizard because she wishes to place her half-witted son, Bulbo,

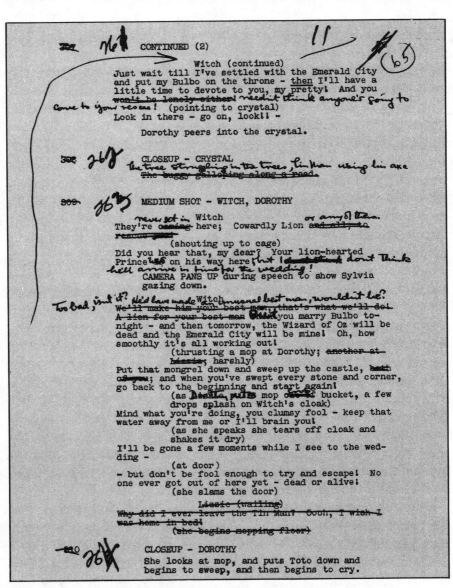

A page from a Noel Langley script mentioning two of his characters, Princess Sylvia and Bulbo (son of the Wicked Witch of the West). Both were later written out.

on the throne. ("There, my darling boy, mother'll kiss it better! Bulbo mustn't cry now; he's going to be King of the Emerald City, and Kings never cry!")

Even when Dorothy *is* involved, it is because of the Witch's plot. The Wizard sends Dorothy to kill the Witch because "the

Emerald City is being threatened." When Dorothy refuses to give up the ruby slippers, the Witch desires to feed her to a real lion. She is saved by the Cowardly Lion, the Tin Woodman, and the Scarecrow, who in the process of rescuing Dorothy get the courage, heart, and brains they have wanted and do not need to have them artificially bestowed by the Wizard. Dorothy melts the Witch because the Witch has hit Toto with her broom. As in Baum's book and the final film, the Wizard intends to fly Dorothy back to Kansas in his balloon. In the final script, the balloon will take off without her. In this script, a woodpecker pecks a hole in the balloon. Then she returns home—as she does in both book and movie—by clicking her magic shoes.

The Kansas framework of Langley's "DO NOT MAKE CHANGES" script consists of Aunt Em and Uncle Henry, Mrs. Gulch and her son Walter, and two farmhands. As in the final film, Mrs. Gulch has a sheriff's order to take the dog, which has bitten her son. She puts Toto in a basket on the back of her bicycle. He escapes and returns to the farm just before the cyclone. When Dorothy—having been hit on the head during the cyclone—wakes up at the end of the movie, she is attended by Dr. Pink, who looks amazingly like the Wizard and who assures her that he will not let the Sheriff take Toto. (By the final script, a great deal of the conversation about the brainlessness of one farmhand who is applying to agricultural college and the heartlessness of the second is reduced to two or three sentences. Walter, too, disappears, while a third farmhand—corresponding to the Cowardly Lion—is added.)

By the time Langley was removed from *The Wizard of Oz*, four other writers had already been assigned to the picture. Herbert Fields worked on the film from April 19 to April 22 but produced nothing. Samuel Hoffenstein worked on the film from May 31 to June 3 and produced a two-page story outline of the Kansas sequence whose main contributions were to rename Dr. Pink "Dr. Miffle" and to rationalize Toto's biting Walter by having Walter burn Toto's ear with a match. Hoffenstein was a poet, a respected writer of light verse, which may explain why someone decided to toss him into the line of succession on a fairy story.

On June 3, Florence Ryerson and Edgar Allan Woolf were officially assigned to *The Wizard of Oz*. The final screen credits on the
film read: "Screenplay by Noel Langley, Florence Ryerson, and
Edgar Allan Woolf. Adaptation by Noel Langley."

Ryerson and Woolf had been working as a team at MGM since
the early thirties. Except for *The Wizard of Oz*, the list of their
films—*Mad Holiday, The Kid from Texas, Moonlight Murder,
Everybody Sing, The Ice Follies of 1939*—evokes no memories.

Woolf lived like a prince. Former MGM story editor Sam Marx
remembers him as "a wild, red-headed homosexual"; writer Allan
Rivkin recalls "a superb cook and a charming man." "Whatever
levity and foolishness there was in *The Wizard of Oz*, Woolf must
have furnished," says Rivkin. "He was a very funny, witty man." To
his friend silent-screen star Carmel Myers, he was "a meticulous,
meticulous man. His kitchen was immaculate. I never kept *my*
kitchen that clean."

Woolf would spend days cooking for his Saturday-night parties.
No producers were allowed. Those parties were limited to the *interesting* people, writers and directors. On Sunday mornings, he would
drive to L. B. Mayer's house at the beach and cook brunch for the
executives and producers whose presence Mayer had commanded.
(Invitations to Sunday brunch were not turned down lightly, although a serious illness in the family or a mother's birthday was an
acceptable excuse.) Woolf had started his career as a sketchwriter for
vaudeville and, at one time, had sixty sketches on the road from
which he was getting royalties. Mayer brought him out to California after being invited to Woolf's house in New York for dinner.

A classic Edgar Allan Woolf story is one that Woolf told on himself. His revue *Mamzelle Champagne* opened on June 25, 1906, at
the Roof Theater of Madison Square Garden, with Woolf's mother
proudly in attendance. Also in the audience was the architect who
had designed Madison Square Garden, Stanford White. Woolf himself was presumably backstage. The revue was dreadful, a fact that
the audience soon made clear enough to discomfort Mrs. Woolf.
Stanford White may or may not have noticed how bad the play was,
since his companion was Evelyn Nesbit, one of the beauties of the
era and, coincidentally, another man's wife. When her husband,

Harry K. Thaw, arrived, pulled out a gun, and killed White, Mrs. Woolf heard the shots, stood up, and shouted, "Oh my God, they've killed my Edgar!"

Woolf died on December 8, 1943. He was walking his dog down the steps of his expensive Spanish house in Beverly Hills when the dog tripped him and he fell. Five days earlier, he had turned in a skit. "Shakespeare in Tap Time," for *Ziegfeld Follies*. The last notation in his MGM file is: "Received no screen credit."

Florence Ryerson is more shadowy. She and her husband wrote detective stories together. She was considered good at writing warm stories for women. Sam Marx remembers that "her first husband ran away with a secretary and went to Tahiti. Four or five months later, the doorbell rang. It was her husband, ready to be forgiven. 'Darling, I've come back.' She slammed the door in his face." Florence Ryerson left MGM and screenwriting in the early forties and now she, too, is dead.

Three days after they were assigned to *The Wizard of Oz*, Ryerson and Woolf turned in four pages of notes. They were distressed by "a total lack of any real emotion" in the Oz sequence. "We feel her [Dorothy's] desperate desire to get home should be dramatized more fully. . . ." "We feel that the menace of the Wicked Witch of the West is not used enough. . . . For instance, we should like to see the witch slinking through the wood whispering to the trees and the trees nodding their heads. . . ." "In at least one place we feel that the straw man should be (apparently) demolished, so that we have, first, the sorrow of thinking him dead, and, second, the joy of seeing him brought back to life again. This is done at least three times in the book. . . ."

Ryerson and Woolf had two further major suggestions. The first was to triple the use of the Wizard character:

. . . If we establish the character in the prologue (perhaps as a quaint old medicine man), then some way should be devised to introduce him in the later sequences.

Perhaps he appears as the gateman who lets them into Oz (wearing green whiskers). As the man who drives the "horse of a different color" (wearing purple whiskers). And again . . . as the guard at the door of the audience chamber (wearing red whiskers). . . . This would give us a chance to use a man like Frank Morgan without having the audience feel cheated because they didn't see enough of him . . . which would certainly happen if he is used only once . . . as in the present script.

Their other major suggestion had the effect of eliminating a Langley scene in which a soldier was deliberately lured to his death. But, luckily, nobody seems to have paid attention to Ryerson's and Woolf's related ideas about the two Wicked Witches.

A small thing . . . but important (we think). The greatest care should be taken to see that nothing actually *dies* in the picture, and nothing is too terrifying for children to see.

This refers particularly to the death of the first Witch (Witch of the East), and, even more so, to the soldier who is deliberately marched to his death and falls into the lion's cage. . . .

Ryerson and Woolf suggested that the Witch of the East should not die when she is hit by Dorothy's house.

If she is turned into something amusing and harmless, or her power is knocked out of her in some way it will avoid an actual death. Perhaps her power really lies in her red slippers. When the house comes down on her she is rendered helpless long enough for Dorothy to pull off the slippers (Dorothy has always wanted red slippers) and once having taken them, the Witch is turned into a nice old lady, a parrot, a white tabby cat, or anything else we choose.

They did not at all object to the melting of the Wicked Witch of the West—an "absurd finish"—but:

We feel that Dorothy's throwing the water on the Witch of the West and melting her is much too casually done. We know it is written that way in the book but it is very flat, even there. The audience should know that water will melt her beforehand, and be hoping Dorothy will find it out. That will give us suspense every time Dorothy touches a pail of water. . . .

Ryerson's and Woolf's first script of June 13, 1938, continued the gentling of Aunt Em. Aunt Em bakes Dorothy a chocolate cake

A page from the Ryerson/Woolf script of July 5, 1938.
Note that at the bottom of the page the description of the image
in the Witch's crystal ball is labeled "trick shot."

Wizard
of Oz

112   FADE IN ON: 60
      WITCH'S CASTLE - INT. TOWER ROOM

      This is the place where the Wicked Witch weaves
      her spells and brews her potions. Just now she
      is compounding something in a cauldron. Beside
      her is a grotesque little figure like a winged
      chimpanzee. This is Nikko, her slave. Nikko
      is unable to speak, but evidently understands
      everything that is said to him, for he fre-
      quently answers in pantomime.

              Witch
              (as she stirs the cauldron)
      ~~Going to the Wizard of Oz, eh? Ha! Well, she'll~~
      ~~never reach there.~~ I want those slippers I must have those slippers

      Nikko dances with evil glee, then hands her
      a flask of some dark liquid. She adds this
      to the cauldron, which causes the other
      ingredients to boil and bubble. Nikko dances
      around, chattering and hissing with fiendish
      glee.

              ~~Witch (in a tense tone,~~
              ~~as she stirs the pot).~~
      ~~I want those slippers.~~
              ~~(she adds another ingredient)~~
      ~~I must have those slippers!~~
      Witch   ~~(she adds another)~~
      Once I get them I'll be more powerful than the
      Great Oz himself!

      She adds a final ingredient. The cauldron
      begins to bubble still more furiously, then
      bursts into flame. The flame spirals upwards,
      making a black smoke which winds its way out
      the window. The Witch.

              ~~Witch (laughing shrilly)~~
      ~~Good! The spell is working!~~
              She lifts a veil and discloses a
              crystal which shows a lovely scene
              at the edge of a wood.
      Witch
      Ha! See that field?
              (Nikko comes and peers into the
              crystal with her)
      They must pass through ~~the field~~ on their way to
      Oz...

113   CLOSER ON CRYSTAL -

      with the Witch's hands visible in the SHOT.
      The grain in the field is waving in the wind.
      Suddenly the black smoke that we saw float out
      the window seems to cross the grain field.

TRICK SHOT

TRICK SHT

to make up for the loss of Toto and tells Mrs. Gulch—as she will in the final script—"Almira Gulch . . . for twenty-three years I've been dying to tell you what I thought of you . . . and now . . . well—being a Christian woman—I can't say it!"

Ryerson's and Woolf's first script also added the Wizard—as Professor Marvel—to Kansas. In another attempt to tie Oz with Kansas, the Professor has a caged lion who is "worse scared than you are." (The lion disappears by the final script in favor of the third farmhand.) The Professor also has a Dwarf. The Dwarf's job is simply to listen so the Professor can talk. (In another Ryerson-Woolf version, the Professor has a daughter who listens instead.) Similarly, in Langley's scripts, the Wicked Witch has had a gorilla, a lion, a Captain, and—of course—her son, Bulbo. In the less complicated final script, the Professor simply talks to his horse and the Witch to the leader of the Winged Monkeys.

But Ryerson's and Woolf's first script still contained echoes of Langley. It was not until their second script, of July 5, 1938, that they eliminated the Wicked Witch's son and began to replace large sections of Langley's dialogue with their own.

Dorothy's first conversation with the Good Witch as written by Langley is as follows:

GLINDA: Are you a good witch—or a bad witch?

DOROTHY: Who, me? Why—my goodness—I'm not a witch at all! I'm Dorothy Gale from Kansas.

GLINDA (*pointing to Toto*): Then is *that* the witch?

Ryerson and Woolf replaced that dialogue with this one:

DOROTHY (*trying to describe Kansas*): Why—it's a state.

GLINDA: A state of mind?

DOROTHY: No—a state—in a big country.

GLINDA (*with a frown*): A *civilized* country?

DOROTHY: Yes. Yes—of course.

GLINDA (*sympathetically*): Poor dear child. There was some talk a couple of centuries ago about civilizing Oz but we put a stop to it quickly I can tell you! Never mind—nobody's going to make you go back.

When Ryerson and Woolf signed off the picture on July 27 and Langley signed back on, he went through the script, crossing out as much of their dialogue as he could and replacing his own. That particular section reads in the shooting script exactly as it did in Langley's final script of May 14. But much of what they had done he could not undo.

On July 28, 1938, when the presumably final script, labeled Ryerson-Woolf-Langley, was typed up and distributed, Ryerson's and Woolf's most obvious contribution was the landing of the Wizard of Oz in the Kansas sequence as Professor Marvel. More subtly and more importantly, they focused their story almost entirely on Dorothy's desire to return home and the Witch's desire for the red shoes. It is their script that introduces the blatant "There's no place like home" motif of the final film. In order to return to Kansas, Dorothy must click the red slippers together and say three times, "There's no place like home!" (An undated stream-of-consciousness memo from Arthur Freed to Ryerson and Woolf implies that it was Freed's idea to have Dorothy literally say "There's no place like home" three times in order to be allowed to go back to Kansas.) And Dorothy's desire to get home is emphasized in such sentimental platitudes as, "Isn't it funny—this is the place I was looking for all the time! And I never knew it! This is the most beautiful place in the whole wide world!"

The script that Ryerson and Woolf turned in on July 27 still had two major plot problems. The first was the Deadly Poppy Field. The second was the ending. The problems that Langley, Ryerson, and Woolf kept having with the Deadly Poppy Field lay in Frank Baum's solution to its danger. In Baum, thousands of field mice pulled the sleeping Lion out of the field. Even for MGM's vast technical resources, such a solution was not possible. Langley simply eliminated the Poppy Field from his final script. The rest of the scripts tried to solve the problem by having one character or another rescue the rest.

[51]

In Baum's book, as in the final shooting script, the Scarecrow and Tin Woodman are not overcome by the scent of the poppies since they are not *meat* characters who breathe. But how could the Scarecrow and Tin Man drag the Lion out of the field? In Ryerson's and Woolf's script of July 5, the other characters pull Dorothy from the field, thinking that she is dead. Shades of *Snow White* and *Sleeping Beauty*, the Tin Man's tears wake her up. Ryerson's and Woolf's final script ignores the problem of breath. Everyone is overcome by the scent of the flowers except the Lion, who rescues all his friends. (In the final film, the travelers are rescued by Glinda, who smothers the scent of the poppies with a snowfall. Baum had turned *The Wizard of Oz* into a play in 1902, and the snowfall is the only device in the movie taken from that play. In 1974, the Broadway musical *The Wiz* simply dressed actors in mouse costumes and had them pick up Dorothy and her friends who had overdosed on the poppies.)

Ryerson and Woolf had dropped all of Langley's nonsense about the Wicked Witch attacking the Emerald City. Their story stayed clean, uncluttered, and relatively simple until the point when Dorothy melted the Wicked Witch. (It was in this script that Dorothy first melted the Witch by accident because the Witch was attempting to set fire to the Scarecrow, a splendid idea that preserved Dorothy's purity of motive.) Then their plot fell apart.

Not only Dorothy but the whole Emerald City discovers that the Wizard is a humbug. Everyone is angry at being tricked. The Wizard tries to placate the angry citizens with a cheap magic act.

oz: . . . You will see that I have nothing up either sleeve. One —two—three—presto! (*He changes his handkerchief into a string of flags.*) Flags of all nations!

He changes the flags into a bunch of flowers, does card tricks with the Scarecrow, and is forced to flee along with Dorothy and her friends.

ONE OF THE CROWD: She's in with him!

SECOND: Maybe they're *all* in with him!

THIRD: How do we *know* she killed the Witch?

FOURTH: Maybe *she's* the Witch herself?

They escape from the Emerald City in the Wizard's balloon, which is then destroyed by Langley's woodpecker. They are saved by Glinda "directing the whole miniature Munchkin Fire Department in a rescue act. All the little Munchkins are holding a huge net and looking up toward the sky." Just before Dorothy leaves Oz, the Scarecrow, Tin Woodman, and Lion realize they have had brains, heart, and courage all the time.

In mid-June, Noel Langley learned that Ryerson and Woolf had been assigned to rewrite his script. He was angry—and astonished, since "everybody had liked my script. That means Freed and Harold

Scripts were revised almost daily—memos like this identified the latest rewrites.

M 72

METRO-GOLDWYN-MAYER PICTURES
CULVER-CITY CALIFORNIA

INTER-OFFICE COMMUNICATION

To MISS E. FARRELL

Subject ~~"BABES IN ARMS"~~ Wizard of Oz – Noel Langley

From ARTHUR FREED Date 10/8/38

Herewith ~~"BABES IN ARMS"~~ "Wizard of Oz" script – You will note there are quite a few changes throughout the script and also additions. Mr. Freed would like all changes mimeographed on yellow paper -- Don't put them in script but send them separately -- One copy to be on Mr. LeRoy's desk and one to Mr. Cannon's desk -- also one to Mr. Freed at 5:30 -- and two extra copies to me.

THANKS.

CECIL ROTH

Arlen and Yip Harburg. And suddenly I find there's another bunch of writers on it."

Langley, perhaps not irrationally, felt both isolated and besieged. He considered LeRoy "a straw boss, a mediocre non-talent." He liked Freed and he felt that Freed liked him. But he also thought of Freed as "a diplomat," skilled in the politics of power at MGM. If LeRoy should insist on the Ryerson-Woolf script, Langley was sure that Freed would not stand behind him.

It was lyricist Yip Harburg who quieted Langley down and kept him from exploding in mid-June. Langley recalls Harburg as "a cuddly chipmunk, a very, very charming man who worried about the worries of the world, but took himself lightly." Harburg persuaded Langley to "wait and see what the thing looks like in the end." Unhappy but quiet, Langley reported to work on *Listen, Darling*.

The end was reached on July 28. "I read their script. Then I had a terrific bust-up with LeRoy. I stormed out of his office and went to [MGM story editor] Eddie Knopf and told him to take my name off the script. That was essentially saying they could blacklist me or boot me out of the business. I refused to come to the studio. And I refused to talk to LeRoy. When he called me at home, I wouldn't answer the phone."

Rather surprisingly, Langley's tantrum brought results. He and his script were the beneficiaries of two lucky accidents. First, songwriter Harburg preferred Langley's version. And Arthur Freed both respected and trusted Harburg, whom he had personally picked to write the score for *The Wizard of Oz*. Second, according to Langley, "the anti-LeRoy executives were using the whole fuss to show what a rump LeRoy was if he couldn't even bring a twenty-six-year-old scriptwriter to heel."

As Langley remembers it, "In the end, Harburg became so militant that Freed supported him. If it hadn't been for Harburg going to Freed and blowing his top . . ." He doesn't complete the sentence. But Harburg was in Freed's office when Freed picked up the phone to call Langley.

"He said I was making it tough for LeRoy by not answering his phone calls. I think I laughed. Then he said, 'Yip is here. At least come over to the studio and talk to us. You don't have to see LeRoy.

47   LONG SHOT (PROCESS)

The house comes spiraling down through the
air toward CAMERA WHICH IS TILTED UP TOWARDS
IT. Eventually it hits CAMERA and blocks
out the SCREEN.

DISSOLVE TO:

48   CLOSEUP - DOROTHY -

with her eyes tight shut. Toto has his
head tucked well under her arm. Slowly
she opens her eyes.

49   FULL SHOT - ROOM

All four legs of the bed are spread-eagled on
the floor and the furniture has been jerked
out of place. A chair lies on its back. There
is dead silence on the SOUND TRACK as Dorothy
gets off the bed and tiptoes to the door.

WIPE TO:

50   MED. SHOT - FRONT DOOR - INTERIOR

As Dorothy opens the door slowly and peers
out a blaze of color greets her. THIS IS
THE FIRST TIME WE SEE TECHNICOLOR. The
Kansas scenes were all grey washes. The
inside of the door is black and grey to
give more contrast. When the door is open
the country is shown - a picture in bright
greens and blues.

As Dorothy goes through the door, the CAMERA
TRUCKS after her and then, over her shoulder,
to a FULL SHOT of the Munchkin Country. It is
comprised of sweeping hills and valleys, and
dips and waves in the ground; the grass is
spangled with daisies, buttercups and red
poppies; flowers grow everywhere, three or
four times life-size so that hollyhocks
stand twenty feet in the air. The sky is
bright blue with little white clouds; the
trees all have blossoms on them, suggesting
a sort of permanent Spring - apple, cherry,
peach and pear trees are everywhere, and a
little stream runs near with huge lily-pads
on it; the lilies are the size of barrel-tops.

Feeding the stream is an exquisite fountain
with water of all colors of the rainbow.
Surrounding the fountain are three or four
steps and back of it is Munchkinland's Civic
Center, a quaint little piece of architecture.
This is all close to the house in which
Dorothy fell from Kansas.

CONTINUED:

The "almost final" script of October 7, 1938, was a blend
of Ryerson, Woolf, and Langley.

10/8

                              Witch (snarling at her)
          Keep out of this! I'm here for vengeance! ~~and vengeance it shall be!~~
                              (to Dorothy)
          So it was you, was it? You killed her, did you?
                              (She is advancing on Dorothy)

                              Dorothy (fearfully)
          No - it was an accident - I didn't mean to kill
          anybody; really I didn't.

                              Witch
          You didn't, eh? Accident, eh? Well, I can cause
          accidents too, my little pretty, and this is how
          I do it -
                              (she raises her hand in the air)

          You're   Glinda (quickly)
          ~~Aren't you~~ forgetting the ruby slippers!

          The Witch stops dead, and then turns quickly.

                              Witch (hurriedly)
          The slippers - yes, the slippers! *and is just about to snatch*
                              (she hurries to the house *and then right up the slippers*
          I've been robbed! ~~a hoarse scream~~ They're gone! (~~She screams and~~ *vanish from under her hand.*
                              (whirling round on Glinda)
          ~~The ruby slippers!~~ What have you done with ~~them? them?~~
          Give them back to me or I'll --
          Glinda: ~~It's too late!~~ *there they are & there they'll*
          Glinda points her wand at Dorothy's feet. *Stay!*
          Dorothy looks down.

          68A   CLOSEUP - DOROTHY'S FEET -

                              in the ruby slippers.

          69 OUT

          70-71   CLOSE SHOT - WITCH, GLINDA, DOROTHY
                                           to both Glinda and Dorothy,
          Thief! Thief! Witch (in a frenzy)
          my slippers! ~~What did you do? You couldn't! You didn't!~~ Give me *back*
          ~~those shoes - please~~ ~~please give me those shoes!~~
          ~~They're mine by right!~~ I'm the only one who knows
          how to use them -- they're no use to you! -- Give
          them back to me -- give them back!

                              Glinda (to Dorothy)
          You keep tight inside of them -- their magic must
          be very powerful or she wouldn't want them so badly!

                                                      CONTINUED:

*The changes on this page of the October 7 script were made a day later.
Although the script was labeled "final complete," two days after that,
several scenes were rewritten by John Lee Mahin when the picture was
already in production. Mahin continued to work on the script for
two and a half months while Victor Fleming was directing.*

You just have to come to us personally. You know that we have never been against your script. We're on your side.' "

Langley went. Challenged by Freed to explain exactly what he considered to be "illiterate mush" in the Ryerson-Woolf script, he picked up a copy of the script and took it apart page by page. He was particularly vitriolic at a sequence in which the Wicked Witch created a magic rainbow with an invisible hole in the middle for Dorothy to fall through. "I said, 'What the hell does *this* do? You know, it's going to give you an extra budget cost of about $120,000 just to do that one shot.' And Freed picked up the phone to the set people and asked them for an estimate. And it was exactly $120,000. And I think that impressed him more than anything else I could have said, that I guessed exactly the extra price of the rainbow."

Ryerson and Woolf had signed off *The Wizard of Oz* on July 27. On July 30, Noel Langley was reassigned to the picture. On August 1, the film's master sheet lists "additions and changes as per script of 5/14/38."

"We replaced my script," Noel Langley says.

That is not quite accurate. The clutter of the Wicked Witch's attempt to conquer the Emerald City never re-entered the script. And although Langley removed "every goddamn thing I could," he was forced to leave in the Professor Marvel sequence. "Everybody thought it was charming." Langley was also required to keep his hands off one other Ryerson-Woolf concept. LeRoy and Freed, both sentimental men, delighted in the uplifting thought that true happiness can only be found at home.

"The picture didn't need that 'Home, Sweet Home,' 'God Bless Our Home' tripe," says Yip Harburg. Yip Harburg's only screen credit on *The Wizard of Oz* was "Lyrics: E. Y. Harburg." But the final shooting script is actually his blend of Ryerson, Woolf, and Langley. "I liked a lot of things Langley had done and threw the other stuff out. I clarified the story. I edited the whole thing and brought back Langley's story, which was simpler. And I added my own."

The major thing Harburg added was the scene in which the Wizard gives the Scarecrow a diploma, the Tin Woodman a testimonial, and the Cowardly Lion a medal. In Baum, the Wizard had provided the Scarecrow with a head full of pins and needles, the Tin Man with a chest full of red silk heart, and the Lion with a drink that had only to be swallowed to turn to courage. In most of the scripts, the Scarecrow, Tin Man, and Lion had discovered they had *always* possessed the brains, heart, and courage for which they had been searching. Harburg "devised the satiric and cynical idea of the Wizard handing out symbols because I was so aware of our lives being the images of things rather than the things themselves."

There were still three more writers who would be assigned to *The Wizard of Oz*. Jack Mintz worked from August 3 to September 2 and turned in four pages of suggestions. Mintz was not a writer but a gag writer, and he was called in to suggest specific jokes for the Scarecrow, Tin Woodman, and Cowardly Lion. Sid Silvers was assigned to the film from October 17 to October 22, the week after it started production. He was to hang around the set and handle any rough spots for director Richard Thorpe. But he left when Thorpe was fired.

The final writer—and the one who spent almost as long a time as did Langley on the picture—was John Lee Mahin. Mahin was assigned to *The Wizard of Oz* from October 27, 1938, to January 10, 1939. Mahin was a close friend of Victor Fleming, and his assignment coincides with Fleming's arrival as director of the film.

Although there is ample evidence of scenes that Mahin polished —and, indeed, he is responsible for the opening scene in the picture— he refused to take any credit. "I thought the script was ninety-two percent great. Fleming felt it was a little bare in spots; and if it didn't play, he wanted me to be there to kind of help fix it up. A lot of the time my changes weren't even written down. I told them to Fleming, and the script girl simply made notes."

Noel Langley's connection with *The Wizard of Oz* was severed on October 31, 1938, when he was dismissed from the film for the second time. He could only wait—perhaps wistfully—for the finished movie to open in a theater.

In the 1930's, writers were never invited to the previews or premieres of their pictures. Noel Langley saw *The Wizard of Oz* "in a cinema on Hollywood Boulevard at noon. And I sat and cried like a bloody child. I thought, 'This is a year of my life.' I loathed the picture. I thought it was dead. I thought it missed the boat all the way around. I had to wait for my tears to clear before I went out of the theater."

THE BRAINS, THE HEART, THE NERVE, AND THE MUSIC

Musical adaptation by Herbert Stothart

Lyrics by E. Y. Harburg

Music by Harold Arlen

Orchestral and vocal arrangements by George Bassman,
Murray Cutter,
Paul Marquardt, Ken Darby

Musical numbers staged by Bobby Connolly

When *The Wizard of Oz* won Herbert Stothart an Academy Award for Best Original Score, the award was really aimed at the forty minutes of songs—"Over the Rainbow," "If I Were King of the Forest," "Ding Dong, the Witch Is Dead," "We're Off to See the Wizard," "If I Only Had a Brain"—all written by Harold Arlen and E. Y. Harburg. That Stothart, who merely composed the incidental music that bridged the songs, picked up the gold statue was typical of the macabre jokes Hollywood played on songwriters during the 1930's. (Under today's Academy rules, the award would have gone to Arlen, Harburg, and Stothart.)

Nearly all the great American songwriters came west during the 1930's. Some stayed in Hollywood for a picture or two. Some, like Jerome Kern, stayed for half the decade. No matter how long or short a time they stayed, nearly all were treated badly by Hollywood —except when it came to money.

The songwriter was hired to write songs that were then used, discarded, or lost according to the whim of the picture's producer. The first time composer Harry Warren played more than one song for a producer, he learned "never to do it again. I thought I was playing part of a score. The man said, 'Well, I think I'll take that first song.' " Of the five songs Harold Arlen wrote for his first film, *Let's Fall in Love* (1933), two were thrown out, two were a meaningful part of the film, and one was used for background music. When Cole Porter's Broadway show *Anything Goes* came to the screen in 1936, it contained only six of Porter's original songs. It had no new Porter songs, but it did have six new songs by such different composers as Hoagy Carmichael, Frederick Hollander, and Richard Whiting. Still, that gave Porter a slightly better batting average than Rodgers and Hart, whose *On Your Toes* (1939) lost all of its songs.

Harry Warren ("Chattanooga Choo-Choo," "Shuffle Off to Buffalo," "Kalamazoo," and seventy movie musicals) once summed up the position of the songwriter in Hollywood with the following anecdote. Lew Brown was summoned to the office of a musically illiterate producer and told how to rewrite his songs. Brown protested that he had written fifteen Broadway shows, to which the producer responded that Brown was still wrong. When Brown finally asked, "How do you know I'm wrong?" the producer blandly replied, "Because you're standing in front of this desk and I'm sitting behind it."

"Hollywood was impressed with songwriters for a minute and a half," said lyricist Johnny Mercer shortly before his death in 1976. "Then the producers decided that songwriters didn't add any money to the box office. The only one of us they ever took seriously was Irving Berlin, and that was because he took himself so seriously. They respected Jerome Kern and Oscar Hammerstein but never paid them too much mind. And they were dazzled by Cole Porter because of his general svelteness and suaveness and because he had a lot more money than they did. A fellow like Harry Warren who made them rich never got any acclaim, not half as much as he deserved."

On Broadway, composers had stayed with their scores through out-of-town tryouts and endless revisions. In Hollywood, they were expected to turn in their songs and pick up their paychecks. If they were curious about how well their songs would be arranged, orchestrated, and used, they could buy a ticket to see the finished film.

Arthur Freed (second from right) at a gathering of songwriters, including Jerome Kern (far left), Irving Berlin (second from left), and Burton Lane (far right). Oz was Freed's first musical. He became the man most responsible for changing the entire nature of the Hollywood musical. It was essentially his idea to blend song and dance with the plot so that all elements fit together. The songs in The Wizard of Oz *not only moved the story forward but helped define the characters.*

*E. Y. ("Yip") Harburg (seated), the lyricist for Oz, and
Harold Arlen (standing), the composer, 1937.*

The songwriter was not the only artist to be handed a stacked deck by the Hollywood dealers, but the case of the songwriters differed subtly from that of .most of the scriptwriters. The composers and lyricists who came west to write the first decade of musical films had enormous artistic and *social* prestige in New York. They expected to be treated well, and their first exposure to Hollywood was almost always painful.

"George was a king in New York," says composer John Green of George Gershwin. "In Hollywood, he was invited to homes where there were no pianos or to homes with pianos where people wouldn't ask him to play or, even if he did play, he was not idolized." Harold Arlen, reminiscing in 1962, made the same point with an exactly opposite illustration. "We had no prestige. We were considered just songwriters. George Gershwin, too. He'd be invited to a party and be expected to sit down and play like a hired entertainer. George liked to play, but he resented being expected to." Gershwin's unhappiness in Hollywood was so great that the symptoms of his fatal brain tumor were first diagnosed as psychological depression.

By the time they wrote *The Wizard of Oz*, Arlen and Harburg had had ample experience with the Hollywood system. Arlen's first painful experience on *Let's Fall in Love* had been followed, in 1934, by *Strike Me Pink* for Eddie Cantor. Harburg had, in 1933, done the lyrics (with Jay Gorney as composer) for a now luckily forgotten film, *Moonlight and Pretzels*. He had spent most of 1934 as a producer-writer at Universal, developing a script from his successful song "April in Paris." The film was never made. When the script was nearly completed, the studio was tottering on the verge of bankruptcy. In 1935, Arlen shared Harburg's rented house in Beverly Hills while they worked at Warner Bros. on *The Singing Kid*. That Al Jolson musical was followed by two more Warner Bros. films on which they collaborated: *Stage Struck* and *Gold Diggers of 1937*, both for Dick Powell and Joan Blondell.

Harburg and Arlen then fled back to New York in the summer of 1937. The Shuberts had agreed to back Harburg's idea for an anti-war musical comedy. The Shuberts kept their promise, and the musical—*Hooray for What!*, starring Ed Wynn as the accidental inventor of a poison gas—made it to Broadway, opening December 1, 1937.

The show was a success, "a great American satire on war" according to one review, and ran for six months. Harburg and Arlen stayed around New York for a while after the show opened and then drifted back to Hollywood in the spring of 1938.

They probably expected nothing more from Hollywood than they had been given before: a chance to write moderately distinguished songs ("You're the Cure for What Ails Me," "I Love to Sing-a," "Fancy Meeting You") for totally undistinguished films. But there was hardly any alternative. The Broadway market for musical revues had been squeezed by the Depression. In Hollywood's lusher pastures, the money was good and the sunshine was even better. (Arlen and Harburg, as a matter of fact, wrote most of the score of *The Wizard of Oz* at night so that Arlen could spend his days playing golf and Harburg could spend his playing tennis.) What neither of them ever expected was to be offered an almost unique opportunity: the chance to write one of the four films of the 1930's in which the music was an integral part of the plot and in which the songwriter was an integral part of the creative process.

Between 1927, when *The Jazz Singer* became both the first talking film and the first musical film, and 1943, when Arthur Freed produced *Cabin in the Sky*, the vast majority of musicals were of the variety best described as "backstage." Not that all the stages where the elephantine, show-stopping dance numbers took place were on 42nd Street. Whether the grand, over-choreographed finale took place in a Broadway theater, a high-school auditorium, a college gymnasium, or a farmer's barn depended on whether the spider-web plot centered on the chorus girl who makes good or the local girl raising money to pay off the mortgage. (In 1974 MGM's *That's Entertainment* underlined the prevalence of such films by splicing together the fatal moment in several Mickey Rooney–Judy Garland musicals when one of them said to the other, "I've got it! Let's get the kids together and put on a show.") At least twenty or thirty movies dispensed with even that much plot, settling for a brief introduction of the characters followed by seventy minutes of show-stopping numbers.

Some of the movies had good songs. Some had brilliant dances. But in almost every case the songs and dances were like raisins in a rice pudding. They could be pulled out without affecting either the plot or the meaning of the film. Even the Fred Astaire–Ginger Rogers movies were based on silly plots that allowed everything to come to a halt while Astaire and Rogers danced. *Follow the Fleet* was about a dancer who joined the Navy when he was jilted and then returned to his old vaudeville partner for the grand finale. And even *Variety* complained that *Top Hat*—about a carefree American dancer meeting and pursuing a girl around London while the girl mistakenly assumes he is married—was almost identical in setting, plot, and characters to *The Gay Divorcee.*

Only three times in the 1930's had a director, a composer, and a lyricist blended songs, dances, and story so that the elements were almost indissoluble. The first time was in Rouben Mamoulian's *Love Me Tonight* (1932), starring Maurice Chevalier and Jeanette Mac-Donald, with a score by Richard Rodgers and Lorenz Hart. Producer-director Mamoulian worked with Rodgers and Hart on a score before he had a script. "Only after the score and all the rhymed dialogue were completed did we put in the dramatic scenes," says Mamoulian. "Music formed the whole structure. Dialogue took second place."

The following year came Lewis Milestone's *Hallelujah, I'm a Bum*, also with a score by Rodgers and Hart. *Love Me Tonight* had been financially and critically successful. *Hallelujah, I'm a Bum* was something of a failure, both because its star, Al Jolson, was no longer interesting to the public and because its story of a playboy mayor of New York with a weakness for gambling and his counter-part, the unofficial mayor of Central Park's hobos, was too indigesti-ble a blend. But both films flowed from music to non-music and back again as coherent wholes; and in both, Hart wrote rhymed dialogue to ease the transitions.

EMILE (*admiring the new suit the tailor has made for his wedding*): It's beautiful . . .
It's a work of art

MAURICE (*the tailor*): The tailor's art . . . for your sweetheart.

EMILE: It's like poetry in a book.
How beautiful I look.

MAURICE: The love song of the needle
Is united with the thread.
The romance of the season . . .

EMILE: So clear that I could wed.

MAURICE: Isn't it romantic?

That section of rhymed dialogue in *Love Me Tonight* was simply a way of leading into Maurice Chevalier singing "Isn't It Romantic?" In *The Wizard of Oz*, Harburg would go Hart one better and write an entire ten-minute scene—Dorothy's welcome to Oz by the Munchkins—in rhyme.

Fifty backstage musicals after *Love Me Tonight* and *Hallelujah, I'm a Bum* came Mamoulian's *High, Wide and Handsome* in 1937. This film, starring Irene Dunne, was an attempt to integrate music into an even more serious and dramatic story—a saga of the Pennsylvania oil country in 1859 that focused on a war between the railroads and men who want to build an oil pipeline. The script and lyrics were by Oscar Hammerstein 2nd; the music, by Jerome Kern. Ten years earlier, Hammerstein had experimented with Kern in trying to make something more than a Broadway musical out of Edna Ferber's *Show Boat*. Six years later, he and Richard Rodgers—with Rouben Mamoulian as director—succeeded in creating a new genre with *Oklahoma!* The success of *Oklahoma!*—the six years it ran on Broadway, the $45 million it grossed in America—helped force the restructuring of the screen musical. But *High, Wide and Handsome*, like *Love Me Tonight* and *Hallelujah, I'm a Bum* before it, had little effect on Hollywood's idea of what a musical film should be.

"There is a kind of built-in resistance to new things with human beings," says Mamoulian. "For the last two weeks before we opened *Oklahoma!* on Broadway, no one even spoke to me. Rodgers thought I was destroying his music. He couldn't accept the singers having their backs to the audience. Everyone wanted me to restage it as an ordinary musical comedy. I refused, and they didn't even invite me to the opening-night party. Besides, it's tremendously difficult to integrate. It's really easy to tell a story and toss in a song or dance here or there."

Arthur Freed and Judy Garland on the set of Little Nellie Kelly, *1940.*
Judy Garland was fifteen when she was cast as Dorothy;
she had been at MGM for two and a half years and had made six movies.
Oz was her first movie with Freed; over the next ten years
they worked together on thirteen more.

Successful musicals—which *High, Wide and Handsome* was not
—were star vehicles, not coherent stories; and every studio had its
own team of stars. At Warner Bros., it was Dick Powell and Ruby
Keeler, or Dick Powell and Joan Blondell, in gargantuan cream puffs
choreographed by Busby Berkeley. RKO had Fred Astaire and Ginger
Rogers, modern and brittle and striking sparks off each other. And
at MGM, it was Jeanette MacDonald and Nelson Eddy, united
against fate as they sang their way through nearly every classic
operetta from *Naughty Marietta*, which Victor Herbert wrote in
1910, to *The New Moon*, which Sigmund Romberg wrote in 1928.
In no sense were the personalities of Powell and Keeler, Rogers and
Astaire, MacDonald and Eddy ever subordinated to the demands of
a plot. A musical was, almost by definition, a film which stopped
every ten minutes so that the audience could watch/listen to the
stars dance or sing, or both.

Arthur Freed changed all that. Even Mamoulian, a strong director who most often considered his producers unavoidable evils,
conceded that "Arthur Freed was a superb producer, a man who absolutely worshiped talent. With talent, he was like a man who can
look at a diamond and say, 'This isn't a piece of glass.'" In Freed's
films, once he got his sea legs as a producer, stars would be used as
actors and actresses, blending into stories that could be most effectively told with the use of music. *The Harvey Girls*, for example, was
intended as a straight dramatic film. When Bernie Hyman, the producer who had bought the story, died, Freed decided to make it as a

Arthur Freed with Vincente Minnelli, a director he worked with frequently.

musical. (The films that Freed made between *Cabin in the Sky* in 1943 and *It's Always Fair Weather* in 1955 are thought to form a golden age of screen musicals. His concept, indeed, remained consistent. His films bloomed with color and with the shockingly masculine choreography of Gene Kelly, who often starred in them. But most of the plots were drearily alike, featuring a brash Kelly getting the girl loved by sweet and timid Frank Sinatra, with a second girl appearing by the final reel to settle into Sinatra's arms for the fade-out. And many of the films were speckled with a most unpleasant sentimentality. *Meet Me in St. Louis* is always referred to as the *perfect* musical, yet it is almost embarrassing to watch today with its wholesome sentimentality capped by a tooth-decaying performance by seven-year-old Margaret O'Brien.)

It was Arthur Freed who hired Arlen and Harburg. On *The Wizard of Oz*, Freed was simply Mervyn LeRoy's assistant. However, LeRoy, who had directed forty pictures of which only three were musicals, had the good sense to leave the musical choices to Freed and, in most cases, to rubber-stamp Freed's decisions.

If *The Wizard of Oz* had been made a year or two earlier, Freed might himself have written the lyrics. Saul Chaplin (one of the dozens of composers, arrangers, dancers, choreographers, designers, directors, and actors—including Gene Kelly, Stanley Donen, Vincente Minnelli, Kay Thompson, Lennie Hayton—that Freed brought to MGM during the 1940's) spoke warmly in 1976 of "the fey and wonderful lyrics" Freed wrote for "The Wedding of the Painted Doll" nearly a decade before *The Wizard of Oz*. That song appeared in the first picture he and Nacio Herb Brown had written for the studio, *Broadway Melody* (1929), which was the second film (and the first musical) to win an Academy Award as Best Picture. But by 1938 Freed no longer thought of himself as a songwriter. In 1937 he was making $1,500 a week; in 1938 his salary was $300: he wanted to be a producer so badly that he bought from L. B. Mayer the right to an apprenticeship by taking a salary cut of $1,200. "By that time, nothing could have induced Arthur to dilute his attempt to be a producer by writing songs," according to John Green, another Freed protégé, who became both artistic and business head of the MGM Music Department in 1949. (After he was established as a producer, Freed did write lyrics for several of his films, including *Yolanda and the Thief* and *Ziegfeld Follies*.)

If Freed no longer considered himself a songwriter, he definitely still considered himself a song connoisseur. He had an extraordinary knowledge and memory of the musical theater. He could almost always recall the tune and lyrics of some piece of incidental music from Act II, Scene 2 of a 1917 Jerome Kern play. Freed never really considered any other songwriters for *The Wizard of Oz,* although he toyed with the idea of hiring Kern. His choice of Arlen and Harburg was instinctive, based primarily on one song they had written—"In the Shade of the New Apple Tree," part of *Hooray for What!* Designed to be sung as an old English madrigal, the song's lyrics went:

> Underneath that shady apple tree
> Things are not what they used to be.
> You don't have to tussle
> Or wrestle with a bustle
> In the shade of the new apple tree.
>
> Though you bob your hair
> And show your knee,
> You are still as sweet
> And quaint to me.
> Your dress may be flipper
> But there's romance in a zipper
> In the shade of the new apple tree.
>
> Granny shied when Granddaddy spoke about that Sacred Flame.
> She blushed through her hoops and her corsets and her skirts
> But he got there just the same.
>
> Hey nonny-o, nonny-o
> No, we haven't advanced, you see.
> In the shade of the new apple tree.*

Freed would tell Harburg and Arlen more than once that the tone of "In the Shade of the New Apple Tree" was the tone he wanted for *The Wizard of Oz.*

* Copyright © 1938 by Chappell & Co., Inc. Copyright renewed. International Copyright Secured. All Rights Reserved. Used by permission.

When Freed asked Harburg to drop by MGM to discuss a project in which Freed was interested, the two men had never met. They knew each other only through their songs. Ideologically, intellectually, and temperamentally, they were complete opposites. Freed was a superpatriot; Harburg was blacklisted through the McCarthy years. Freed was a good businessman, an expert at studio politics; Harburg has been described by half a dozen of the people who knew him as "fey." "Yip was out of *Alice in Wonderland*," says Noel Langley. "He wasn't here. He didn't understand about people on this planet. He thought he should correct it so we could all lead ideal lives." Freed was almost painfully inarticulate. Harburg was both an intellectual and a wit.

Thirty-eight years later, Freed remained "an enigma" to Harburg. "He knew how to work the angles, how to get things done, how to put things together so they made sense economically. Politically, he was a flag-waver of the first order. He was a reactionary and he detested everything I stood for. But that didn't stop him from respecting me artistically. After I was blacklisted, he tried like hell to get me back." Nor did Harburg ever come to understand Freed's artistic sensibilities. "He appreciated a good idea, but he was just as in love with the crud. He loved sentimentality, loved the drippy lachrymose situation. He was really a very insensitive man. Except in one area. He had a real feeling for all musical things. Underneath that crude, brusque exterior was that lovely sensitive feeling for music and lyrics."

Harburg's relationship with Freed was punctuated by violent quarrels over politics. Harburg says his parents "had forecast the future in my name. *Yipsel* is a Jewish nickname of endearment. It also stood as an abbreviation for Young People's Socialist League. I was never a member of the Communist Party. I was a Socialist. I was involved in China. And I aided the Loyalist cause in Spain. But anybody who was anti-Fascist was considered pro-Communist."

Freed found Harburg's political ideas insufferable. But he had not hired Harburg's vision of an ideal world. Despite the fact that neither man ever really understood the other, they worked well together, tied by an almost grudging mutual respect. "Arthur had sensed my love of whimsey. And he was right. He told me to read *The Wizard of Oz*. I read the book and loved it. It was my sort of thing."

Freed also respected Harold Arlen's music. Unlike most popular songwriters, Arlen rarely wrote songs that lasted the standard thirty-two bars. As often as not, he would write what songwriters called tapeworms, songs whose melodic lines were long and intricate. One of his most famous screen songs, "The Man That Got Away," from Judy Garland's 1954 *A Star Is Born*, is sixty-two bars long. "One for My Baby" from *The Sky's the Limit* (1943) has a forty-eight-bar melody. "Blues in the Night" is an authentic blues song with a twelve-bar form, and "Stormy Weather" has no repetition of any musical phrase in the entire first statement of the melody. (It was the analytical George Gershwin who pointed out that fact to the less analytical Arlen.) Both Johnny Mercer, who wrote with Arlen through the 1940's, and Harburg named Arlen as one of the two truly original American songwriters (the other being George Gershwin). "All the good songwriters had very high standards," said Mercer. "But with Harold there was something more. He liked to be original. He tried very hard to have his melodies not sound like anyone else's. At first it was very difficult to work with him. But I got used to it."

Harburg and Arlen were hired on May 19, 1938, on a "flat deal," a fourteen-week contract. They were paid $25,000, with one-third advanced against royalties. When they signed the contracts and were given the keys to a bungalow at MGM, the script was four months away from its final form, and the only actor already cast was Judy Garland. Instead of being attached to the film after the fact, they were, so to speak, in on the ground floor with a chance to help design the building that was rising around them.

Arlen and Harburg wrote an integrated score in which every song commented on character or advanced the plot. The Freed Unit at MGM in later years polished and perfected the integrated musical form. But Harburg does not remember that Freed ever asked him for an integrated score "although he accepted the integrated concept quickly and was very encouraging." Harburg was well aware of *Love Me Tonight, High, Wide and Handsome,* and earlier attempts in the same direction by Ernst Lubitsch. "The trouble was, those stories didn't give the lyric writer enough leeway. This story did."

They first tackled what Arlen called "the lemon-drop songs." Those were the light songs, emotionally undemanding and generally easy to write: "Ding Dong! The Witch Is Dead," "We're Off to See the Wizard," "The Merry Old Land of Oz." Nor was the song that set up the characters of the Scarecrow, the Tin Woodman, and the Cowardly Lion difficult to write. The tune for "If I Only Had a Brain . . . a Heart . . . the Nerve" came out of the proverbial songwriter's trunk. Under the title of "I'm Hanging On to You," it had been written for *Hooray for What!* but not used in the show. Harburg simply wrote new words for the tune.

Whether a composer sets a lyricist's words to music or a lyricist writes words to fit a composer's tune depends on the two artists and their relationship. Most composers work one way with one lyricist, another way with a second. Richard Rodgers always wrote music to which Lorenz Hart later added lyrics. When Hart died and Rodgers started his collaboration with Oscar Hammerstein 2nd, he adapted to Hammerstein's way of working and composed the music after Hammerstein wrote the words. Both Yip Harburg and Johnny Mercer usually added words to Arlen's music. For Mercer, "Harold was a strong writer. He knew where he was going." With Harburg, it was more of an intellectual decision. He was always extremely concerned "about boxing a composer in." Although the subject matter and meaning of a song were usually discussed in advance, Harburg refused to corner Arlen with a lyric or even with a title before Arlen had written at least part of a tune. Usually, Arlen gave Harburg the first eight bars. Harburg listened to them and came up with a title. Then Arlen completed the song before Harburg started on the lyrics.

Arlen rarely wrote his songs at the piano. He felt that tunes created at the piano were contrived and mechanical. Arlen, more than most songwriters, believed in inspiration. The idea for a melody would sometimes come when he was in a store or on the golf course, more often when he was aimlessly walking or driving. He would catch the melody by jotting a few notes in his notebook. Later, at the piano, he would develop the tune. Harburg would sit in the room while Arlen wrote a song. "He'd keep playing a line over until I learned it by heart. There was something about a composer playing a tune over and over for you. You couldn't get away from it. Now I use a tape recorder. I capture everything the composer does, even if it's going to be thrown away. Sometimes the asides give me an idea. I started using a tape recorder during my last collaboration with Arlen, when we did the title song for Judy Garland's *I Could Go On Singing* in 1963." When Arlen played a song over and over, Harburg "could hear words." When the words didn't make sense, he would go out in the garden and plant something while Arlen disappeared to look for a golf course. (In similar circumstances, Johnny Mercer and Arlen—who worked a more businesslike noon-to-6-p.m. day—would solve the problem of feeling stale by driving down to a Beverly Hills delicatessen for something to eat.) When Harburg was surfeited with the music, he would leave Arlen's house, go home to try to fit in the words, "turn dull," telephone Arlen and go back to Arlen's house to listen to him play.

By the time they started to work on *The Wizard of Oz*—Arlen was thirty-three and Harburg was forty—they were close friends and comfortable collaborators. Both friendship and collaboration had started with Harburg's respect for Arlen's music. In 1932, Harburg's song "Brother, Can You Spare a Dime?" had become almost the battle hymn of the Depression. In the spring of 1934, the Shuberts had come to Harburg and asked him to do the lyrics for a new revue. He could choose his own composer. He chose Arlen, with whom he had casually written a few songs (including, with another collaborator, Billy Rose, "It's Only a Paper Moon"). Arlen was so disturbed at the idea of turning his back on his usual lyricist, Ted Koehler, that he could not bear to tell Koehler about Harburg's offer. He wrote and handed Koehler a letter describing it. Koehler's response that Arlen would be a fool not to take the job was not enough to assuage Arlen's conscience. He took the job, but first he went out and got drunk.

When Harburg picked Arlen to compose what became *Life Begins at 8:40,* Arlen was a gay and funny young man of twenty-nine with a tinge of mysticism and a penchant for reading Marcus

Aurelius. His father was a cantor, and he had been born Hyman Arluck into a rigidly Orthodox Jewish home. A promising piano student at ten, he had dropped out of high school to play piano. He had no idea then of becoming a composer. Arranging songs and playing the piano were means to the end of a career as a jazz singer. Extraordinarily handsome, outrageously spiffy in his blazers and foulard scarves, his spats, his homburg, and his cane, he probably could have been successful, "really successful as a singer," said Mercer, "like Bing Crosby, who also started as a band singer around the same time." But his singing career was over when, at twenty-four, he improvised a tune that lyricist Koehler turned into "Get Happy." (Arlen is still considered the songwriter who could best sell his own songs by singing them, with the possible exception of Mercer.)

What John Green calls "the tragic metamorphosis of the happy young man" into the reclusive old one began with his marriage in 1937 to Anya Taranda. Anya, a showgirl, was not Jewish. Given the unspoken horror of his family, it took Arlen five years to ask Anya to marry him, although John Green doubts that Arlen ever had a date with anybody else. Even then, he did not really ask her. He simply handed her a note telling her they would get married the next day, just as he had handed Koehler a letter telling him of Harburg's offer. The marriage ended with Anya's death in 1970, after years of mental illness.

But in the spring of 1938 Anya was still well and Arlen was still what Green remembers as "the greatest laugher I ever knew." The lemon-drop songs had come easily to Arlen. The ballad was something else. "The ballad is always the hardest song to write in any structure," according to Harburg, "because a ballad is pure melody. Also, the ballad is the one that has to hit the Hit Parade, the one everybody sings, the one that must be easy enough to sing. The ballad has to step out. A song's life will depend on how good the show is. If it's a good show, a song will step out. Even in a not-so-good show, a song *can* step out if it's given a chance to breathe and a lot of luck." Arlen and Harburg had agreed that the ballad in *The Wizard of Oz* would be "a song of yearning. Its object would be to delineate Dorothy and to give an emotional touch to the scene where she is frustrated and in trouble."

Then came the week-long struggle to find a melody. When the "broad, long-lined melody" did take possession of Arlen's head, it was ironically attached to some peculiarly Hollywood symbols. He was on his way to the most garish of movie theaters—Grauman's Chinese, where movie stars cemented their footprints in the forecourt—to see a movie. And he was exactly opposite Schwab's drugstore when he told his wife to stop the car so he could jot down a tune. Schwab's was already being fictionalized as the magic soda fountain where any good-looking girl who wanted to be a movie star would be handed an agent's card before she finished her milkshake. It is doubtful whether any movie star was ever discovered inside the drugstore, but the melody of "Over the Rainbow" was composed outside the front door.

When the song was three-quarters finished (Arlen had not composed, nor did he at that time intend to compose, the childishly simple middle part), Arlen played it for Harburg. Harburg's disappointment was obvious. He respected Judy Garland's capabilities, but he thought the song too symphonic for any sixteen-year-old girl: "A song that's done for a movie is custom-made. You have to write something that will fit a singer's style and ability, but you also have to know the character that is being played. Today, young composers beat out a tune with rhythm and energy without any differentiation for character. Everything depends on the beat. Everything sounds the same. Somebody did a rock version of one of my plays. The young guy sang rock. Fine. So did his boss. When the hippie and the big executive both sing rock songs, the big executive loses his dignity and you lose the differentiation between the two. That's why you're not getting shows on Broadway except *Godspell* and *Hair*. They're just infantile charades, all the characters drumming out the same yah-yah-yah. A songwriter, like a tailor, has got to measure his customer. Dick Powell was just a juvenile singer with a tenor voice. We could only give him a ballad with a nice sentimental strain. We couldn't give Bert Lahr a ballad at all unless it was satiric. Judy had a wide range. She could go from torch song to high humor. She ran the gamut of emotion. I knew Judy could sing 'Over the Rainbow,' but I thought it was too old for the character."

Remembering, Harburg was sure that "I was fooled by the

Judy Garland recording the sound track for Oz.

majestic and serious way Harold played the song." Ira Gershwin, a customary arbiter, was asked to come over and listen. By the time Gershwin arrived, Arlen's initial euphoria had been blunted by Harburg's response. When he played the tune for Gershwin, it was with a certain embarrassment and hesitation. The melody sounded plainer, less important. Harburg changed his mind before he heard Gershwin's favorable opinion. "Even so, it was a daring song for a little girl. The songs in Disney's *Snow White* had all been little jingles. 'Some Day My Prince Will Come,' 'Heigh Ho, Heigh Ho.' If you play 'Over the Rainbow' symphonically, it will stand up. If you play 'Heigh Ho, Heigh Ho, It's Off to Work We Go,' it won't."*

To please Harburg, Arlen wrote the melody for the tinkling middle section of the song:

Some-day I'll wish upon a star
And wake up where the clouds are far behind me.
Where troubles melt like lemon drops
Away above the chimney tops
That's where you'll find me.

It was an almost automatic thing for Arlen to do. "We'd instinctively give each other clues about what we were thinking," says Harburg nearly forty years later. "I'd incorporate his ideas into my lyrics. He'd incorporate my ideas into his music."

Sitting on a straight-backed kitchen chair in the California garden of a friend, eyes closed, a sun worshiper still, a small man as elflike as the leprechaun he created for *Finian's Rainbow*, Harburg remembered bits and pieces of what had happened when Arlen left the ballad in his hands. "The girl was in trouble, but it was the trouble of a child. In *Oliver*, the little boy was in a similar situation, was running away. Someone thought up a song for him, 'Where Is Love?' How can a little boy sing about an adult emotion? I would never write 'Where Is Love?' for a child. That's analytical adult thinking, not childish thinking. This little girl thinks: *My life is*

---

* The music in *Snow White* did, however, serve much the same purpose as the music in *The Wizard of Oz*. From the beginning, Walt Disney intended to use the songs to advance the plot.

messed up. Where do I run? The song has to be full of childish pleasures. Of lemon drops. The book had said Kansas was an arid place where not even flowers grew. The only colorful thing Dorothy saw, occasionally, would be the rainbow. I thought that the rainbow could be a bridge from one place to another. A rainbow gave us a visual reason for going to a new land and a reason for changing to color. 'Over the Rainbow Is Where I Want to Be' was my title, the title I gave Harold. A title has to ring a bell, has to blow a couple of Roman candles off. But he gave me a tune with those first two notes. I tried *I'll go over the rainbow, Someday over the rainbow.* I had difficulty coming to the idea of *Somewhere.* For a while I thought I would just leave those first two notes out. It was a long time before I came to *Somewhere over the rainbow.*"

When, after the first sneak preview, L. B. Mayer removed "Over the Rainbow" from *The Wizard of Oz*, Harburg, Arlen, and Freed were outraged. Losing "Over the Rainbow" did not simply mean losing a pretty ballad; it meant losing the dramatic point of the whole Kansas preface—a consideration that escaped the numerous producers who complained to Mervyn LeRoy and L. B. Mayer. "Why does she sing in a barnyard?" they asked. Those complaints began almost as soon as "The End" was flashed onto the screen in San Bernardino. San Bernardino is seventy miles from Los Angeles, but it was typical for MGM producers to show up at previews of their rivals' films. (Arthur Freed, during the days when he was trying to get a handhold as a producer, rarely missed a preview and never missed an opportunity to give his opinion of the picture.) And LeRoy, the interloper from Warner Bros., was not one of the MGM producers' own. Their virulent response to "Over the Rainbow" may have been more an attempt to embarrass LeRoy than reasoned musical judgment.

Harburg remembered that first preview as "unbearable. You were always working with people who knew nothing, working with the ignominy of ignorance. Those ignorant jerks. Money is power. Money rules the roost. The artist is lucky if he can get a few licks in." In 1976, LeRoy's and Harburg's memories diverged quite strongly over what happened next. LeRoy insisted that *he* had known the worth of the song and refused even to try the film with the song out.

Harburg remembered that the song was removed and that it was Arthur Freed—pleading with Mayer, shouting at Mayer, using every bit of leverage his friendship with Mayer could give him—who forced the song's return.*

The San Bernardino preview came in June of 1939—long after the song had been written. In the summer of 1938, Harburg was "living the life of royalty." He had a beautiful office, which he didn't have to use. He was allowed to work at home, and his weekly paycheck was delivered to his house by a messenger on a scooter. While it is true that the studios were factories, they were not all the same *kind* of factories. Harry Warren, who worked at Warner Bros. during the 1930's and at MGM in the Freed Unit during the 1940's, used to entertain at parties with a song describing the differences between the two studios. To a number of metallic sounds, including the rat-tat-tat of his fingers drumming on a table, he would begin with, "At Warner Brothers, you come in the gate at seven in the morning. The guards on the walls keep their guns aimed at you. At 7:05, Hal Wallis calls. 'Have you written that song yet?' " In contrast, the section about MGM would be accompanied by gentle piano music. "At Metro, the birds sing. The grass is green. Everybody smokes a pipe and has the Book-of-the-Month under his arm. Nobody works at Metro. You watch the flowers grow."

In his thirty-three years as a Hollywood songwriter, Warren worked at every studio except RKO. "Each studio was, in a sense, a Fascist state," he says. "Because then they were one-man studios. Harry Cohn ran Columbia like a dictator. Jack Warner ran Warners like a dictator. Zanuck ran Fox like a dictator. They say L. B. Mayer ran Metro that way, but I never saw it. I liked Mayer, probably because—of all of them—he liked music the best. Life was more leisurely at Metro. Nobody pressured you. At Warner Brothers, you couldn't even buy a newspaper or get a cup of coffee in the afternoon."

Harburg says whenever he did show up at the studio, "Mayer

---

* Both Edward Jablonski's biography of Harold Arlen, *Happy With the Blues* (Garden City, N.Y.: Doubleday, 1961), and Hugh Fordin's biography of the Freed Unit, *The World of Entertainment* (Garden City, N.Y.: Doubleday, 1975), insist that the song was cut from the film and was cut more than once. Both books credit Freed with its retrieval.

would always flatter me up, put his arm around me, introduce me as one of his geniuses." Harburg and Arlen valued sunshine too much to work in the daytime. Often they would work all night, Arlen at the piano, Harburg sitting in a corner listening, the process of creation somehow purer and less disturbed with the extraneous sounds of the day filtered out. They shared the comfort of working for someone who appreciated them. "Freed felt my lyrics had a poetic value," said Harburg. "The average producers didn't refer to it that way. They told me, 'You write college stuff.' " (Harry Warren goes even further in praise of Freed. "Freed was the only producer who understood anything about songwriters. He never said, 'I have to have the song by nine o'clock Wednesday.' The rest of the producers ordered a song like they were ordering a steak dinner.")

There were, however, some false starts and disappointments. Harburg and Arlen started to write "Horse of a Different Color," then realized there was too much music during the entrance into the Emerald City to sustain another song. Their musical elaboration of "We're Out of the Woods" was dropped, as was most of a song— "Lions and Tigers and Bears"—that they wrote for the Scarecrow, Tin Woodman, and Dorothy just before their meeting with the Cowardly Lion. The music surrounding Dorothy's triumphant return to the Emerald City after the Witch's melting was cut along with that whole sequence. Harburg fought hard for a reprise of "Ding-Dong! The Witch Is Dead" after the melting of the Witch. The Winkies and Winged Monkeys would sing, "Ding-Dong, she met her fate/We liqui-dated her." But he was overruled.

Beyond that, only one major song was deleted from their score. On their way to the Witch's Castle, the Scarecrow, Lion, Woodman, and Dorothy were attacked by Jitter Bugs invented by Harburg. The Jitter Bugs looked like pink and blue mosquitoes, and Harburg probably got the idea for them from the stinging bees the Witch had sent to destroy the travelers in L. Frank Baum's book. The background of the song was what the script described as "spooky music." Throughout, the music was accompanied by a persistent mosquitolike whine.

DOROTHY: Did you just hear what I just heard?

LION: That noise don't come from no ordinary bird.

DOROTHY: It may be just a cricket
Or a critter in the trees.

TIN MAN: It's giving me the jitters
In the joints around the knees.

SCARECROW: I think I see a jijik
And he's fuzzy and he's furry.
I haven't got a brain
But I think I ought to worry.

TIN MAN: I haven't got a heart
But I've got a palpitation.

LION: As Monarch of the Forest
I don't like the sitchy-ation.

DOROTHY (*to Lion*): Are you gonna stand around
And let him fill us full of horror?

LION: I'd like to roar him down . . .
But I think I've lost my roarer.

TIN MAN: It's a whozis.

SCARECROW: It's a whozis?

LION: It's a whatzis.

SCARECROW: It's a whatzis?

TIN MAN: Whozat?

LION: Whozat?

DOROTHY (*singing chorus*):
Who's that hiding
In the tree top?
It's that rascal
The Jitter Bug.

Should you catch him
Buzzin' round you,

Just look out for
The Jitter Bug.

Oh, the bees in the breeze
And the bats in the trees
Have a terrible, horrible buzz
But the bees in the breeze
And the bats in the trees
Couldn't do what the Jitter Bug does.

So be careful
Of that rascal,
Keep away from
The Jitter Bug.*

It had taken five weeks and $80,000 to film "The Jitter Bug." The number was cut from the film immediately after the first preview. Harburg protested, but this time Freed did not back him up. The film was too long. Something had to be removed, and "The Jitter Bug" was less necessary to the plot than most of the other songs. Besides, the word "jitterbug" was already attached to a popular dance. "When we wrote the song," Harburg recalled, "the word had no meaning. Our 'Jitter Bug' was a bug who gives you the jitters. But they began to worry that 'The Jitter Bug' might date the picture."

Despite the loss of "The Jitter Bug," Harburg had been allowed to manipulate the script with a freedom that had been given to no other lyricist. Mamoulian had brought in Rodgers and Hart to do the score of *Love Me Tonight* before a script had even been written, but Mamoulian was notorious for keeping complete control over every element in his films. He had come to *Love Me Tonight* with the idea of making "architecturally a perfect musical." He had succeeded well enough for both Stanley Donen and Vincente Minnelli to tell him decades later that they often ran a print of *Love Me Tonight* before starting new films of their own. No one was trying to make a *perfect* musical of *The Wizard of Oz*. The film's director, Victor Fleming,

INTER-OFFICE COMMUNICATION

To Mr. LeRoy - cc to Messrs Chic, Stothardt, Freed, Cannon, Busch

Subject _____ WIZARD OF OZ

From Keith Weeks   Date Dec 20 1938

METRO-GOLDWYN-MAYER PICTURES
CULVER-CITY CALIFORNIA

Is the present existing sound track which was recorded for the Jitterbug Number, the correct track for Mr. Fleming to photograph to on the set?

If not, and any changes are to be made, such as the substitution of Haley's voice for Ebsen's, it should be recorded Thursday of this week, when there would be no interference with the shooting company.

Keith Weeks

Above: Memo from Keith Weeks, production manager, to Mervyn LeRoy about planning the re-recording of Buddy Ebsen's songs by Jack Haley, who had replaced Ebsen as the Tin Woodman.

Below: Weeks's memo to LeRoy, Freed, et al., about the sound track for the ill-fated Jitter Bug number.

INTER-OFFICE COMMUNICATION

To Messrs. Le Roy, Freed, Stothardt, Stoll

Subject   WIZARD OF OZ

From   Keith Weeks   Date Dec 27 - 1938

METRO-GOLDWYN-MAYER PICTURES
CULVER-CITY CALIFORNIA

It is my understanding that the sound track with corrections, which is now available for the Jitterbug Number, is the proper one to which Mr. Fleming photographs the Jitterbug Number.

It is also my understanding that starting tomorrow, work will begin on the recordings for Emerald City. It is important that this be carried out as we will get into the Jitterbug Forest this week and Emerald City is the next set.

Keith Weeks

had no part in the preparation of the script. As a matter of fact, he was the second director assigned to the film. The film's producer, Mervyn LeRoy, had had limited experience with the musical form and, besides, was producing two other films simultaneously. LeRoy's assistant, Arthur Freed, had to be careful not to stand too firmly astride the project. In addition, his own experience with scripts was negligible.

When there was trouble with the script, Harburg simply stepped in to fill the vacuum. "Songs seem simple," according to Harburg. "They're not. The process of putting music in is very intricate. The function of song is to simplify everything, to take the clutter out of too much plot and too many characters, to telescope everything into one emotional idea. You have to throw out the unnecessary. And lots of things not in the script have to be invented to make the songs work."

AUNT EM: Now, Dorothy dear—stop imagining things . . . you always get yourself into a fret over nothing. You just help us out today and find yourself a place where you won't get into any trouble!

DOROTHY: Some place where there's no trouble . . . do you think there is such a place, Toto?
(*dreamily to herself*)
There must be. Not a place you can get to by a boat or a train. It's far far away . . .
(*music starts*)
Behind the moon
Beyond the rain.

It was Harburg who cued in "Over the Rainbow" during one of the "day after day" script sessions at Florence Ryerson's house in the San Fernando Valley. Although Lorenz Hart had used such rhymed dialogue twice before, it was Harburg's daring innovation to throw out an entire prose scene and replace it with a scene written in rhyme.

DOROTHY (*puzzled*): But, if you please, what *are* Munchkins?

GLINDA: The little people who live in this land . . . it's Munch-
kinland . . . You're really their national heroine, my dear.
  (*Glinda calls to the Munchkins*)
It's all right—you can come out and thank her!
  (*She starts singing in a conversational tone so that it is hard
  to realize, at first, that a number has begun.*)

GLINDA (*singing*): Come out, come out wherever you are
        And meet the young lady who fell from a star.
        She fell from the sky, she fell very far
        And KANSAS she says is the name of the star.

CHORUS: KANSAS she says is the name of the star.

From the moment Glinda asks the Munchkins to come out of hiding
until the explosion that signifies the arrival of the Wicked Witch of
the West, all the conversation is in rhyme and song.
  Love Me Tonight achieved its unity through the outline in

*Memo from Weeks to Freed, et al., about the midgets recording the
Munchkinland number (their voices were not used in the final sound track;
the voices of professional singers were recorded and then electronically distorted).*

FORM 72

INTER-OFFICE COMMUNICATION

To Messrs. Freed, Cannon, Stothardt,
        Stoll, Highsmith
Subject   WIZARD OF OZ
From Keith Weeks   Date Dec 21   1938

METRO-GOLDWYN-MAYER PICTURES
CULVER CITY, CALIFORNIA

        We should have by Friday of
this week, the correct sound track on
disc of "You're Off to See the Wizard"
number as done by the midgets, on page
35, script, WIZARD OF OZ.

        When may we expect this correct
track to which we are to photograph?

        Keith Weeks

Rouben Mamoulian's head. *An American in Paris, Singin' in the Rain, Meet Me in St. Louis* would achieve their special unities through Arthur Freed overseeing the sensibilities of such directors as Donen and Minnelli. In *The Wizard of Oz*, it was Harburg's involvement with the script "which allowed a song to lead everywhere. All a director had to do was follow the lyrics." "We're Off to See the Wizard" became a motif. "Follow the Yellow Brick Road" led to Dorothy's meeting with the Scarecrow. "If I Only Had a Brain . . . a Heart . . . the Nerve" moved the procession to the Deadly Poppy Field. "The Merry Old Land of Oz" took care of the Emerald City. And "The Jitter Bug" counterpointed the Haunted Forest. The primer provided by Harburg's lyrics must have been something of a relief to Victor Fleming, a chauffeur turned cinematographer turned respected director of Clark Gable and Spencer Tracy melodramas— a man with a rough-hewn masculine affect and little musical delicacy. It was definitely a relief to choreographer Bobby Connolly, who telephoned Harburg to ask where to fit in the dances. "But he couldn't go wrong," Harburg said. "Since the songs were there before the choreography, Connolly just had to fill in with dances." (Also eliminated after the first preview was one of Connolly's best pieces of choreography. "My dance was originally ten or fifteen minutes long," says Ray Bolger. "I was on wires. The winds came and blew me up in the air and down and up again. It was a fantastic dance that didn't mean anything overall to the picture.")

When the score was finished, Arlen sat down at a piano in a small room at MGM and played his way through his songs, accompanying himself by singing the lyrics. Herbert Stothart listened. The score was now his baby. That the final film would contain all but two of the numbers Harburg and Arlen had written and that it would sound reasonably similar to their hopes was either accident or luck. (When MGM was making *Till the Clouds Roll By*, the life story of Jerome Kern, Kern and Harry Warren went to the studio to listen to some of the songs being recorded. According to Warren, Kern, disturbed by one arrangement, diffidently requested a change, and was ignored.)

Commonly referred to as the dean of the MGM Music Department, Stothart was a Thalberg man. "He loved to eat," says Ken
Darby, who did the vocal arrangements for *The Wizard of Oz.* "He
loved to drink. He loved to fly a gang up to San Francisco to feast
at some favorite restaurant. He was an epicurean, a gourmet, a great
conductor, and a very generous man." Less than six months earlier,
Darby had come to Stothart's office—twenty-seven years old, $7,500
in debt, and with two fifteen-minute records he had made under his
arm. Darby was musically talented but couldn't get work as a singer
because of contract problems with band leader Paul Whiteman, and
he was desperate. Stothart listened to his records, hired him at
$12,000 a year, and advanced him $7,500 to clear up his debts. He
worked on two Jeanette MacDonald–Nelson Eddy musicals, but
The Wizard of Oz was his first screen credit.

In 1945, Stothart was the subject of a four-page pictorial essay
on elegant entertaining in *Life* magazine, which began, "The Herbert
Stotharts are wealthy." The article itemized Stothart's $50,000-a-
year salary, his cook, butler, swimming pool, Studebaker, Ford, and
Chevrolet. All in all, composers did well financially in Hollywood.
Harry Warren, for example, was under contract to one studio or other
nearly every week from 1932 to 1965 at an average salary of $2,500
per week and had a Beverly Hills estate complete with tennis court
to show for it. Composers Jimmy McHugh, Sammy Fain, Harry
Revel, Richard Whiting, Nacio Herb Brown wrote scores for picture
after picture for two or three decades, as did lyricists Leo Robin,
Sam Coslow, Al Dubin, Mack Gordon, Johnny Mercer, Gus Kahn.
The fame wasn't nearly as great as the fame that could be achieved
on Broadway, but the money was excellent, the security was better,
and only rarely did one of them end up broke before he died. Johnny
Mercer credited the lifelong affluence of successful songwriters to
ASCAP (American Society of Composers, Authors, and Publishers)
and abstinence. Directors and screenwriters, discarded by an industry
whose needs had changed, had a tendency to end up poverty-stricken,
often with a large assist from a bottle. "But there were no drinking
songwriters," said Mercer. "And nobody else in our business had
anything like ASCAP. If we made $75,000, ASCAP provided another
$75,000 from live and radio performances of our songs."

Herbert Stothart was a house composer. Every studio had three or four of them, men whose job it was to write the scores for the studio's dramatic films. They called themselves screen composers, although they were often referred to by songwriters as "background-music men." Their music had to be good—but not too good. "When you went to a picture, you heard the music for the first time and, usually, the last," says Murray Cutter, who spent his first eight years in Hollywood arranging for Stothart at MGM and his last sixteen arranging for Max Steiner at Warner Bros. "If the composer was really great, there would be too much in his music for the audience to grasp. It would be too complex. At one time there was a story at

Herbert Stothart, house composer for MGM, conducting the studio orchestra as Dorothy, the Scarecrow, the Tin Woodman, and the Cowardly Lion return to the Emerald City with the broomstick of the Wicked Witch of the West (cut in the final version).

MGM that L. B. Mayer wanted to hire Igor Stravinsky to do a picture. By the time he got to Stravinsky, it was thirty years after *The Firebird*, and he wanted him to write 'another *Firebird.*' It was absurd."

According to John Green, "Stothart had a felicitous feeling for combining background music with dialogue. He was an effective composer for the screen, although not in the same league as Max Steiner." Steiner and Erich Korngold, both at Warner Bros., and Alfred Newman at Fox were considered the best of the screen composers.* "There was a million miles difference between Korngold and most of those guys," says Murray Cutter, who arranged and orchestrated the songs for *The Wizard of Oz.* "Korngold was a real composer. There isn't one thing anyone had to do for him. He wrote operas; he wrote symphonies. Those other guys were just songwriters." According to Cutter, Stothart was, "above all, a good showman, a gifted musician with very little technical knowledge." He could not do his own orchestrations. Steiner, whose technical knowledge was greater, could when it was necessary. Ironically, Stothart's score for *The Wizard of Oz* took the Academy Award away from Steiner's *Gone With the Wind* score, the one category in which *The Wizard of Oz* defeated that picture.

Herbert Stothart is credited with "Musical Adaptation" on *The Wizard of Oz.* George Bassman, Murray Cutter, Paul Marquardt, and Ken Darby were given screen credit for "Orchestral and Vocal Arrangements," while George Stoll is listed as Associate Conductor. Actually, Bassman, Stoll, and Robert Stringer composed several bits of incidental music. The MGM conductor score for the film lists "Additional Composition" by Stoll. Bassman, and Stringer. "Stothart would conceive the idea and give it to Stoll or Bassman or Stringer to develop," Darby recalls. "He might just hand them a lead sheet, a two-line piece of music with a melody, a bass part, and some harmony symbols." Bassman wrote the music for the cyclone, Stringer the music in the Deadly Poppy Field. The credit on the MGM cue sheets for Dorothy's first meetings with the Scarecrow and the Tin

---

* Steiner won three Academy Awards; Korngold, two; and Alfred Newman, nine. Stothart's only award came for *The Wizard of Oz.*

Woodman and much of the music in the Emerald City and the Haunted Forest reads "Stothart-Stoll-Bassman."

Stothart was known as a composer who borrowed liberally from the classical composers. Indeed, he borrowed so liberally from Delius for *The Yearling* that Delius had to be given screen credit. His score for *The Wizard of Oz* contains a little of Schumann's piano piece for children, "The Happy Farmer" (during the opening scene on the Kansas farm); Mendelssohn's Opus 16, #2 from Three Fantasies (during Toto's escape from the Witch's Castle); and Moussorgsky's "Night on Bald Mountain" (during Dorothy's rescue from the Witch). Borrowing from well-known composers was hardly unusual in Hollywood. In accepting his Academy Award for *The High and the Mighty* (1954), Dimitri Tiomkin thanked Brahms, Bach, Beethoven, Richard Strauss, and Johann Strauss. It was hard to be creative when scoring ten to twelve films a year, so Stothart, like other Hollywood studio composers, learned how to derive.

In the pieces of music which he wrote for *The Wizard of Oz*, George Bassman made one joke. He used six bars of "In the Shade of the Old Apple Tree" during the scene in which the apple trees fight Dorothy and the Scarecrow. Whenever possible, Bassman chose to embroider on thematic music from Harold Arlen's songs. In "If I Only Had a Brain . . . a Heart . . . the Nerve," Arlen had used a little fill, a ruffle of music without lyrics. Bassman took that fill—which was one bar long—from Arlen's original piano copy, elaborated on it, and used it as thematic music for the scenes in which Dorothy met the Scarecrow, the Tin Woodman, and the Lion. The cyclone, on the other hand, was not derived from Arlen. The cyclone lasted one and a half minutes on the screen. Bassman worked on the music for three weeks. "I wrote it and scrapped it five times. Herb Stothart told me to work on it until I was happy with it. I wasn't happy until the sixth version. Then it took me three or four days to lay out the sixth version for orchestration and two more weeks to score it."

Scoring is the process of telling each instrument exactly what is expected of it. A page of score is laid out vertically with the woodwinds on top, followed by flutes, oboes, clarinets, bassoons, French

FORM 73

INTER-OFFICE COMMUNICATION

To **Mr. LeRoy - cc to Messrs.Chic,Freed, Stothardt.**

Subject _____ **WIZARD OF OZ - Prod 1060**

From **Keith Weeks** _____ Date **Dec 21 193**

The decision reached by Messrs.
Fleming, Stoll and Connolley on Stage #27
this morning, following the discussion about
the music for the end of the Munchkinland
Sequence, was -

1. Fleming wants Stoll to work
   the details out today with the
   music writers - He wants some
   additional music and lyrics
   to get the effect he desires.

2. Mr. Stoll is to present his
   ideas tomorrow on the set in
   the form of a piano recording.

3. If these ideas, lyrics and music
   are approved and work satisfactorily,
   Mr. Stoll will make the final sound
   track as quickly as possible, probably
   Thursday evening or Friday of this
   week. This will be the track to which
   Mr. Fleming will photograph the action.

   Keith Weeks

Memo from Weeks to Freed, Stothart, et al., about writing additional music and lyrics for the Munchkinland sequence.

horns, trumpets, trombones, tuba. Halfway down the page come the percussion instruments, including tympani, bells, chimes, xylophones, and all kinds of traps. They are followed by harps, piano, violins, violas, cello, and bass. To record the cyclone, MGM used "an immensely large orchestra," says Bassman. "Ninety instruments. Fifty was more common. But it was an important piece of music. It took the picture from the simplicity of Kansas to the beauty and grandeur of a different world and from black-and-white to color." Horizontally, a page of score has four bars on it. Vertically, it has as many lines as the instruments one is scoring for. That ninety-instrument orchestra had, as far as Bassman can remember, "six French horns, four trumpets, four trombones, perhaps thirty violins."

Each trombone needed its own line on the page of score, since each trombone played a different part. But a single line sufficed for most of the violins, since up to twenty of the violins played a single melodic line. For the cyclone, each sheet of score had thirty-six lines from top to bottom. It was two feet in length and ten inches in width. When Bassman was finished, he found it had taken sixty pages to score his minute and a half.

"Theoretically, the cyclone could have been done in ten different ways," says Bassman. "At least, ten different composers would have each done it differently. I chose to do it very much along the lines it would have been done in a Disney film. The Witch had her theme. The dog had his theme. Music essentially is like a match or candle. You hold it to the film and it warms the scene. Or use a cool low flute and it can make the scene colder. Then, music either helps accelerate the action or retards the action or makes the action stand still. With the cyclone, we were accelerating the action—the house twisting and whirling—especially with the change in the film which would come afterward."

At another studio, the cyclone would have sounded quite different. Just as films from different studios had a different look during the thirties and forties, so they also had a different sound. Warner Bros. accompanied the harsh and grainy look of their films with dissonant musical scores full of brass. You could always hear the trumpets and the horns in a Warners movie. Producer David O. Selznick once sent a memo to an assistant asking him to find out why Warner Bros. films sounded better than those from any other studio. The assistant discovered that Warners alone recorded their musical scores at top volume and then played them downward to the desired level. The 20th Century-Fox sound was also brassy, but it was more strident than Warners, a kind of booming sound that was brassy and shrill. The lush look of MGM films was duplicated in the lush, sweet sound of their musical scores. At MGM, it was strings, strings, and more strings—what someone best described as "a great wash of mush." The background treatment of the themes in *The Wizard of Oz* was done in an impressionistic style that was popular during the late thirties, the dreamy idiom of such French composers as Debussy and Ravel.

A page from the score for the cyclone (it took sixty pages to score this minute-and-a-half sequence). As in the Disney movies, all the characters in Oz—the Witch, the dog, etc.—had individual themes that were heard as the wind carried them past Dorothy's window during the cyclone.

According to Murray Cutter, Stothart held a very loose rein on his arrangers. Cutter was told, "This song should be two choruses, this song three, this song is for the Tin Man, so make it sound metallic." Then he was left on his own. His arrangement—"the first arrangement ever"—for "Over the Rainbow" was "as pretty as I could make it, lots of strings and a touch of woodwind." For the "metallic sound" of the Tin Woodman's "If I Only Had a Heart," Cutter says, "I tried to make it sound orchestrally like the tin outfit he was wearing. It's always a matter of color, something like coloring a picture. I used wood blocks, percussion, and brass mutes. The mutes were not to make it sound soft but to make it sound nasal."

It was the vocal arranger, Ken Darby, who was given the job of creating the voices for the Munchkins and the Winkies. "In those days," says Darby, "we didn't have the technical facilities we have now, like speeding up tape. I had to figure out how to make the Munchkins sound high-pitched. I worked it out mathematically, using a metronome. Then I went to the head of the sound department, Doug Shearer. I told him that if we could record at sixty feet per minute instead of the normal ninety feet per minute and if we sang at a slower pace in a different key, when we played it back at ninety it should sound right. He said there was no way to do that because we didn't have a variable-speed recorder. Then he said he would try to manufacture a new gear for the sound-recording machine. And it worked. I had the singers sing very slowly and distinctly so the words would be clear when we played it back at a faster speed. *Ding . . . Dong . . . the . . . witch . . . is . . . dead.* When we played it back, it was a perfect one-fourth higher. None of the midgets did any of the singing. None of them could carry a tune. Among the singers were the three men who had been with me in the King's Men quartet—Bud Linn, Rad Robinson, and John Dodson. They sang for the little toughies of the Lollipop Guild. "I sang the part of the mayor and Rad did the coroner. On the Decca album, Harold Arlen sang the coroner." There was a group of three girls called the Debutantes who did the Lullaby League. Later the Debutantes sang the song in the Poppy Field when the spell was broken."

For the voices of the Winkies, Darby used exactly the opposite technique. "I got men with deep voices and had them singing in a fairly low register while we recorded it at a faster-than-normal speed. When we played it back at normal speed, it dropped a perfect fourth lower and made them sound like monsters."

When Stothart, Bassman, Stoll, Cutter, Marquardt, and Darby were finished, thirty-five or forty minutes of songs had been elaborated into seventy-six minutes of music. *The Wizard of Oz*, completed, was an original musical with an integrated score. But—like *Love Me Tonight* and *High, Wide and Handsome*—it had absolutely no effect on the Hollywood musical. Not until Arthur Freed followed five conventional films with *Cabin in the Sky* in 1943 and *Meet Me in St. Louis* in 1944 did the direction in which *The Wizard of Oz* pointed become familiar territory. As for Arlen and Harburg, Hollywood paid them well while casually mistreating them. When they had finished *The Wizard of Oz*, Mervyn LeRoy hired them to write songs for his Marx Brothers film, *At the Circus*. That was followed by a song for *Rio Rita*, an Abbott-and-Costello comedy. Arlen wrote *Blues in the Night* and *Captains of the Clouds* with Johnny Mercer while Harburg presented his talents to Arthur Freed for *Babes in Arms*, *Babes on Broadway*, and *Presenting Lily Mars*, all starring Judy Garland. Together they wrote some songs for *Cabin in the Sky* in 1943 and *Kismet* in 1944. Many of the songs were good, some were much better than that. For *Star Spangled Rhythm* in 1942, Arlen and Mercer wrote "That Old Black Magic." For *The Sky's the Limit* in 1943, Arlen and Mercer wrote "My Shining Hour" and "One for My Baby and One More for the Road." But, in every case, these were just songs—to be sprinkled like bits of coconut onto an already baked cake.

Arlen got his chance to compose the score—from beginning to end—for one other classic film. With Ira Gershwin, in 1954, he did the Judy Garland *A Star Is Born*. But during the height of the integrated musical, Harburg was not working in Hollywood. "We did *The Wizard of Oz*," he said, "and then they never used us for another fantasy film. Sam Goldwyn did hire me to do *Hans Christian Andersen* in 1952, but when I was on my way to the airport, they telephoned me and told me not to come." By that time, Harburg had been blacklisted for four years. He had been working on a musical version of *Huckleberry Finn* for Arthur Freed when the blacklisting began. Donald Ogden Stewart, another victim, was taken off the script and Harburg was called in by MGM's New York lawyer Robert Rubin and told he was being paid off. Harburg convinced Rubin not only that he had never been a Communist but that he had been a passionate worker for Roosevelt. Rubin told him to write a letter "which should clear you." But it didn't. He was blacklisted another seven years.

He found the blacklisting "very traumatic although it didn't floor me." He weathered it very well; he had never been one to squander money, never been one to live lavishly. He retreated from Hollywood to "my old haunts on Broadway." He had been extraordinarily successful on Broadway in the mid-forties when he had turned one of his socialist ideas into a musical comedy "for which we had to raise the money ourselves. Nobody wanted to direct it, choreograph it, or act in it. Nobody wanted to be connected with it. 'What the hell kind of a musical is a white man turning black?' everyone asked." But the play was *Finian's Rainbow*, and it made the reputation of its unknown choreographer, Michael Kidd, and revitalized the reputation of the fading singer Ella Logan, who were willing to get involved.

Eventually, Hollywood invited him back. In 1962 he and Arlen did the unsuccessful feature-length animated cartoon *Gay Purr-ee*. Harburg still muses about the missed opportunities, about *Hans Christian Andersen* and *Doctor Dolittle*, "all those movies up my psychic alley." In the spring of 1975, he began tentatively to work with Arlen again. Arlen, though depressed, had gone back to the piano "and written some lovely songs." Perhaps they would do a musical operetta of *The Informer* together. But would anything they do be accepted by a Broadway lashed by rock and rhythm? Harburg had gone to see *The Wiz*, the black rock version of *The Wizard of Oz*, almost as soon as it opened. "I was horrified by it. They had taken the beautiful imagination children have at a certain age—the one age when they have idealism—and thrown rotten eggs and mud at it. When a child sees the real *Wizard* after *The Wiz*, he's already made fun of it, so he has to see the real thing with a cynical eye." To sum up his feelings, Harburg wrote a jingle.

> From Roosevelt to Nixon,
> From *The Wizard* to *The Wiz*,
> My God, it can't be possible!
> But, oh my country, 'tis.

In the end, Harburg will, at least posthumously, have the last laugh. *The Wizard of Oz* (1939) will outlast *The Wiz* (1974). What is most remarkable about *The Wizard of Oz*—and perhaps the mark of its success—is that one doesn't really think of it as a musical at all. Because the songs are integral to the plot, they don't intrude as songs. The ballads from most musicals are so rootless that one can hardly remember the play or movie to which they were originally attached. Because the Arlen-Harburg songs are evocations of personality, they have not become dated in nearly forty years.

Production #1060	4.

CASTING

From MGM's 120 stars and featured players (the "Ingenues, Characters, Comedians, Comediennes, Juveniles, Child"—and Leads)

In 1938, MGM had under contract some 120 "stars and featured play-ers." From those 120 actors and actresses were cast six of the ten major roles in *The Wizard of Oz*. The studio had to go beyond its high white walls only for the Wicked Witch of the West, the Cow-ardly Lion, Dorothy's Aunt Em, and the dog Toto. Yet 1938 was hardly a peak year at MGM. In 1935 there had been 253 actors and actresses under contract. By the early forties the rolls were swollen again. "MORE STARS THAN THERE ARE IN HEAVEN!" was the MGM slogan, and casting director Billy Grady once reflected that "it cost the studio nearly a million on the red side to carry the load."

George Chasin, an actors' agent, describes the studios of the thirties as "vast storage bins of talent." The constantly replenished contract list was a symbol of MGM's status. "In the middle thirties," said Chasin in 1976, "actors ran for security, and the most pros-perous studio was MGM." Under the weight of the Depression, RKO reorganized, Universal teetered on the brink of bankruptcy, United Artists was inactive, Fox merged with 20th Century, and Paramount went into receivership. Only Warner Bros.—which had suffered through its problems a few years earlier—and MGM prospered. "If we were able to say of our clients that they had worked at MGM," said Chasin, "it was tantamount to saying they were fine actors."

Lionel Barrymore, Freddie Bartholomew, Wallace Beery, Joan Crawford, Nelson Eddy, Clark Gable, Greta Garbo, Helen Hayes, Myrna Loy, Jeanette MacDonald, the Marx Brothers, Robert Mont-gomery, Eleanor Powell, William Powell, Luise Rainer, Norma Shearer, Robert Taylor, and Spencer Tracy were all under contract to MGM in 1938 and labeled as stars. Among the "featured players" under contract were Robert Benchley, Bruce Cabot, Melvyn Douglas, Betty Furness, Reginald Gardiner, Judy Garland, Edmund Gwenn, Fay Holden, Guy Kibbee, Hedy Lamarr, Una Merkel, George Mur-phy, Basil Rathbone, Mickey Rooney, Rosalind Russell, Ann Ruther-ford, James Stewart, Franchot Tone, Johnny Weissmuller, and Dame May Whitty. There were CONFIDENTIAL red notebooks that further stratified the two lists. According to L. B. Mayer's personal copy of Hitchcock's *Who's Where in Hollywood's Show World* for April–May–June 1938, the featured players were divided into Ingenues, Characters, Comedians, Comediennes, Juveniles, and Child, while the stars were always Leads. Some of the handsomer featured players were Leads, too, among them Walter Pidgeon, Ilona Massey, George Murphy, Dennis O'Keefe, Florence Rice, and Robert Young. Stars were too valuable to be wasted in the low-budget films that would make up the bottom half of a double bill. If the film wasn't strong enough for Robert Montgomery or Robert Taylor, the part could always be given to Robert Young.

In general, MGM's actors were expected to earn their money. Between 1931 and 1935, Clark Gable made twenty-eight movies. In 1938, Robert Young appeared in five pictures, Walter Pidgeon in six, and Mickey Rooney in eight. Not that all contract players were shoved into film after film. There were always a few comediennes like Fanny Brice to be salted away for the one picture a year for which her special talents were suited. Similarly, there were always a few $100-a-week ingenues and juveniles to be dangled before the public in one or two films so that Mayer and Thalberg could appraise the results.

MGM's stars were not used indiscriminately. Scripts were written for them; books were rewritten for them. Their parts were as carefully tailored as their clothes—and with much the same purpose: to exaggerate strong points, to disguise flaws. A potential star was not treated with the same gentleness. A young actor or actress was clay for molding. Robert Taylor was given a singing role in *Broadway Melody of 1936* in the hope that he might make a leading man for musicals. Taylor's voice made that experiment a failure, but Eleanor Powell's success as a dancer in the same film allowed the studio to shift Joan Crawford to exclusively dramatic roles. Powell could take over all those dancing ladies previously reserved by necessity for Crawford.

Once an actor was a star, the clay was considered permanently fired. Although there were subtle changes—in the late thirties, as Robert Montgomery grew older and his screen presence solidified, Robert Taylor inherited the rakish roles Montgomery had played a few years earlier; all that dancing on tables seemed out of place for a woman of thirty-three, so Joan Crawford's flapper turned into a career girl—there were very few experiments. Occasionally, however, a star himself demanded to cross the artificial boundaries the studio had set. Robert Montgomery insisted on playing the murderer who kept his victim's head in a hatbox in *Night Must Fall.* Unable to dissuade him, the studio went so far as to make a trailer telling prospective audiences that Montgomery had chosen the role for himself. When critics praised the film, the trailer was withdrawn. But Mayer remained uneasy with Montgomery's unpredictability; Robert Taylor was groomed to replace him.

Grooming was the specialty of the house at MGM. It was as though that whole vast contract list contained the names of racehorses, each a potential prize-winner (if the race was properly chosen) for any trainer with time, patience, and intuition. Even the character actors were used so audiences could hardly avoid becoming fond of them. Marjorie Main. Reginald Gardiner. Edmund Gwenn. Edna May Oliver. Nat Pendleton. "We used those characters as often as we could in major roles, and the public loved them," recalls Leonard Murphy, a casting director at MGM in 1938. Their presence on the screen always meant a few more dollars at the box office. And sometimes the characters themselves became approximations of stars. Van Heflin managed it, as did Marjorie Main a decade later in the Ma and Pa Kettle series. And the low-budget Andy Hardy films constructed around Lewis Stone and Mickey Rooney were largely responsible for making Rooney a star.

For the grooming of a pretty young actor or actress, MGM's usual procedure was to try the young player in a picture or two and wait for the audience's response. Thalberg was so sensitive to the nuances of an audience that he could tell when those at a preview became involved with a personality on the screen. For executives with less sensibility, there were the twin barometers of preview cards and fan mail. If enough preview cards mentioned a new male contract player or if he got a surprising amount of fan mail, he was cast as quickly as possible in as many pictures as possible opposite the studio's established female stars. For example, during his first year at MGM, Clark Gable played opposite Norma Shearer, Greta Garbo, and Joan Crawford.* Crawford and Shearer could hardly complain,

---

* MGM was not the only studio to use this technique. During his first year at Paramount, Cary Grant was cast in seven pictures, playing opposite Sylvia Sidney, Mae West, Carole Lombard, and Marlene Dietrich, among others.

since the studio had done the opposite thing for them six years earlier. They had been the first two stars to be created by the newly formed Metro-Goldwyn-Mayer.

An actor or actress to whom audiences did not respond quickly had his option dropped. (Most of the players let go by MGM were never heard of again, although there were a few who, like Deanna Durbin, were picked up and turned into stars by another studio.) Mayer and Thalberg were in agreement that "The public makes the stars." Oddly, though Thalberg could develop stars by casting an actor or actress with an almòst Proustian delicacy, it was Mayer who had the surer instinct for clay that would take firing: it was he who brought over from Europe Greta Garbo, Hedy Lamarr, Greer Garson. According to Sam Marx, Thalberg's story editor, "When Thalberg discovered unknowns, they had a disconcerting way of remaining just that."

Thalberg was still alive when Judy Garland entered the MGM system—as one of the 253 contract players—on September 27, 1935, three months after her thirteenth birthday. But it was Mayer who signed her and who directed her career. She was signed to a standard seven-year contract, forty-week guarantee, with seven options. For the first six months she would be paid $100 a week. If her first option was picked up in February 1936, she would be given $200 a week for the next six months. If at the end of the first year the studio still desired her services, she would be paid $300 per week for the next year. In the fall of 1937 her salary would rise to $400 per week; in the fall of 1938 to $500. By September 1939 she would be making $600 each week. In 1940, the summer after her eighteenth birthday, her salary would be increased to $750. The last year of the contract she would be earning $1,000 a week.

The last two options of that seven-year contract were never exercised. On August 28, 1940, the original contract was torn up and a new one was written paying her $2,000 a week for the next three years. It had taken MGM exactly five years to turn Judy Garland into a star.

If there seemed a certain mechanical exactness to taking a seven-

*Louis B. Mayer gives a party for Judy Garland's seventeenth birthday,
June 11, 1939. From left: Ann Rutherford, Betty Jaynes, Mayer,
Garland, Mickey Rooney, Leni Lynn, June Preisser.*

teen-year-old Lana Turner, stuffing her into a sweater, and setting
her out for inspection in *Calling Dr. Kildare* and *Love Finds Andy
Hardy*, there were no rules to follow for Judy Garland. Shirley Tem-
ple and Jackie Coogan had been stars before they were six; Freddie
Bartholomew and Jackie Cooper, stars before they were ten. Judy
Garland was too old to be a child star, too young to be an ingenue.
At thirteen, her figure was dumpy, her features ordinary at best.

There are two totally contradictory and equally well verified
accounts of how she got to MGM. In the first account—the details
vary—she was brought onto the MGM lot by either her agent, her
father, or an interested bystander to audition for Mayer or anybody
who would listen to her sing. In the second account, Mayer found
her himself when he dropped in at a Hollywood nightclub where
she happened to be singing.

Forty years later, half a dozen people remembered or were sure they knew someone who remembered Judy Garland coming onto the MGM lot to audition. In Arthur Freed's version,* it was Jack Robbins, the head of one of MGM's music-publishing firms, who brought the plump thirteen-year-old in; and it was Freed who listened.

"Arthur Freed never met Judy until after she was signed," said Al Rosen, Judy Garland's first agent. "I knew Sam Katz was the head of the studio while Mayer was in Arrowhead recuperating from a cold. Mayer had turned her down before, but I got Katz and Robbins to listen. Katz signed her. When L. B. Mayer came back and saw she was signed, he raised hell."

Gerold Frank in his 638-page biography of Judy Garland† credited Mayer's assistant Ida Koverman with summoning Judy to the studio and insisting that Mayer listen to her sing. In that account, she sang for Mayer one day in his office and returned the next to sing for Mayer, Freed, and a roundup of other executives on Stage 1. Freed, Koverman, and Mayer's nephew Jack Cummings badgered Mayer into signing her.

Benny Thau remembered it differently. In Thau's version, Mayer did not need any badgering. "Mr. Mayer gave a little party at a nightclub called the Trocadero," said Thau, a former MGM vice-president who had the responsibility for negotiating contracts. "I was there. Judy Garland was singing, with her mother playing the piano. A test was made of her. Her voice was good, and even at that age she had personality."

In signing Judy Garland, MGM had bought an extraordinary voice unfortunately attached to a mediocre body and a badly flawed face. In the next seven years, the voice would be trained, the teeth capped, the nose restructured, the thick waist held in by corsets, and the body reshaped as well as possible by diet and massage. In greater or lesser measure, the same things happened to everyone the studio put under contract. If nothing had to be done to improve Lana Turner's breasts, there was certainly enough to be done by the studio's hairdressers and dramatic coaches. MGM's actors and actresses responded to the ministrations of the studio in different ways. To June

* As reported by Hugh Fordin in *The World of Entertainment* (Garden City, N.Y.: Doubleday. 1975).

† *Judy* (New York: Harper & Row, 1975).

Allyson, MGM was a haven. "The only parental authority I had was the studio. Until I got married, it was really the only home I knew. I wasn't unhappy when they worked me hard. I needed to be wanted, and work meant I was wanted. When I went out on the streets, I was never alone. There was always a guard. I felt protected." Peter Lawford, who came to the studio at eighteen, was more ambivalent. "Metro really was a star-builder, and you had no choice about it. If they signed you, you were put into that machine—wrapped in cotton wool, looked after, looked over, looked under. If you survived, you were a star." Lawford never quite became a star, possibly because he refused to dress the part. He was urged to imitate Robert Taylor, who "came into the studio every day of his life in a suit and tie and a pin through the collar. They were very high on pins through the collar." Lawford continued to wear denims and continued to play second leads.

During her vaudeville childhood, Judy Garland had come to perceive herself as the undesired repository of her voice. The years at MGM would only intensify that feeling. "Mr. Mayer used to love to show his stars off," says his ex-secretary, Sue Taurog. "When Joan Crawford came to have lunch with him once without dressing up, he sent her home. He wanted to walk on the lot with one of his stars and have everybody say, 'Isn't she gorgeous?' " MGM did indeed want Judy Garland solely for her voice. Even a glance at the other young girls who came to the studio as contract players made that obvious. Ann Rutherford. Lana Turner. Hedy Lamarr. Gloria de Haven. June Allyson. Deanna Durbin. Durbin was lost to the studio by accident in 1936 after being paired with Garland in a short film, *Every Sunday*, that was really a contest. Which girl should the studio keep? Which would give evidence of that magical rapport with an audience? Deanna Durbin's lean, long-legged prettiness convinced many of the executives who judged the film, although Judy's voice tilted the balance back to dead center. To the end of her life, Judy Garland would remember those early years when the wardrobe women circled her, discussing her flaws between themselves but never once speaking directly to her. "She got her revenge," says costume designer Mary Ann Nyberg. "When I was designing for Arthur Freed, she showed me how she could stand a certain way for a fitting, and when the dress was made and brought back, the waistline would be one inch too short. She could also distend her throat and make the neckline stand out." During those first seven years, Judy Garland's sense of physical unattractiveness—and, by extension, sexual unattractiveness—became an obsession.

In five of the six movies she made before *The Wizard of Oz*, the studio unerringly used Garland's physical awkwardness to advantage. Part of MGM's luck in developing stars was actually skill at matching performers to roles that reflected their emotional scope. On her way through the smooth digestive tract of the system, Garland was surveyed and computed and very accurately appraised. In *Pigskin Parade*—on loanout to 20th Century-Fox—she played Sairy Dodd, frumpish and freckled little sister to a country bumpkin skilled at throwing a football. In *Broadway Melody of 1938*, she was the stolid daughter of stage mother Sophie Tucker. Her big number was a song pouring out her unrequited love for Clark Gable. That song, "Dear Mr. Gable," exploited the vulnerability latent in her personality but always near the surface of her voice. Vulnerability and sincerity formed the bedrock upon which a majority of her roles would be constructed. The sincerity became apparent in *Thoroughbreds Don't Cry*, the first of her eight films with Mickey Rooney: she was steadfast, loyal, and dowdy. In *Everybody Sing*, she had improved her billing. Her name was equal to those of Allan Jones and Fanny Brice in the credits at the beginning of the film and second only to Jones at the end. It was the only one of Judy Garland's first six films in which her plainness was a disadvantage.

It is *Love Finds Andy Hardy* that gives the clearest picture of the persona invented for Garland by MGM. Judy played Betsy Booth, deep in puppy love with Rooney, who considers her "swell" and allows her to polish his car so he can take another girl to the dance. At the end of the film, Garland is revealed as a singer of almost professional ability whose voice finally allows her to impress—and even to awe—Rooney. She played the same role or some variation of it in most of her pictures with Rooney—the unglamorous, steadfast, vulnerable girl left unnoticed or left behind, at least until the last five minutes of the movie. She played the same role in other pictures, too—in *Little Nellie Kelly* and *Presenting Lily Mars* and even, as late as 1944, in *Meet Me in St. Louis,* in which Lucille Bremer was her older, dazzling sister, and Garland was in love with the seemingly unattainable Boy Next Door.

By the time Judy Garland made *Love Finds Andy Hardy* in the spring of 1938, she had already been cast in *The Wizard of Oz.* On February 24, 1938, *Variety* had carried a small item announcing the purchase of *The Wizard of Oz* from Goldwyn and the casting of Garland as Dorothy. She had been at MGM almost exactly two and a half years.

From the first, Judy had had her admirers—chief among them Arthur Freed and musical arranger Roger Edens. L. B. Mayer might jokingly refer to the fifteen-year-old girl as his little hunchback, but

The Gumm sisters: left to right, Mary Jane, Frances (Judy Garland), and Virginia Gumm, late 1920's.

Freed and Edens were aware of the potential in the voice Edens had spent more than two years developing. Throughout the 1940's, Garland would be Arthur Freed's creation, his star or guest star in fourteen movies. But without Edens she might not have stayed at MGM long enough to be cast in *The Wizard of Oz*. A great many people had been mesmerized by Garland's voice in the second-rate theaters where she had sung as one third of the Gumm Sisters. Edens, her vocal coach, was the first person in the movie industry to come fully under its spell: it was he who wrote the song of yearning for Clark Gable that she sang at the birthday party the studio gave for Gable's thirty-sixth birthday. And it was the response of the captive executives at that party in February 1937 that caused the studio to put Garland—and the song—into *Broadway Melody of 1938*. Garland was Edens' protégée. Edens was Freed's protégé, his musical arranger, and—later—his associate producer. Edens, a debonair Southern gentleman, would win Academy Awards for scoring *Easter Parade*, *Annie Get Your Gun*, and *On the Town*. He would end his career as the producer of *Funny Face* and *Hello, Dolly!* Until close to the end of her life, Judy Garland would trust him as much as she trusted anybody. "Roger Edens was responsible for giving Arthur his taste," says lyricist Yip Harburg. Arranger Saul Chaplin, who joined the Freed Unit in 1949, amends the thought to read, "Arthur admired Roger's taste and leaned on him heavily." In either case, one can probably not overestimate how much Edens stimulated Freed's interest in Judy Garland.*

Both Arthur Freed and Mervyn LeRoy claimed credit for casting Judy Garland in *The Wizard of Oz*. "Some of the producers at Metro wanted Shirley Temple," says LeRoy. "But I always wanted Judy Garland. On account of her voice. On account of her personality. She *looked* more like Dorothy than Shirley Temple did. I insisted we had to make a test of her, and she was sensational. I fixed all her teeth in front. She had big wide spaces. That was the first thing I did with Judy Garland."

The executives who wanted the box-office insurance of Shirley

---

* On *The Wizard of Oz*, Edens supervised some of the pre-recording. He also wrote four songs, including a welcome to Dorothy from the Munchkins. None of his songs was used.

Temple may or may not have included Mayer, but they definitely included Loew's president, Nick Schenck. Temple, ten years old, had been the No. 1 box-office attraction in 1935, 1936, and 1937—with MGM's own Clark Gable a distant second. If it had come to a show-down between Judy Garland and Shirley Temple, Garland would undoubtedly have lost. But when Mayer tried to borrow Shirley Temple from 20th Century-Fox, Darryl Zanuck refused to loan her out. (Ironically, *The Wizard of Oz* caused Zanuck to star Temple in a fantasy, Maeterlinck's *The Blue Bird*, a year later. The film was dismal, called by studio jokesters "Dead Pigeon." The failure of the film essentially ended Shirley Temple's career.)

Unable to borrow Temple, MGM fell back on the techniques it had honed during the preceding fourteen years. In March 1938, Garland was sent on tour. Accompanied by Roger Edens, she appeared on stage—as often as possible to accompany the newly released *Everybody Sing*—in Pittsburgh, New York, Chicago, Miami Beach, and a dozen smaller cities. By the time she returned from the tour in April, the script of *Love Finds Andy Hardy* had been written to showcase both the awkwardness of her adolescence and the pre-cociousness of her voice. She finished *Love Finds Andy Hardy* on June 25. When the starting date of *The Wizard of Oz* was delayed from July to October, she was rushed, sixteen days later, into another picture. *Listen, Darling* was a quintessential B picture, but Garland had top billing. Freddie Bartholomew's name—equally large—came second. The names of Mary Astor, the widowed mother Garland managed to keep from marrying mean-spirited Gene Lockhart, and Walter Pidgeon, the handsome bachelor she found for Mary Astor instead, were farther down in the credits and in considerably smaller type. It was obvious that MGM was trying to build a star. How well the public would respond remained to be seen.

Dorothy was the pivotal role in *The Wizard of Oz,* but it was not the only role. In March 1938, Ray Bolger was called into Mervyn LeRoy's office and told that he was to play the Tin Woodman. His response was less than enthusiastic. "It wasn't my cup of tea. I'm not a tin performer. I'm fluid."

Ray Bolger, the Scarecrow, in 1939.

It was not that Bolger didn't want to be in *The Wizard of Oz*. It was just that his eye was on the Scarecrow. "Fred Stone, who played the Scarecrow in the original 1902 play of *The Wizard of Oz*, was a kind of idol of mine. When I was fifteen or sixteen years old— around 1919 or 1920—I saw him in *Jack O'Lantern* at a theater in Boston. We were Boston Irish. Dorchester Irish, to be exact. I grew up in an Irish-Jewish neighborhood and spoke pretty good Yiddish. All I remember now is that I saw this man save a girl from a fate worse than death. He bounded on a trampoline out of a haystack looking just like a scarecrow, put his hand on his head, and said, 'Just in time!' I've never forgotten it. That moment opened up a whole new world for me. Up until then, the theater had nothing to do with me. I was going to high school mornings and making a living afternoons. My father was a house-painter, and he had gotten sick, and his sickness had used up all our money. Me, I was just after survival, after making a living for myself. That moment in the theater changed all that."

Bolger had moved from Dorchester to vaudeville and then—a longer jump—from vaudeville to Broadway. In 1935 he had come to MGM for one picture at $20,000 a week for seven weeks. When he signed his long-term MGM contract for $3,000 a week on April 11, 1936, he was the star of several Broadway shows, including *Life Begins at 8:40* with Bert Lahr and *On Your Toes*.

He never took movies very seriously, somehow realizing quite early that he would never be a star in them. On the set of *The Wizard of Oz*, he occupied himself with his racing form. His bookie was an ex-vaudeville dancer who showed up every Friday to collect. "I don't ever remember winning," mused Bolger years later. "But I don't regret one single solitary penny of it. And it had its advantages. One day in Chicago, I realized it was stupid and I quit. So that by the time I started to work in Vegas, I was never hooked the way lots of others were."

The month after *The Wizard of Oz* was finished, Bolger asked to be released from his contract. The money was good, but the long waits between pictures were intolerable for a man who in 1976, at seventy-two, was still dancing for an hour every morning to keep his joints from stiffening. Bolger's greatest success would come a decade after *The Wizard of Oz* with *Where's Charley?* (a musical version of *Charley's Aunt*), in which he would star—on Broadway, on the road, in a movie—for nearly four years.

Nobody paid much attention to Bolger's complaints about the Tin Woodman. Three thousand dollars a week or not, he was an MGM employee, and MGM employees usually did what was requested of them. The studio had several ways of enforcing discipline. An actor could always be suspended without salary. Or loaned out to another studio. Some loanouts were merely trades, a way of acquiring a square actor for a square hole while providing some other studio with a round actor for a round hole. More commonly, a loanout was a way of pawning an actor for whom you had no immediate plans. Judy Garland's first picture had been on loanout. The receiving studio would usually pay the actor's full salary, plus an agreed-upon bonus, which went to the lending studio, not to the actor. But other loanouts were deliberately intended as punishment, a guaranteed way of bringing a young actor to heel. It worked unless the punishment (being sent to Columbia for *It Happened One Night*) brought an Academy Award to the actor being disciplined (in this case, Clark Gable).

It was a lanky young juvenile, Jimmy Stewart, under contract to MGM in 1938, who changed the system. When he returned from World War II as Air Force Colonel James Stewart, he was talked into free-lancing by his agent, Lew Wasserman. The great agent of the 1930's, Myron Selznick, had set out to punish the studios for bankrupting his father, Lewis J. Selznick, and pushing him out of the film business. Myron's revenge consisted of forcing the studios to pay large salaries to the actors and actresses who were his clients. Wasserman, the great postwar agent—soft-spoken where Myron Selznick was abrasive, soberly conservative where Selznick was drunkenly expansive—was more interested in getting his clients a piece of the action, a percentage of a picture's gross after the break-even point, deferring salaries over seven or ten years. Eventually, Wasserman even came up with the idea of having his clients take no salary; instead, they owned 50 percent to 100 percent of a picture's profits.

It was the studios' fault that actors were able to get away with such demands. With the almost simultaneous advent of television and the Justice Department's decision in July 1949 that the studios could no longer own the theater chains in which their pictures played, the market for B pictures collapsed. Like frantic fishermen afraid that the fish they had hooked would swamp the boat, the studios cut loose their vast contract lists. The result was that in 1952 Clark Gable finished off his MGM contract at a salary of $7,200 a week for the standard forty weeks. Ten years later, Elizabeth Taylor was paid $1 million for *Cleopatra*.

In the 1930's, a studio's most powerful weapon was the inviolable seven-year contract. This is not to imply that MGM used the power of its contracts with cruelty. No other studio treated its actors as tenderly as MGM did. Moving to another studio for a picture was often the equivalent of roughing it. When Darryl Zanuck borrowed Wallace Beery to co-star with George Raft in *The Bowery* in 1933, Beery was horrified at the picture's twenty-five-day shooting schedule. "MGM," he told the director, "never runs anything under sixty days." During her last desperate years, Judy Garland blamed MGM for everything that had gone wrong with her life. Whatever responsibility the studio bore for Garland's amphetamines and sleeping pills and dramatic attempts at suicide, it was certainly nowhere near full responsibility. And it came from neither wanton destructiveness nor indifference. On September 28, 1950, MGM fired the twenty-eight-year-old Judy Garland it had made into a movie star. After several psychiatric hospitalizations paid for by the studio and multiple suspensions because of her unwillingness or inability to perform, the contract between Judy Garland and MGM was canceled. "She was just too much trouble and too costly," according to songwriter Harry Warren, who suffered through several of her films. "So Metro let her go. But she was treated better at MGM than she would have been treated at any other studio. If she had been at Warners, they would have dropped her years earlier."

In the end, Ray Bolger got to play the Scarecrow. But in the beginning the studio had someone else in mind. The cast list attached to Noel Langley's script of April 4, 1938, lists only three actors:

Buddy Ebsen, seen here on the set of Broadway Melody of 1938, *was LeRoy's original choice for the Scarecrow. When the filming began, he had been cast as the Tin Woodman. Nine days later, he was hospitalized and never appeared in the movie at all.*

Judy Garland as Dorothy, Ray Bolger as the Tin Woodman, and Buddy Ebsen as the Scarecrow. Buddy Ebsen was 6' 3" tall and thirty pounds underweight. In *Broadway Melody of 1938*, a joke had been built around his appearance at a health club where he came to lose weight, while the club naturally assumed he was there to gain weight. Ebsen unequivocally looked like a scarecrow. He had done ballroom dancing with his sister Vilma, and he had also tap-danced his way through *Captain January* with Shirley Temple.

In April 1938, Buddy Ebsen was on the second year of his second two-year contract at MGM at a salary of $1,500 a week. During the first three years of his contracts, MGM had assigned him to three or four roles, but had also made a tidy profit on him by loaning him out for *Banjo on My Knee, Captain January, My Lucky Star*. He had come to the studio in December 1934 with his sister. In the contract he and Vilma signed, there were a few lines of fine print of which the twenty-seven-year-old dancer was unaware. "It turned out that MGM had the option of keeping one of us and letting the other one go," says Ebsen. "Which was a very unpleasant realization when MGM kept me and dropped Vilma. Vilma went back to New York with her husband. I stayed in Hollywood." Of such small points are careers made. The eight television years as oil-rich Jed Clampett of *The Beverly Hillbillies* made Ebsen a millionaire. At sixty-six, he once more became a television star—as private investigator Barnaby Jones.

Even after Ebsen began costume fittings and dance rehearsals for the Scarecrow, Bolger did not give up. In 1976, his memory was that a clause in his contract gave him the right to play the Scarecrow if MGM were ever to make a movie of *The Wizard of Oz*. "Otherwise, I can't imagine that the studios would let me tell them what to do." But his contract was signed two years before MGM bought the book from Samuel Goldwyn, and it contains only one extraordinary clause, which was added *after* the filming of *Oz*. This clause—dated July 12, 1939—says that any imitation doll of the Scarecrow must include a tag that "The Scarecrow in *The Wizard of Oz* was played by Ray Bolger." It seems more likely that Bolger's insistence that he was miscast as a tin man eventually wore the studio down. And Ebsen didn't object to changing roles. Scarecrow or Tin Woodman, it was all the same to him: "I wanted to be in the picture because I knew it would be a very big one. And it's always good to be associated with a big project."

Ebsen was not to be associated with that big project for very long. Two weeks after the picture began, he was replaced by Jack Haley; and his career—whether coincidentally or not—went into a slump. He did not resurface with any permanence until 1956, when he appeared as the sidekick to Fess Parker in Disney's *Davy Crockett*.

Bolger and Ebsen were both under contract. "We wouldn't miscast a role just to put a contract person in," said casting director Leonard Murphy in 1976. "Particularly under Mayer's regime," he added, perhaps remembering the compromises and shortcuts taken by several of the regimes that followed Mayer, including the sale of most of the studio land and properties by James Aubrey in order to build a Las Vegas hotel. "But the first thing you do is think about who you have under contract who could play the role."

MGM tried to fill all but two of the major roles in *The Wizard of Oz* from the 120 actors it had under contract. It had to go beyond the contract list for the dog, Toto. And LeRoy always intended to go beyond the list for his Wizard. There was something in the character of the wizard who is not a wizard, the sorcerer who is only a humbug, that caused the men connected with the film to search for the perfect actor. To Mervyn LeRoy, the perfect choice—what Yip Harburg calls "the wished-for one"—was comedian Ed Wynn. To Freed and Harburg, it was W. C. Fields. Fields' *Wizard* would have been a con man, blustering and boisterous. Wynn's Wizard would have been emotionally and physically zany. "We would have had to give him a lot more puns," says Harburg. Frank Morgan, the Wizard who was finally picked from MGM's contract list, created a frightened little man ensuring his survival through humbugging. Morgan made sixty-eight films at MGM between 1933 and 1949, when he died in his sleep at the age of fifty-nine. In most of them, he was an endearingly befuddled Milquetoast perpetually stammering his way through life. The befuddlement was quite real, since the briefcase he carried onto the set in the morning contained martinis. One of eleven children born to the family that owned the formula for Angostura

Bitters, he had followed his older brother Ralph onto the stage. It is hard to imagine him as a dramatic actor, and yet becoming a comedian had been an accident: he was offered a dramatic role and a comedy part at the same time, and the comedy paid $50 a week more.

Since LeRoy was the picture's producer, Ed Wynn was given first chance at the role. Wynn, a vaudeville comic who had become a radio star, turned the part down. So did Fields, although not until after Harburg had written the Wizard's main speech to fit Fields' massive cynicism as he handed out a diploma in place of brains, a plaque in place of a heart, and a medal in place of courage. Fields is supposed to have refused the part because MGM wouldn't pay him enough. "They offered Fields $75,000 and he wanted $100,000," says Harburg. "To do that little part. A man gives up immortality for a few lousy dollars he doesn't need." According to a letter in *W. C. Fields by Himself,** the situation may have been a bit more complicated. The letter bears the signature of his agent, but Fields' grandson thinks that it was written by Fields himself and given to the agent to sign. The letter states that Fields "has not accepted $5,000 a day from Metro-Goldwyn-Mayer to play in 'The Wizard of Oz' in order to devote his whole time to writing the script of 'You Can't Cheat an Honest Man.' " The letter also states that Fields was promised that "The picture would start immediately the story was turned in." But, although Fields finished the script, *You Can't Cheat an Honest Man* didn't go into production. The letter complains that Fields has lost "MGM's $115,000" for nothing.

According to screenwriter Noel Langley, Frank Morgan was not even third choice for the role. "He begged for it. He said, 'Let me go onto a stage and do an ad-lib test.' He did all the scenes as they were in the script. He knew the script backward. He did it all by himself with nobody there but himself and an assistant director. Harburg and Arlen and Freed and I watched the test afterward. And it was marvelous, as funny as Buster Keaton."

The casting of *The Wizard of Oz* dragged along for months. Throughout the spring, dozens of memos from Freed and MGM cast-

* (Englewood Cliffs, N. J.: Prentice-Hall, 1973).

ing director Billy Grady ended up on Mervyn LeRoy's desk. At the beginning, the memos centered on MGM contract players. What about old Charley Grapewin as Dorothy's Uncle Henry and May Robson as Aunt Em? Would he consider Fanny Brice as the Good Witch and Edna May Oliver as the Wicked Witch? Those were February questions. In May came a more urgent, "I suggest you make a decision on Edna May Oliver for the Wicked Witch, as she is usually in demand." Charley Grapewin, Freed's first choice in February, would—one year later—do the one-week role of Uncle Henry. For Aunt Em, the studio would hire an outside bit player, Clara Blandick. She, too, would work one week. "It was too minor a role to cast from our contract players," recalls Leonard Murphy, "and we really had nobody under contract who fit the part. We

Top, from left: Frank Morgan (Professor Marvel; the Wizard), Charley Grapewin (Uncle Henry), Bert Lahr (Zeke; the Cowardly Lion); bottom, from left: Judy Garland (Dorothy), Ray Bolger (Hunk; the Scarecrow), Jack Haley (Hickory; the Tin Woodman), and Clara Blandick (Auntie Em).

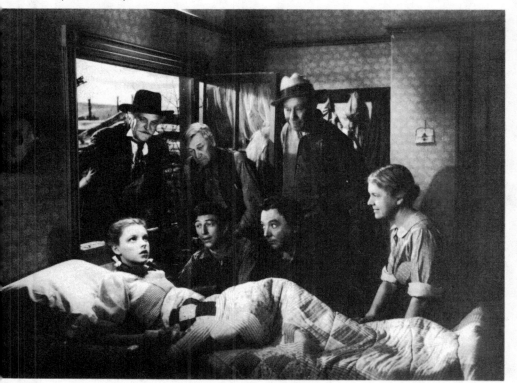

Gale Sondergaard, LeRoy's first choice for the Wicked Witch, whom he originally envisioned as a glamorous, "fallen" woman.

weren't like Warner Brothers. They'd put their whole contract list in every picture, whether an actor fit or not. You couldn't even find a Warner Brothers picture without Pat O'Brien and Alan Hale in it. We always asked who fits into a picture, chemically speaking."

Interested as Freed was in Edna May Oliver as the Wicked Witch, Mervyn LeRoy had a different idea. He had decided on a glamorous witch, a fallen woman wearing green eyeshadow and a witch's hat made out of black sequins. To be played by Gale Sondergaard.

In 1936, Mervyn LeRoy had directed Gale Sondergaard's first picture, *Anthony Adverse*. She promptly won the Academy Award as Best Supporting Actress, a fact that allowed LeRoy to congratulate himself on his eye for talent. She then—coincidentally—arrived at MGM about the same time he did, having signed a one-year contract. He cast her immediately in *Dramatic School* and looked around for other roles she could play.

"Mervyn and I did the entire Witch's wardrobe," says Sondergaard. "I would wear sequins everywhere—a tight black sequined dress, a black sequined hat. The makeup would be very glamorous and thus, subtly, very wicked. Then Mervyn came to me and said, 'Gale, the people around me say I absolutely can't make the witch a glamorous witch. The children need that wicked, hateful witch. And I don't want you to be an ugly witch.' I said, 'Fine, Mervyn. I really don't want to be an ugly, hateful witch.' And that was the end of it. In those days, I was not about to make myself ugly for any motion picture."

Gale Sondergaard, nearly forty years later, had "no regrets. Absolutely no regrets." Nor did Margaret Hamilton, who accepted the role of the ugly, hateful witch and who was even then—Ray Bolger struggles to put it tactfully—"not the most beautiful woman in the world, although she had a beautiful interior."

"When I was six years old, I played Sleeping Beauty in a production an older girl concocted to raise some money for a sewing group so we could all sew diapers for a children's hospital. That was my first acting appearance and the last time, if I may say, that I ever played a beauty of any kind." Margaret Hamilton, sitting in a Los Angeles hotel room, laughed. The laughter was without bitterness. She had accepted her lack of beauty long ago, made the best of it, made—in fact—a career of it.

In 1938 she was thirty-six years old, newly divorced, earning a living for herself and her three-year-old son by drifting from studio to studio and never letting her salary go above $1,000 a week. "At $1,200 or $1,500 a week, I knew I wouldn't work much. And I had my young son and I wanted to work all I could. So I never let them pay me more. And I never went under contract. If you were under contract and you looked like me, you got all the parts where you opened the door and said, 'I'm sorry, he's not here, good-by,' and shut the door. Even so, I got a lot of those parts. I did a one-woman show once, and I had one number called 'Aprons I Have Worn,' bits from all the different maids I had played."

By 1938 Margaret Hamilton had already played the Witch in *The Wizard of Oz* twice, for the Junior League in Cleveland. At twenty-one, when she first played the Witch, she was already, quite obviously, a character actress. As a matter of fact, she was a character *actor* even earlier, in the senior play at Hathaway-Brown Girls School in Cleveland. The morning after her triumph as an elderly Englishman, she told her mother, over breakfast, that instead of going to kindergarten teachers' training school she would be going to New York to be on the stage. "My mother never even missed a bite of her toast. She said, 'You'll do nothing of the kind, dear. You'll go on with kindergarten training school the way you've always planned. And when you learn how to earn your living, then you can fool around with the theater all you want.' And that was that."

Margaret Hamilton opened her own nursery school in Cleveland, joined the Cleveland Playhouse, and did eventually get to New York. A few years later, MGM brought her to Hollywood along with most of the supporting members of the cast of *Another Language*, the play in which she was appearing. When the play was bought by the studio, the leads stayed behind, to be replaced on the screen by Helen Hayes and Robert Montgomery.

It was Leonard Murphy who interviewed Margaret Hamilton and then sent her along to Mervyn LeRoy. Murphy had little to do with the stars of a picture. Their names were usually attached to the script that was sent down for him to budget. Every department did a script breakdown. For the Wardrobe Department, it was how many costumes each character would need and how much the clothes should cost. The Casting Department estimated how long each actor would be necessary and approximately how much each role should be worth. Margaret Hamilton's $1,000 was on target for the Wicked Witch and, besides, Murphy liked her work. He thought she would fit, "chemically speaking."

"Mr. LeRoy and I talked a little bit about the part and it was very pleasant and I supposed that I was probably going to get the part, but there was nothing definite," Margaret Hamilton remembers. "I'd only been in pictures about six years, but I already realized that you can't ever count on much of anything until it is signed

Margaret Hamilton, the Wicked Witch of the West (and Miss Gulch), 1940.

on the dotted line, as it were. And, luckily, I *didn't* count on it. Because about two weeks later I read this article that they'd decided to have a *beautiful* witch and Gale Sondergaard was going to play it. I was a little disappointed, but it wasn't the blow of my life by any means because it had happened several times before. So I simply thought, 'Well, too bad, but that's that!' "

Margaret Hamilton asked her agent to find her another part. He refused because he didn't know when *The Wizard of Oz* was going to start. "And I said, 'Jess, haven't you been reading the papers?' And he said, 'You've been in this business six years and you still believe what you read in the papers?' And a few weeks later they began to negotiate back and forth."

She was asked to make a screen test. "I think I had them put big, heavy eyebrows on and rings under my eyes and lines on my face. In those days they had to put the lines in, and now I take them out. Then I picked the oldest, crummiest-looking clothes I could find, some dirty things that sort of hung on me like a Mother Hubbard. And then a little shawl. There was no witch's hat and I really looked more like an old hag. And I cackled and screamed and said a few lines from the script."

The screen test must have been satisfactory because the negotiations became serious. But MGM balked at the time guarantee that Hamilton's agent demanded.

"I never did work for less than a two-week guarantee, which was not extravagant, not beyond the pale, but respectable. This time Jess asked the studio for six weeks, and they didn't want to give it to him. They were perfectly willing to guarantee three weeks, but they were adamant about six. And I begged my agent, 'Jess, don't lose this part. You know nobody gives me six weeks unless they're sure it's going to be eight. Don't hold out, Jess. I *want* this part.' But he insisted on holding out. And then Jess and his wife and some beau I had were with me at a football game and Mervyn LeRoy comes down the aisle and takes a big cigar out of his mouth and says, 'Glad you're going to be with us.' And Jess says, 'Not definite.' And Mr. LeRoy says, 'What do you mean, *not definite?*' And Jess says, 'Meet me outside at halftime.' And that was that."

Margaret Hamilton got her six-week guarantee. It was, as it

turned out, hardly worth fighting about since she worked on the picture for four months.*

The search for the good witch, Glinda, was not as complicated. Under contract were eight Characters and Comediennes who might be suitable. The choice could be made from Fanny Brice, Billie Burke, Constance Collier, Gracie Fields, Una Merkel, Edna May Oliver, Helen Troy, and Cora Witherspoon. According to Murphy, "We all said, 'Let's have Billie Burke.' There was no contest." Burke's more than slightly fey quality would play well against the acidulous menace of Margaret Hamilton. She would lighten the menace by treating it as an incomprehensible annoyance.

Mary William Ethelbert Appleton Burke, daughter of a Barnum and Bailey circus clown, had grown up to be a Broadway star. She had married Florenz Ziegfeld in 1914 and had turned down a $10,000-a-week offer from the movies in 1915 in order to stay married to the outrageously handsome, outrageously philandering impresario. ("I perceived that I was destined to be jealous of the entire *Follies* chorus as well as the *Follies* star list for the rest of my married life," Billie Burke wrote in her autobiography,† though one of Ziegfeld's more famous ladies, Marilyn Miller, had once observed, "She waves her baby at him like George M. Cohan waves the American flag.") Ziegfeld died in 1932, leaving debts of half a million dollars; and Burke's friends put her to work playing addled matrons—what she called "my silly women"—who had their basis in her own personality.

One of Margaret Hamilton's strongest memories of the picture was of the very marked differences between herself and Billie Burke: "She had a pink and blue dressing room, with pink and blue powder puffs and pink and blue bottles filled with powder and baby oil. And pink and blue peppermints. And an infinite number of perfectly beautiful clothes, all lace; and everything was pink and blue. And one day she left the set when she was waiting for a costume test. When they were ready for her, no one could find her anyplace. Eventually up to the door of the set came a limousine and out

* Garnering a salary of exactly $18,541.68.
† *With a Feather on My Nose* (New York: Appleton-Century-Crofts, 1949).

Billie Burke. She was picked to play Glinda, the Good Witch of the North, from MGM's "Characters and Comediennes" then under contract—among them Fanny Brice, Gracie Fields, and Edna May Oliver.

stepped the fairy lady, and the first assistant director said, 'Miss Burke, where have you been? It's been very expensive and costly and uncomfortable for all of us.' And I couldn't believe my eyes. Her reaction was the most amazing thing. Those blue eyes of hers were filled with tears, and the tears were dropping down her cheeks. And she said, 'You're . . . you're browbeating me!' "

It was Yip Harburg who acquired a Cowardly Lion for the film. When Langley's fourth script provided a lion who was not an enchanted prince but merely a lion, Harburg suggested Bert Lahr, a seasoned burlesque comedian who had worked his way up through vaudeville to star in Broadway musicals. Harburg had worked with Lahr in the revue *Life Begins at 8:40*, and he thought him a very funny man. More than that, Harburg knew that Lahr could play the pathos beneath the Lion's bluster; he was confident he could write for Lahr; and he sensed that both Lahr's broad comedy and his sweetness would be irrepressible even when Lahr himself was hidden under a seventy-pound lion skin.

Lahr, whose education had ended abruptly when he failed the eighth grade, had never even heard of *The Wizard of Oz*. But he read the script and was enthusiastic. MGM offered a guaranteed three weeks at $2,500 a week. Lahr's vanity made him insist on a guaranteed five weeks of work. He had already been under contract to and released by Universal and 20th Century-Fox—essentially because his enormous comic energy made his screen presence almost distasteful. He was bewildered and hurt by what Hollywood was doing to him. According to his son, novelist and critic John Lahr,* "Generally, he was slated for second-banana parts, not handsome enough for the love interest; and too grotesque in close-up (his energy made him grotesque) to work in full form in films. It's very important to stress that he was so large a comic figure, I mean he radiated such energy and size, that the camera could only accept it as 'real' if he was an animal and not human."

The pathos beneath the Lion's bluster was something that was

---

* In a letter to the author.

Bert Lahr, circa 1939. Yip Harburg, who had worked with him in Broadway musicals, suggested him for the part of the Cowardly Lion.

quite real. Lahr was a man who had plowed all his emotional under-standing into his work, and not into the people who were part of his private life. In 1938, his wife and former partner was hopelessly ill mentally, and he could not rid himself of the fear that his ambition, his lack of empathy, had been the cause of her illness.

The Cowardly Lion was the only screen role in which Bert Lahr fully exploited his gifts. Yet it took MGM a month to agree to the five-week guarantee he demanded. The irony is that, including tests and rehearsals, Lahr worked on *The Wizard of Oz* for six months. Five weeks of that time were spent doing "The Jitter Bug," the musical number that was cut from the finished film in order to shorten it.

It was not a human actor but the dog, Toto, for whom the longest search was made. The Property Department was handed a copy of L. Frank Baum's book and told to find a dog that looked like the dog in W. W. Denslow's drawings, just as the Wardrobe and Makeup departments were handed copies of the book and told to create a Scarecrow and a Tin Woodman who resembled the pictures in the book. No one in the Property Department could recognize the breed Denslow had drawn.

Hollywood animal trainers are almost always identified in juxta-position to their most famous animals. Rudd Weatherwax's name is never mentioned without adding "Lassie." In the 1930's, Lee Duncan was known as the trainer of Rin-Tin-Tin, while Carl Spitz's name was always placed next to that of Buck, the St. Bernard he had trained to star with Clark Gable and Loretta Young in *Call of the Wild*.

Spitz had acquired Terry, the female Cairn terrier who would play Toto in *The Wizard of Oz*, nearly four years before the picture was made. "A lady had come to me and said, 'Carl, I have here a dog. Will you train it for me?' She was a breeder, and she had sold this dog to an elderly couple in Pasadena. And the dog was so shy that for three weeks it didn't come out from under the bed. The people called her and said, 'Missus, give us our money back and come get the dog out from under the bed.'

[131]

"So she asked me to train the dog. I knew she didn't have much money, but she talked me out of a down payment. She said she would pay me when she picked up the dog. And the dog was really shy. It took me seven weeks to train it. When the dog was finished, the lady came for it and tried to outtalk me for the money. But this time I didn't fall for her tricks. I said, 'You don't bring the money, you don't get the dog.' Eight days later, she came and said, 'Here is a car.' I took one look at the car she brought and I said, 'Lady, I'm not the best mechanic, but I know enough I'd have to pay ten bucks to tow it *to* the wrecking yard.' So she took the car away and never came back for the dog."

Spitz had no intention of working his new dog in pictures. But MGM director Clarence Brown saw her at Spitz's kennels and chose her for a film. At first Spitz refused, on the basis that the dog was too shy to work. When Brown insisted, Spitz refused to work the dog. Brown agreed to work her himself. Says Spitz, "I told him he would have to live with the dog for two months before the dog would work for him. I was wrong. He worked her through the whole picture, and I was amazed at how the dog progressed. And so then she was a picture dog."

Spitz had come to America from Germany in 1926, a fireman by vocation and a dog trainer by avocation. He was thirty-three years old, and he had not wanted to emigrate. But the loss of his job in the German Depression and his inability to find another had forced him to go to New York. He spent one day in New York before realizing it was too close to Germany. "I was so homesick I might just get on a boat and go back home." So he went inland to Chicago, where he opened a kennel. Chicago had "too cold a winter for my profession." A customer told him to go to California. He left Chicago on November 10, 1927, in a two-door Chevy sedan and arrived in Los Angeles twenty-one days later.

He was successful almost immediately. In Germany he had trained a few dogs to react to silent commands for deaf people. He was one of the first movie animal-trainers to see the necessity for silent cue commands in talking films and the first to train all his animals to respond to silent orders. "Up to then, we hollered and shouted at the dogs."

Carl Spitz on a public appearance tour in 1940. From left: Promise,
the pointer in The Biscuit Eater; *Buck, the St. Bernard from* Call of the
Wild; *Terry, the Cairn terrier who played Toto; Prince, the Great Dane*
in Wuthering Heights; *Mr. Binkie, the Scottie of* The Light That Failed;
and Musty, the mastiff in Dangerous Days. *The six dogs were valued*
at $120,000.

Spitz learned about the search for Toto quite late. He was
handed one of the copies of Denslow's drawings that had already
been sent to Switzerland and New York. He was sure the drawings
were intended to be a Cairn terrier, and he brought Terry to the
studio. After a stop at the Property Department, he was sent to the
Thalberg Building. "The producer was there, the writer was there.
Everyone. And someone right away hollered, 'That's the dog we
want.'"

Unfortunately, during his brief stop at the Property Department, Spitz had agreed to a salary of $125 a week. "I didn't know
then how badly they needed the dog. I could have gotten $500 a
week, but I only got $125." Of the ten major actors in *The Wizard
of Oz*, Terry was paid the least. Judy Garland, at $500 a week, re-

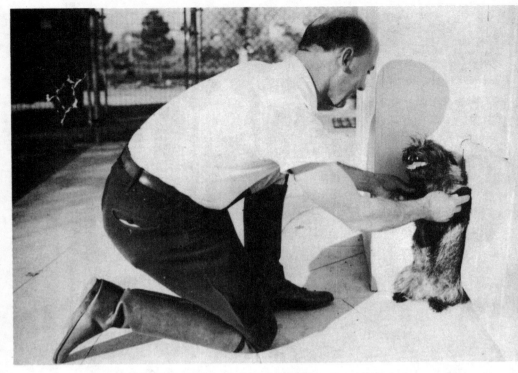

Carl Spitz training Terry for the part of Toto.

ceived the next lowest pay. Charley Grapewin and Clara Blandick got $750, Billie Burke $766.67, Margaret Hamilton her usual $1,000. Ebsen was paid $1,500, Bert Lahr and Frank Morgan $2,500 apiece. Ray Bolger's $3,000 topped the list.* Their salaries totaled $13,391.67 each week.

They were the skillful or lucky ones. The back door of the casting department at MGM opened onto an alley outside the studio. Every day, hopeful actors waited in the alley. There might be as few as twenty people in the alley or as many as one hundred. Each week, some were hired to fill the backgrounds on the immense sound stages. Occasionally, for a big costume film, all of them would be given work. But if they expected to become stars, no one ever did.

* When Jack Haley replaced Buddy Ebsen, his salary too was $3,000 a week.

THE DIRECTORS

RICHARD THORPE
Before *Oz,* twenty-one movies including *Tarzan* and *Night Must Fall;*
after *Oz,* fifty-five movies including *Above Suspicion* and *Follow the Boys*

GEORGE CUKOR
Six years after *Dinner at Eight, Oz* for three days,
Gone With the Wind for two weeks, then *The Women*

VICTOR FLEMING
En route to *Gone With the Wind*

KING VIDOR
Twenty years after *The Big Parade*

Richard Thorpe directed *The Wizard of Oz* for two weeks, George Cukor for three days, Victor Fleming for four months, and King Vidor for ten days.

None of the four men can be considered the creator of the film in the sense that D. W. Griffith created *Birth of a Nation* in 1914 or Robert Altman created *Nashville* in 1975. MGM directors were well fed and well paid, but they were kept on a tight leash. Irving Thalberg and L. B. Mayer, hostile about so many other things, were in agreement that a director was simply one more tool to be used in the making of motion pictures. MGM story editor Sam Marx once tried to get Thalberg to hire an aging and poverty-stricken D. W. Griffith. He refused. "I could never work with Griffith," Thalberg said, "nor he with me."

With rare exceptions, an MGM director was assigned to a picture much as the actors and scriptwriters were assigned. A director could try to convince Benny Thau or L. B. Mayer that he wasn't right for the assignment. He could even refuse to do the picture and take the small risk of being suspended without salary. (Studios used suspension as a way of controlling their actors but rarely bothered to use it on their directors.) But once a director accepted the assignment, he was handed a script that had already been written and was told to shoot it with actors who had already been chosen on sets that had already been designed. Noel Langley began work on the script of *The Wizard of Oz* in March 1938. The last of the casting was completed in August. On September 17, Richard Thorpe was officially assigned to direct, and the picture went into production three weeks later.

"You'd always get the script after it was written," Thorpe said in 1972. "You'd change words once in a while. And if some scene didn't play, didn't seem to belong or work out right, you could ask the producer to have the writer take another whack at it." Of course, the producer could—and sometimes did—refuse.

Thalberg himself was unfailingly gentle and courteous to his directors; and most of them loved him. But he expected to have *his* pictures shot the way *he* visualized them. The directors with whom he worked most often—Jack Conway, W. S. Van Dyke, Clarence Brown, Robert Z. Leonard, Sam Wood, Victor Fleming, Sidney

Franklin, Harry Beaumont—were craftsmen rather than artists, and not unwilling to do what they were told. At MGM, the interchangeability of directors, like that of certain automobile parts, was taken for granted. Thalberg might ask the original director to do any necessary retakes. But if the original director was assigned elsewhere, Thalberg was hardly concerned—some equivalent director was sure to be available.

Thalberg died in 1936, but he had done his philosophical work well. Fifteen years later, MGM was still a producer's studio. According to Sam Marx, "As late as 1950, if there was a quarrel between a producer and a director, the producer was backed to the hilt." MGM pictures and actors won the lion's share of early Academy Awards. Yet, of the first thirty Academy Awards given for Best Director, MGM films won only two—and one of those was the Oscar given to Victor Fleming for *Gone With the Wind* (1939), an MGM film only in the sense that the producer, David Selznick, was "blackmailed" into allowing MGM to release it.

Working over at Columbia on Hollywood's Poverty Row, ten miles from MGM's rolling acres, Frank Capra was nominated as Best Director five times between 1933 and 1940. He won three times. The directors at MGM were "the crème-de-la-crème," Capra wrote in his autobiography.* But they were also "organization men, as anonymous as vice-presidents of General Motors." Capra had been at MGM, too. Briefly. In 1931, he had been loaned to that luxurious studio. Even then, MGM was "the Mecca for filmmakers," but Capra still found himself the victim of "a queasy, uneasy feeling" whenever he entered MGM's East Gate. The queasy feeling came from the gulf between his own rebellious passion for controlling his films and the "many films, many assembly lines" system at MGM. At Columbia, that smelly rabbit warren of a studio on Poverty Row, Harry Cohn would go to any cutthroat lengths to keep his studio above water, even if it meant giving his directors the power to choose and produce their own films. In 1927, Cohn had offered Capra $1,000 to direct a film at Columbia. Capra had agreed—but only on the condition that he also be allowed to write and produce the film. For no

* *The Name Above the Title* (New York: Macmillan, 1971).

Richard Thorpe (left), the first of four directors to work on Oz
(here with Wallace Beery on the set of Wyoming *in 1940). Thorpe stayed
at MGM for twenty years and directed more than 200 movies. After
two weeks on* Oz, *he was replaced by George Cukor.*

extra money, of course. When Capra had signed his contract at
Columbia, he had deliberately "traded money for power I couldn't
get at any other studio."

Capra's first trip to MGM ended abortively. He was shipped
back to Columbia for shooting a scene differently from the way he
had been instructed to shoot it by his executive producer. During
the 1930's, that crosstown journey was rather like the one-way passage in a Hollywood prison picture. Columbia was "the germ of the
ocean," the "Siberia" to which obstreperous major-studio stars were
banished for a picture or two. If Mayer had an actor he wanted to
punish, he picked up the phone and called Cohn. Eventually, mav-
erick directors who wanted to shape their own films flocked to Columbia. Harry Cohn outlasted Louis B. Mayer.

At MGM in 1938, the white administration building named for
Irving Thalberg had just been opened, and one of the elevators was

reserved "FOR PRODUCERS AND EXECUTIVES ONLY." That elevator was opened to everyone after a few liberal producers protested that the restriction was needlessly embarrassing to their favorite directors.

In 1938, Richard Thorpe was the quintessential studio director. Says one of his peers, "He was a company man, a very pleasant, good-looking, nice, well-behaved guy who took pride in being efficient like some businessman would take pride in the way he ran his bank." He did what he was asked to do—usually four days ahead of schedule. He stayed at MGM over twenty years, and only once did he try to turn a picture down. "It was a picture with Gene Kelly," Thorpe says, "about the Mafia or something [*Black Hand*]. I talked to Dore Schary for an hour and a half. I didn't think I could handle Gene Kelly because he had been a director. And after an hour and a half, Schary said, 'Well, you go ahead and do it.' So I went ahead and did it." Thorpe directed *Night Must Fall*, the first four of Weismuller's Tarzan films, *The Great Caruso*, and nine Robert Taylor films, including those beautiful, stilted historical romances of the 1950's like *Ivanhoe* and *Knights of the Round Table* and *Quentin Durward*. And Benny Thau once told him that his movies made more money for the studio than the movies of any other director.

By 1976, Mervyn LeRoy could not remember why he chose Richard Thorpe to direct *The Wizard of Oz*, nor does Thorpe know why he was chosen. Hugh Fordin's book on Arthur Freed, *The World of Entertainment*, implies that LeRoy's first choice was Norman Taurog (who was probably considered because he was regarded as Hollywood's top director of children). Taurog, whose 1938 films included *Boys' Town* and David Selznick's *Adventures of Tom Sawyer*, was the Academy Award–winning director of *Skippy* (1931). The choice-of-director log, according to Fordin, reads:

July 12, 1939*   No director
July 27   Norman Taurog set

* July 12, 1939, is an obvious error to begin with, since the film was started in October 1938. There are other errors in that same chapter of Fordin's book. He assigns Florence Ryerson and Edgar Allan Woolf to the film on February 25, 1938, four months before they actually went to work on it. He credits them with Noel Langley's adaptation; brings Langley in as a scriptwriter after Ryerson and Woolf rather than before; and gives the Wizard the character of Professor Marvel as of late February instead of early June.

August 16	Taurog off, Richard Thorpe set
August 29	Thorpe off, Taurog returns
September 2	Thorpe returns
September 16	Taurog returns for one day
September 17	Thorpe officially engaged to direct

If Taurog was indeed penciled in for *The Wizard of Oz*, it was only on a scratch pad in someone's office. In 1976 he remembered the summer of 1938 very clearly. No one approached him to direct *The Wizard of Oz*. He never even heard a rumor that he was being considered.

Thorpe started directing the picture on October 12, 1938. Twelve days later, he was fired. It was not Mervyn LeRoy who broke the news to Thorpe. LeRoy left that task to Benny Thau. Then Thorpe was spirited to Palm Springs by MGM publicity director Howard Strickling. Thorpe remembers Strickling hiding him in Palm Springs for a week or two "so that no reporters could get to me." The newspapers and trade papers were told that Thorpe was "ill," and no one seems to have questioned that diagnosis. On November 21, well tanned from the desert sun, Thorpe returned to the studio to start directing *Huckleberry Finn*.

Thorpe never knew why he was fired. "Somebody was going to chop a door down.* I remember when Mervyn said to me, 'Why did you have him chop it that way? Why didn't you have him chop it this way?' And I didn't argue. Because I already *knew* I was off the picture. But if you're going to split a board, the easiest way to split it is my way, not his way. Which I don't think Mervyn is practical enough to know."

Mervyn LeRoy squirms with embarrassment. Direct confrontation is not his style. "He was a wonderful guy, Dick Thorpe. He made some fine pictures. But to make a fairy story is a different type of thing entirely. He didn't quite understand the story. He just didn't have the . . . the warmth or the feeling. To make a fairy story, you have to think like a kid."

---

* The Tin Woodman, who was attempting to free Dorothy from the Wicked Witch of the West.

Although Thorpe stayed on the picture two weeks, LeRoy's dissatisfaction was evident by the end of the first week. "He called us all in," Buddy Ebsen recalls, "and said that everything looked terrible. He said it was utter confusion, that the rushes looked like *Ladies' Night in a Turkish Bath.* He started berating the actors. We were only doing what we were directed to do, so we were startled, to say the least. We didn't feel we deserved it."

Buddy Ebsen's own exit from the picture came a day or two before Richard Thorpe's. This coincidence would lead to the assumption that Ebsen, like Thorpe, was fired. But he was not fired. Nor was anyone else. "Each time we started with a new director, I thought, 'Oh-oh, this is where I get the ax,' " says Margaret Hamilton. "But there was never a hint that the new director disapproved of any of us. It was Mr. LeRoy who made the casting decisions."

Thorpe's two weeks had been spent shooting scenes in the Witch's Castle with Dorothy, the Tin Woodman, the Scarecrow, and the Cowardly Lion. He had also shot immense amounts of film of Toto escaping from the Castle and returning to help rescue Dorothy. "He was a fine fellow, Richard Thorpe," according to the dog's trainer, Carl Spitz. "He loved the little dog so much that the dog was finally the star—not Judy Garland. But it left a bitter taste between the actors and the dog after they threw all that film out. And I was disgusted. So when they changed directors, I gave the dog over to another trainer to work. He worked three or four weeks and got suddenly very ill because the picture was so strenuous. And then I took over again." Before the picture was finished, both Spitz and his dog were on the edge of nervous breakdowns.

Richard Thorpe left for Palm Springs on October 25. Victor Fleming brought everyone back to the Witch's Castle on November 3. In the interim, there was George Cukor. Cukor was an anomaly at MGM. Originally a stage director, he had come to MGM under the wing of L. B. Mayer's son-in-law David Selznick. He had directed *Dinner at Eight* and *David Copperfield* for Selznick. Then Thalberg had entrusted him with his wife, Norma Shearer, in *Romeo and Juliet* and Greta Garbo in *Camille.* An exquisite director of polished, liter-

George Cukor (with Joan Crawford during the filming of Susan and God, *1940). Cukor was reluctant to take over the direction of* Oz *but finally agreed to make some costume and makeup tests for Mervyn LeRoy.*

ate comedy, Cukor would eventually become known as a "woman's director."

Cukor was asked—not told—to do *The Wizard of Oz* by Mervyn LeRoy. "I wouldn't have *dreamed* of doing it," says Cukor. "I was brought up on grander things. I was brought up on Tennyson."

But Cukor, like nearly everyone else at MGM, was a team player. Directors would mop up pictures that other directors had started, without asking for or receiving credit. Occasionally, they even worked on two pictures at the same time. Richard Thorpe had done that once or twice, running from stage to stage in order to finish the last week of one film while shooting the first week of another. Despite the fact that Cukor considered *The Wizard of Oz* to be "a minor book full of fourth-rate imagery," he agreed to look at the film Thorpe had shot and to help LeRoy out by doing three or four days of tests. He was appalled by the footage he saw. "Judy Garland looked artificial. She was too made up, too pretty. She was also very young and inexperienced—although very gifted—and so she was too *cute*, too inclined to act in a fairy-tale way. The whole joke was that she was this little literal girl from Kansas among all the freaks. If she is real, it makes the whole picture funny."

Cukor took off Judy Garland's blond wig* and half of her makeup. Then he took her aside and told her "not to act in a fancy-schmancy way." She must always remember, he said, that she was "just a little girl from Kansas." He directed her tests with the new makeup and departed with a sigh of relief, leaving Mervyn LeRoy still in search of a director.

At first glance, Victor Fleming seems an odd choice for LeRoy to have made. If Cukor was to be labeled a "woman's director," Fleming was the "man's director" par excellence. *The Virginian, Test Pilot, Red Dust* with its sexual banquet of Jean Harlow and Clark Gable, *Treasure Island, Captains Courageous*—those were Fleming's pictures. Fleming had a grammar-school education, an ugly-handsome face, rough manners, and fingers that were long and delicate. "He had the fingers of an artist," recalls his drinking and motorcycle buddy, John Lee Mahin. Nothing else in his outward appearance or personality suggested an artist in the least. When the wild cats in the hills above his Bel Air home kept him from sleeping, he shot them and lined the bodies up outside his bedroom door. To show his disgust at his wife for bringing her marmoset monkey into a restaurant, he killed a fly, mashed it with his knife, sprinkled it with salt and pepper, and licked the knife clean. To prove he had actually eaten the fly, he opened his mouth. One black leg was still on his tongue.

His older daughter, Victoria, remembers him as a blend of Gen-

---

* The studio's official still photographs of scenes in the Witch's Castle show Garland in her blond wig. They also show Margaret Hamilton with a different makeup from the one she wears in the film. During the respite from directors, the Witch's nose and chin were restructured.

10/31/38
original Dress—
own Hair & fall
before darkening

eral George Patton and General Douglas MacArthur. When an alley cat tried to mate with K.C., Victoria's calico cat, Fleming took his star-gauge Springfield rifle and shot the alley cat while it was mounting K.C. 150 feet away. "He knew what would have happened if he had missed and killed my cat," says Victoria. "But he knew he wouldn't miss."

He piloted his own plane, rode a motorcycle twenty years before motorcycles were fashionable, wore clothes well enough to have gotten a job as a model. He was equally fascinating to women and to men. He had his pick of the women he knew, and once or twice a month there was one he didn't know hiding in his car in the studio parking lot. Women warmed his bed, but men provided companionship. Flanked by Ward Bond and Clark Gable, Fleming rode off through the hills every Sunday afternoon on his Ariel Square Four. Even after his marriage, he spent his Sunday afternoons with the Spit-and-Polish Club he had founded.

He looked flamboyant but was basically a conservative man. He drove a dove-grey Cadillac and envied his next-door neighbor, Howard Hawks, who had the dash to buy a Duesenberg. He was staunchly Republican, and after the war he would organize an anti-Communist group with John Wayne and Ward Bond.

Fleming had quite literally tinkered his way into films around 1912. Some fly-by-night movie company was making two films a week in Santa Barbara, a hundred miles up the coast from Los Angeles. The budget was $500 a film, and the camera was broken. "Vic was a chauffeur for a rich old lady," says John Lee Mahin. "A chauffeur in those days was quite somebody—like a pilot is today. He could fix the old lady's Locomobile, and he could fix the camera for the movie company. Later, when the cameraman got drunk, they asked Vic if he could operate a camera. He said, 'I fixed it. Yeah, I'll operate it.' They gave him 35 dollars a week and the director was only getting 40."

Inset: Judy Garland, wearing a blond wig and heavy makeup, stands with Munchkins for a color test during Thorpe's reign as director. At left: as she appeared after Cukor's three days on the picture.

[145]

In 1938, he was getting $2,500 a week. He was fifty-five years old and—although he was still arrogant enough to turn around and drive home if a new gateman at the studio didn't recognize him and asked him to show his pass—he had quite perceptibly mellowed. The mellowing had nothing to do with age. In 1933, he had married for the first and only time. He had picked for his wife a forty-year-old married woman who had been his friend for at least twenty years. "Victor used to come by our house every single afternoon for years and years," says his stepdaughter, Helene Bowman. "He was my father's best friend, and Mother was his confessor. He used to fly her to Indianapolis for the races and talk to her about his crush on Clara Bow or some other girl. Eventually, I guess, the intimacy got a little more intimate."

It was a strange marriage by any standards, an even stranger one for a man who had waited until he was fifty years old. At his wedding in Yuma, Arizona, he told the justice of the peace "to leave the *love* out of the ceremony." At premieres of his movies, he would walk down the red carpet with his female star while his wife walked ten paces behind—"a frog in his wake," says their daughter Victoria, who recalls her father toying with her mother at the dinner table "like a cat with a mouse." He didn't even take her into his house until she got pregnant with Victoria in 1934: until then, she lived in the Beverly Hills house she had shared with her first husband, Arthur Rosson. Yet he was, despite the sexual swath he had previously cut through Hollywood, faithful to Lu Rosson Fleming until 1948 and *Joan of Arc* and Ingrid Bergman.

If it had not been for his two daughters, Victoria and Sally, Fleming would probably not have directed *The Wizard of Oz.* "Here Vic was, a man of, oh hell, fifty-two, and he suddenly had two little girls. And all his joy was in them," according to John Lee Mahin. He was, says Helene Bowman, "so madly in love with those two little girls that it was unbelievable." He was home for breakfast with them in the morning. He was home for dinner with them every night at 6:30. If he had to shoot at night, he went back to the studio after dinner. But under no circumstances and for no reason did he skip dinner. To keep them safe from polio, he spent the summer with them on an island he had bought in British Columbia. To keep them safe from Hollywood, he put them in a private Catholic day school, although he himself had no apparent religion. He gave them horses, taught them to fish, supervised the buying of every item of their clothing, including their school uniforms. He built them a magnificent house on Moraga Drive in Bel Air and, in his basement workshop there, carved them a perfect penguin out of ivory. "We had the best of everything until he died," says Victoria. "He was a very, very tender person," says Sally, a judgment that would probably have shocked most of the people who knew him.

Mervyn LeRoy was looking for a director "with the mind of a child." On the screen, Fleming's world had been one of rough men, rough skies, rough seas. Fleming hesitated. LeRoy insisted. Fleming still hesitated. Fleming and LeRoy drove down to L. B. Mayer's beach house. There was a long walk on the sand. Fleming was flanked

Victor Fleming with his family, May 1937.

by LeRoy on one side, by Mayer on the other. LeRoy started talking, "selling him. What a wonderful thing it was to make this picture, this classic book." Mayer was no more subtle. "He was doing the same thing I was," LeRoy recalls. Except that Mayer's very involvement was "using his finger in Victor's nose." Even so, Fleming almost refused, feeling that he would be quite literally out of his elements. "I think he did it for *them*, for Missy [Victoria] and Sally Fleming," says John Lee Mahin. "I was with him on the set and I could see his whole love for them poured into the picture."

All the film that Richard Thorpe had shot was swept out, disposed of in storage vaults and wastepaper baskets. Buddy Ebsen was replaced by Jack Haley, but there were no other cast changes. Haley chopped down the door to Dorothy's prison without a single frown from LeRoy. Victor Fleming was at the helm.

Exactly what Fleming contributed to *The Wizard of Oz* is hard to assess. Since the early 1960's, it has been fashionable to regard the director as the author of his film. The actors, cameramen, and screenwriters are seen as his robots, performing a simple mechanical function in helping him translate his internal vision to the external screen. Although Robert Altman has most often been the *author* of his films in the sense that he raised money by showing the studio a conventional script and then, money in hand, threw away the conventional script (written by someone else) to replace it with the improvisations of his antic unconscious; although Preston Sturges was the *author* of his films in the sense that he literally wrote them, and Fellini the *author* of his films in the sense that both content and images were the mixed memories and emotions of his past, most studio directors have never been *auteurs*. The studio system made everything, everybody, subservient to the studio. At MGM, there was even a sign on the desk of Eddie Mannix, L. B. Mayer's jovial assistant, that read: "THE ONLY STAR AT MGM IS LEO THE LION."

Inevitably, those directors who considered themselves artists found themselves at war with the studios that considered them employees. It was a war that the studios did not always win, but victory for a director—when it came—was usually the result of tenacity, coincidence, and astounding good luck.

Says Alfred Hitchcock, "I was able to be independent because, although I was under contract to David Selznick, I only made three Selznick films. David kept loaning me out. Because I didn't belong to the studio to whom I was loaned, I was one step away from the studio umbrella. I could even work as my own producer. The producer's name on many of my films was just a name put there to satisfy studio policy. When I went to Fox to make *Lifeboat*, I asked William Goetz, 'Do you want me to have a producer?' He said, 'If you don't mind.' I said, 'Not at all.' "

At MGM, Thalberg tried occasionally to work with independent directors whose talent he admired. With one exception, the result was to make everyone miserable: Josef von Sternberg fled from MGM as soon as *The Exquisite Sinner* was finished; Maurice Tourneur walked out before *The Mysterious Island* was completed; Erich von Stroheim and Ernst Lubitsch lasted through two films apiece before they departed. The exception was King Vidor. Only with Vidor (*The Crowd, Our Daily Bread, Hallelujah*) was Thalberg willing to allow a director almost unlimited freedom.

Vidor, eighty-one years old in 1976, a courtly and kind gentleman, sat in the office of his Beverly Hills home and wondered why. Perhaps, he said, it was because of *The Big Parade*. "I made *The Big Parade* [1926] very early in the history of MGM. It was just supposed to be a program picture, a starring vehicle for John Gilbert. But it turned out to be successful—so big, so successful that maybe they thought, 'If we leave him alone, he might make another *Big Parade*.' "

It was tenacity, rather than luck, that bought Rouben Mamoulian his freedom. "If you fought long enough, argued long enough, you could get what you wanted," says Mamoulian. "You could always do what you wanted if you delivered, if your films made money. I take responsibility for every film I have made. Any faults in my films are my own."

Mamoulian started out at Paramount, a studio somewhat less fixated on the producer system than MGM. From the beginning,

King Vidor directing Northwest Passage, *1939. He was considered the most independent of the MGM directors, but he agreed to wind up* Oz *when Fleming was hired away by David Selznick to direct* Gone With the Wind.

Cecil B. DeMille served as his own producer at Paramount; and, for a brief time, director Ernst Lubitsch was even head of production there. Mamoulian got his first lesson on the status of a director with his first film. Paramount president Adolph Zukor was so excited about that film, *Applause* (1929), that he insisted Mamoulian sit in his chair. Mamoulian sat, and Zukor proceeded to tell him that *Applause* was the greatest film Paramount had ever made. He gave Mamoulian a two-week vacation, urged him to hurry back, and assured him that "It doesn't matter how the film's received." When *Applause* got sensational reviews but fell on its face at the box office, it was months before Zukor would even answer Mamoulian's telephone calls.

When Mamoulian moved to MGM, he simply refused to sign a contract to direct Greta Garbo's *Queen Christina* (1933) unless Walter Wanger's name was written into the contract as producer. "I knew I'd have no trouble with Wanger. He had been at Paramount." Mayer was aghast at this bending of the MGM system. "We can't do that. We can't put a particular producer into your contract. What if Wanger dies?" Mamoulian smiled innocently. "If he dies, then *I* become the producer."

It was harder at 20th Century-Fox. "Darryl Zanuck was the worst of the studio bosses, a real tyrant. For years he said, 'Mamoulian will never work on my lot. He's too independent.' Then my agent called and told me Zanuck would like me to remake *The Mark of Zorro*. I had seen the Fairbanks version when I was eighteen and loved it. So I read the script Fox had. I hated the script. 'That ends it,' said my agent because he knew Zanuck had worked on that script. But the next day I was summoned to the studio. I walked into that Mussolini-like office. There Zanuck stood with that polo mallet in his hand. 'I've worked on this script for two years,' he said. I started to walk out. He told me to stay. He agreed that I could have the script rewritten. Then came the question of putting the finished picture together. I said, 'Darryl, I understand that on this lot a director finishes a picture and you cut it. Unless you see my cut, you don't know what I intended.' 'When John Ford finishes a picture,' Zanuck said, 'he goes to Catalina and I cut it and he likes it.'* I said, 'I don't work that way.' He said, 'I can't establish a precedent.' I started to walk out again. 'How long will it take you to cut the film?' he asked. 'Eight days.' 'When you're through with the film, I'll go to Palm Springs for eight days. Of course, I can't start cutting until I get back.' So I cut the film while he was in Palm Springs and we ran a preview and the audience loved it. The next night we ran it in a projection room with Zanuck and fifteen yes-men, including his barber. Every time Zanuck would make a suggestion, the fifteen men would say, 'Oh, great! Oh, great!' They stayed in that room saying, 'Oh, great!' until four-thirty a.m. Zanuck cut the film his way. We had a second preview. I thought the picture was absolutely awful and it laid an egg. When we left the theater, Zanuck put his arm around my shoulder and said, 'We're the best cutting team in the business. Put it back the way it was and ship it.' "

If Zanuck had chosen to send out his version of *The Mark of Zorro*, there was nothing Mamoulian could have done except take his name off the picture and refuse to honor his contract with Zanuck for *Blood and Sand*. Fortunately, the Hollywood sovereigns' desire for power warred with their greed. Creative directors often made pictures that made money. And almost always there was some overseer —like MGM's Nick Schenck—in New York who was concerned only with profit and loss. So long as their pictures made money, independent directors were, at most studios, at least tolerated.

Most of the studio directors of the thirties did not attempt to buck the studio system. But it would be incorrect to assume that none of them had the talent to impress their personal visions on their films. Many good directors simply did not have the stamina to fight the system. "I used to say to myself, 'no more pictures that come out of my guts,' " recalled King Vidor, who wanted to make *Hallelujah* so badly that he offered to give his salary back to MGM if the studio would allow him to do the film. "The fight to make your own films was such a difficult and painful thing. So I'd give in and make a few of the others. Things like *Northwest Passage*. Or I'd take Brian

---

* John Ford was the only important Hollywood director who didn't at least try to edit his own films. "He used to go off on his boat and get drunk instead," says King Vidor. "And brag about letting someone else cut the film." However, Ford, like Hitchcock, edited through the camera, and it was almost impossible for his pictures to be put together in any way other than the way he had intended.

Donlevy for *An American Romance* when Mayer begged me to, instead of fighting him and holding out for Spencer Tracy. But after a few of those studio films, I'd find that I couldn't stand it; and I'd start to fight again to make my *own* films."

The studio system was not deliberately cruel. Directors were usually assigned to the stars and subject matter and writers with whom they felt comfortable. Clarence Brown directed Greta Garbo three times. Victor Fleming directed Clark Gable and Spencer Tracy half a dozen times apiece, while King Vidor was never allowed near Garbo, Norma Shearer, or Joan Crawford. "I was not the guy who was given the star vehicles," Vidor says wryly. But MGM was, after all, making forty-two pictures a year. Like members of any team, directors had to play where they were most needed.

Victor Fleming never really objected to this philosophy. In 1938, he was used to being handed projects that had been planned and designed by someone else. Later in his career, after he won his Academy Award for *Gone With the Wind*, he would demand more freedom. "Because Vic felt that Selznick never gave him enough credit on *Gone With the Wind*, he made a deal with MGM that no producer would take credit on his pictures," says former MGM production manager Joe Cohn. "But he didn't stick to it. When he made *Tortilla Flat*, he even asked that Sam Zimbalist be given credit."

Despite his Academy Award, Fleming is not a director about whom monographs have been written, nor are there demands for retrospective showings of his work. Perhaps he died too early. He died of a heart attack in 1949, in the front seat of a car, on his way to a hospital in Flagstaff, Arizona, with his wife holding him in her arms. He had directed over fifty motion pictures.

Some of them are great motion pictures; few are bad. Fleming's talent was peculiarly suited to the studio system. "He never prepared his own scripts," says King Vidor. "But he would always come in fighting and arguing against being forced to do something with his film that he didn't want to do." "There aren't two people in Hollywood today who could make *Captains Courageous*," remarks Joe Cohn. "He made that whole movie on a sound stage in front of an eight-foot screen, without a boat or an ocean in sight." "I remember *Boom Town*, which I wrote," says John Lee Mahin. "Jack Conway started out as the director. Jack attempted to stage a real fight between Clark Gable and Spencer Tracy without using doubles. Gable didn't draw back, and he got hit in the lip. It split his lip. They had to shoot around him for a week—it cost a lot of money—before his lip healed. And that ruined Jack. He took right to his bed, and Vic took over the fight. 'Now look here, Clark and Spence,' he said. 'We've got one actor with a lot of fake teeth and one actor with too big a belly. You boys just go home, both of you. We'll put this on with doubles, and we'll get your faces, and everything will be fine.' And Gable and Tracy went home."

When Fleming inherited *The Wizard of Oz*, he had little room to tamper with the actors, the costumes, or the sets. But he did have the right to supply himself with one of MGM's contract writers as long as the writer he wanted wasn't assigned elsewhere. He immediately asked for John Lee Mahin. Mahin had been brought to Hollywood in 1930 by Ben Hecht and Charles MacArthur, who had offered him $200 a week " 'to help write our pictures while we write our plays. Nobody will know. You'll be our secretary.' " But "Ben Hecht wasn't the kind of guy who would let anybody write anything for him. For eight or ten weeks, I really did nothing except keep people away from him so he could work. Then Ben got me *Scarface*. He wrote an outline. I said, 'Gee, this is great.' He said, 'You'll find it's full of holes, kid. Don't let it fool you.' And I turned it into a script."

Mahin had already written the scripts for four Fleming pictures: *The Wet Parade, Red Dust, Treasure Island,* and *Captains Courageous.* Although Fleming did not prepare his own scripts, he did—as often as he could—team up with Mahin. Most of the good studio directors eventually found some writer under contract to their studio whose ideas or sensibilities were close to their own. The most independent directors went further. Hitchcock and Mamoulian insist that they *never* made a picture in which they did not work extensively on the script, and Hitchcock's wife was the credited screenwriter on most of his early films. King Vidor wrote or helped to write the scripts for all of his personal films, but accepted studio-manufac-

John Lee Mahin (with Jean Harlow and Victor Fleming on the set of Bombshell, *1933). Mahin had been brought to Hollywood by Ben Hecht and Charles MacArthur as a secretary (his real job: to write their pictures while they wrote their plays). By 1939, he had worked with Fleming on four pictures (including* Red Dust *and* Captains Courageous*).*

tured scripts for his studio-manufactured films. Between 1934 and 1940, Dudley Nichols wrote nine of the pictures directed by John Ford, including *The Informer, Stagecoach,* and *The Long Voyage Home.* And Frank Capra usually retreated to the desert to live with his screenwriter, Robert Riskin, for the six weeks they collaborated on each film.

Mahin's presence on the set of *The Wizard of Oz* meant little fundamental change in the script. Mahin was making $2,000 a week, but his largest contribution was to rewrite completely the picture's first scene. The first page of the script which had been handed to Fleming was all long shots and medium shots of barns and silos. Dorothy wasn't mentioned until the second page and didn't appear until the bottom of page 3. When she did appear, she was riding a pony, talking to a scarecrow, and grinning—not the slightest bit concerned that Miss Gulch had thrown her out of school "just because Toto took a little nip out of her leg." Fleming was uncomfortable with the script's deliberate coyness. Mahin replaced whimsey with reality. He started the picture with a "breathless and apprehensive" Dorothy whose first speech was:

> She isn't coming yet, Toto . . . Did she hurt you anywhere? She tried to, all right! Come on—we'll go tell Aunt Em and Uncle Henry . . .

Mahin also invented a reason—other than pure meanness—why Aunt Em and Uncle Henry refused to listen to Dorothy. The five-hundred-chick incubator had broken down and they were working frantically to save the baby chickens.

There was little Mahin could do to change whimsey to reality in the Oz sequence. He never even tried. Thirty-eight years later, Mahin, casual, open-handed, was generous in his praise of the script and belittled his own additions to it. "Most of the writing I did was for Bert Lahr. Because there never seemed to be enough of a reaction for him in the script. So I'd get together with Jack Haley—he was an old vaudevillian—and say, 'Come on, Jack, let's have some jokes. And we'll turn them into Frank Baum language so poor Frank won't roll in his grave.' And Jack would feed me these old stale jokes. Like, 'Don't you remember that guy that did the prizefighter's skit? He kept saying, "I'll kill him. I'll kill him. There's only one thing I want you guys to do. Try to stop me." ' So we gave that to Bert—to add a little laugh."

The actors were not unhappy to find that Victor Fleming was their new director. Actors liked Fleming. "He was understanding, sensitive, kind; and he had time to tell stories," says Jack Haley. The stories Haley remembers best were yarns; they centered on Fleming's early days in the flamboyant world of silent movies. The wildest story concerned a cross-country train trip with Douglas Fairbanks and a suitcase of valuable bonds, a trip complete with false mustaches and locked compartment doors. Although Fleming could

*From left: Ray Bolger in Scarecrow costume, Victor Fleming,
dance director Bobby Connolly, and Mervyn LeRoy.*

be cold and sarcastic with his actors, the sarcasm did not alter what
they felt to be his genuine concern for them. "We loved him," says
Ray Bolger, "because he was such a good director. He was a competent man. But he was also like an army officer. He was a disciplin-
arian. He stood for no foolishness."

Actresses were more ambivalent about Fleming. On the set of
The Wizard of Oz, Fleming's streak of sadism would show itself
twice—with disastrous results for Margaret Hamilton and her stand-
in, Betty Danko. Hamilton had been directed by Victor Fleming
once before, in *The Farmer Takes a Wife* in 1935. She was amazed
to discover how much gentler a person he seemed almost four years
later. Even so, she says, "Although he was a very pleasant person
when everything went right, he could be very sarcastic. And he did
have a real dilly of a temper."

Inside the immense concrete vaults where movies were made, a director could afford to lose his temper. Or he could, as Fleming did, insist that one of the laborers who roamed the high catwalks above *The Wizard of Oz* show off the six-inch scar on his stomach. (Fleming was fascinated by illness, perhaps because his own body was less sturdy than it appeared to be. And he called the workman down to display his incision to all visitors.) The huge sound stages, taller and wider than the airplane hangars they resembled, were a director's territory. "Your producer would see the rushes and come down to the set and say, 'I just saw the rushes. I thought they were fine,' " says *The Wizard's* first director Richard Thorpe. "Or he would say, 'Let's make another close-up of So-and-so.' Then he would leave." "Mervyn would make a token visit to the set," says John Lee Mahin specifically of *The Wizard of Oz.* "But a good producer trusted his director and knew the director didn't want some guy peering over his shoulder."

There was, in the end, more than status reflected in those thickly carpeted, tastefully decorated offices reserved for producers in the Thalberg Building. The "eight-by-ten-foot office with two chairs, a desk, and a telephone," that had greeted Richard Thorpe on his arrival at MGM in 1934, was—like the waiting room at a railroad station—merely a place to stay until it was time to board the next train. Sitting behind his walnut or mahogany desk, an MGM producer controlled script, costumes, sets, and chose his actors. But most of his control stopped at the door to the sound stage. He could make suggestions. He could complain. He could even, if he felt it necessary, ask Benny Thau or L. B. Mayer to remove his director. But as long as the director was on the stage, the camera, the arc lights, and the actors belonged to him.

Even though the actors on *The Wizard of Oz* belonged to Fleming, there was not terribly much he could do with them. "It was very, very strange work playing those characters," says Jack Haley. "There was no acting. It was all movement. We were running all the time. We were always afraid. We had three lines and then we were off to see the Wizard. We were running all over the joint—putting out fires, chopping down doors, cutting the rope that held the Witch's chandelier. The only scenes that had any acting value were in black-

and-white when Judy met Frank Morgan and he looked in his crystal ball."

Haley, Bolger, and Bert Lahr created their characters out of their vaudeville personalities. "I was always a weakie," says Haley. "My character in show business was always a Milquetoast who was filled with fear. So the Tin Woodman was a very easy part." Bert Lahr had started out as a Dutch comedian in burlesque—a dialect comedian, the most physical and unsophisticated type of comedy. His Cowardly Lion was the summation of his early career, allowing

Dorothy (Judy Garland) and the Scarecrow (Ray Bolger) find the Tin Woodman (Jack Haley) longing for a heart.

Bert Lahr in the Cowardly Lion costume.

him to give full vent to the bow-wow braggadocio of his personality. Since Yip Harburg and Harold Arlen had written for Lahr before, each of the Cowardly Lion's songs was a specific comment on Lahr's stage personality, incorporating mannerisms he had already made famous on Broadway. Beyond *Oz,* Lahr did increasingly subtle work; and he ended his career with Aristophanes and as Estragon in Samuel Beckett's *Waiting for Godot.* Ray Bolger's stage personality was less defined than the personalities of Haley and Lahr; but the good-natured, almost lazy physical grace that had caused Walter Winchell to label him "America's Soft-Shoe Man" dominated his Scarecrow. "I kind of made myself go limp," recalls Bolger. "I thought, 'I have no bones. I have nothing in me. It's just the wind that's holding me up.' I walked on the side of my ankles so I would be as floppy as possible. As far as my brain was concerned, I knew I didn't have one. So I had to make a character without a brain but with logic of a sort, with common sense."

It was Haley who created the breathless, slightly stilted way the Tin Woodman and Scarecrow would speak to Dorothy. "I gave

Fleming the key. He was troubled about how the characters should talk. I said, 'I want to talk the way I talk when I'm telling a story to my five-year-old son.' And he said, 'Give me an example.' I started with, 'Well, there was this big frog. And he had great long legs.' Sort of breathless. And then I said the Tin Man's first speech in that same voice. 'Well, a long time ago I was standing here, and it started to rain. . . .' And he said, 'That's it.' And then Bolger followed my key." "I tried to get a sound in my voice that was complete wonderment," says Bolger. "Because I was so new, so newly made." Lahr, of course, chose to be as guttural as possible, growling his words with mock menace, while Frank Morgan created another version of the frightened little man he had played in a dozen films.

Nor did Margaret Hamilton find much need for direction from Fleming. "Miss Gulch was just like a hundred other parts I'd done.

Ray Bolger played the Scarecrow as if he had nothing inside of him, as if he were being held up by the wind.

The Wicked Witch of the West (Margaret Hamilton) with her servant Nikko.

She was thin and she was skinny and she was mean and she was funny in her audacity and in her feeling of being just appalled at the simplest things. She was funny in her strictness and her hewing to the line and her insistence on certain things, regardless of whether she was right or wrong." Margaret Hamilton, endlessly voluble—memories from seventy-four years scattered like edible tidbits in her head—does not like to talk about Miss Gulch. "When I watch her on television, I think she's too fast and too jerky. There's something about that characterization that I never really liked very well. Maybe I just don't like the lady. Maybe I don't like her taking that dog."

The Wicked Witch of the West is a pleasanter memory. For the Witch, there was "a feeling inside that you get. One word: *skulduggery*. She enjoyed every single minute of whatever she was doing, whether she was screaming or yelling about the fact that Dorothy had those slippers, or sending the monkeys after them all. And the other thing was her utter and complete frustration. She *never* got what she wanted. She didn't want Dorothy and she didn't want any of those other characters. She just wanted those slippers. And today, according to law, she probably would have had them. They were her sister's, and she would have been in line to inherit them. But she didn't get there fast enough. The audience had to feel a certain anxiety about what she would do, but it couldn't be anything terribly frightening or really disastrous."

She can watch her performance as the Witch with equanimity. "There are some little things, some gestures, that I wish I hadn't done; but I can't say I dislike a lot of it. Because I think Mr. Fleming had a very good firm hand on things. Although I don't have any consciousness of his changing anything really for any of us. He seemed to accept what we were working at. I don't remember him ever saying, 'Don't do that,' or 'Don't do this,' or 'Try to do this.' If he did make changes, he did it so gracefully and so diplomatically that you didn't even know it was being done."

Fleming could not keep a tight rein on most of his actors because the queerness of their characters defied a realistic approach. He could, and did, keep a tight rein on Judy Garland. And it is Garland's obvious belief in what is happening to her that keeps the film credible. "You believed that she *really* wanted to get back to Kansas," says Jack Haley. "She carried the picture with her sincerity."

The first confrontation between Fleming and Judy Garland came late in November when she first met the Cowardly Lion on the Yellow Brick Road. John Lee Mahin was on the set that day, and the moment stuck fast in his memory. "She slapped the Lion and he broke into tears. And she was to continue bawling him out. But Lahr was so funny that she burst into screams of laughter instead. Vic was patient at first. She went behind a tree. I could hear her saying, 'I will not laugh. I will not laugh.' Then she'd come out and start laughing again. They must have done the scene ten times, and eventually she was giggling so much she got hysterical. She couldn't stop laughing. And Vic finally slapped her on the face. 'All right now,' he said, 'go back to your dressing room.' She went. And when she came back, she said, 'O.K.' And they did the scene."

There is no cuteness anywhere in Garland's performance. The Judy Garland from Kansas flows into Oz as though the Yellow Brick Road is just one step beyond the Kansas prairie: there are no rough edges where the two performances were stitched together. And yet the Kansas sequences of *The Wizard of Oz* were directed by a more eccentric and more gifted director than Victor Fleming.

"It was a Monday when I took over the picture," King Vidor recalls. "I went to Fleming's office across the hall from mine. We had lunch together, but we didn't talk about the picture. Fleming was a close friend, but he played the part of being gruff, brusque, taciturn. So instead of telling me what I wanted to know, he'd say, 'Oh, you know what to do.' I'm not even sure that he took me down to see the sets."

It was a curious coincidence that made Vidor, the most independent of MGM's directors, eager to mop up a film another man had started. Vidor says he had "a certain loyalty to MGM," but he was "also afraid of getting swallowed up by Mother MGM, by Papa Mayer." He was "afraid of losing my identity in that nest." So he constantly ran away from the studio. "Over and over I fled. Every time my contract ended, I would leave. The other guys stayed so long they got a pension. I never got one." Three days earlier, Vidor had been called by David Selznick. George Cukor had been fired from *Gone With the Wind,* and they were stopping production. "David wanted me to read all the *Gone With the Wind* scripts," says Vidor. "So I went by his house and picked up all the material. Masses of material. As I left, David told me that he wanted to start shooting again in one week. I picked up the stuff on Friday, and I spent the whole weekend reading it. To take the best scenes out of every script in one week seemed an impossible job. My most intense work was always done before I started shooting. I figured this would take four months. So Monday morning I went over to Selznick's house. I was going to put up a big argument over doing the film so quickly. But over the weekend—without telling me—Selznick had made a deal with Mayer to get Fleming. Because Clark Gable had asked for Victor. So David asked me if I would take over *The Wizard of Oz.* I was so relieved to get out of undertaking *Gone With the Wind* that I said, 'Sure. That'll be great.' "

When asked what he contributed to *The Wizard of Oz,* Vidor shrugs. What can you say about a film that another man has shaped?

There was only one special thing—a small point perhaps, but, decades later, it still gives him great pleasure to watch it. "I staged 'Over the Rainbow' with Judy walking. Previous to this, when people sang, they stood still. I used 'Over the Rainbow' to get some rhythmical flow of movement into a ballad."

Except for Richard Thorpe's feelings, none of the directors was much hurt by the game of musical chairs played on *The Wizard of Oz*. And Thorpe recovered quickly enough to direct *Huckleberry Finn*, which he later labeled "a stinkeroo." King Vidor avoided having to face *Gone With the Wind*. Victor Fleming became director of record on both *The Wizard of Oz* and *Gone With the Wind* in the same year, 1939. Though he completed neither film—he collapsed after ten weeks on *Gone With the Wind* and Sam Wood took over temporarily—he won his one and only Academy Award that year. Since George Cukor refused *The Wizard of Oz* and was fired from *Gone With the Wind*, he was free to take over MGM's *The Women* and was acclaimed for his handling of the all-woman cast. He also, secretly, coached both Olivia de Havilland and Vivien Leigh for their roles in *Gone With the Wind*. The game of musical directors didn't quite end there. Ernst Lubitsch had been scheduled to direct *The Women*. A new assignment had to be found for him and he was switched to *Ninotchka*. What did it matter since they were all MGM pictures.

Production #1060

THE STARS
AND
THE STAND-INS

"I couldn't lie down in that costume. I couldn't even sit in it. I could only lean against a reclining board. . . ." They were not allowed to eat in the commissary. They tried it once . . . their faces covered with rubber and fur and aluminum paste. . . . If they would eat in their dressing rooms, the studio would pay for lunch.

From October 12, 1938, to March 16, 1939, Ray Bolger, Jack Haley, Bert Lahr, Margaret Hamilton, and Judy Garland lived within the confines of a nightmare in which they were joined occasionally by Billie Burke, Frank Morgan, and 124 midgets.

Time has not softened the edges of the bad dream. The survivors still look back on that endless fall and winter as conscripts might remember their years in the army or ex-convicts their years in jail. And each day was—in a very real sense—an imprisonment.

"My makeup took one hour and forty-five minutes to put on in the morning," says Haley. "One hour and forty-five minutes to sit in that chair. A dentist's appointment takes less time than that. And this was six days a week."

"I came home exhausted," says Ray Bolger, "and had two bourbon old-fashioneds. The drinks were therapeutic. I needed the alcohol to let me down, and they had enough sugar to give me a kind of a lift so I could manage to eat my dinner and fall into bed." Bolger remembers nothing of those months except "going to bed and getting up and going to work. And half the time I don't even remember that."

Bolger was up by 5 a.m., at the studio by 6:15. During August, a plaster cast had been made of his face. The cast had then been photographed. A piece of clear plastic had been placed over the eight-by-ten photograph. Working to some extent from the W. W. Denslow drawings of the Scarecrow in *The Wizard of Oz*, the Makeup Department had sketched changes in Bolger's face onto the plastic. After Mervyn LeRoy approved the sketch, wax was molded onto the plaster cast. A negative impression was made, then another positive. And the wax was replaced by foam rubber baked in the oven of the makeup laboratory. The result was a rubber bag wrinkled to simulate burlap. The bag covered Bolger's entire head except for his eyes, nose, and mouth and then extended down his neck, where it was tied with a piece of rope. It took an hour each morning to glue the bag to Bolger's head and another hour to blend the brown makeup on the center of his face to the color of the rubber mask and to paint by hand the lines that would make his nose and mouth seem a continuation of the burlap. The process did not bother him as much as it bothered Haley, since Bolger productively spent the time studying a racing form and choosing the six or eight horses on which he would place bets that afternoon. It was after the process was over that his pain began. "The mask wasn't porous, so you couldn't sweat. You couldn't breathe through your skin. You don't realize how much you breathe through your skin until you can't do it. We felt like we were suffocating."

The feeling of suffocation was intensified by the huge arc lights that were necessary because of the large sets and the primitive Technicolor film. "We had enormous banks of arc lights overhead," says cinematographer Harold Rosson. "We borrowed every unused arc light in Hollywood. It was brutally hot. People were always fainting and being carried off the set." When the temperature became unbearable, Victor Fleming would order the lights turned off and the twenty-foot-wide stage doors opened. The actors would stand outside gasping for breath until the stage cooled off enough for them to continue shooting.

Each evening it took an hour for the makeup man to peel from Bolger's face—as gently as possible—the rubber bag he had glued on so carefully that morning. If he was lucky, the bag could be used for a second or even a third day. Eventually, 100 bags would be baked, used, discarded. In March, when Bolger removed his bag for the last time, he discovered that both corners of his mouth and part of his chin were permanently lined from his months as the Scarecrow.

Jack Haley did not wear a mask, but his makeup was "no less awful. They pulled my hair back as flat as they could and put some sort of rubber skin over my head and glued it down behind my ears. They covered my face with cold cream. Then they took a white chalklike salve and painted my face white. The idea of the white stuff was to close my pores so the silver paste that made me look like I was made of tin wouldn't damage my skin. They painted my face silver and glued on a silver nose. They glued a strip of rubber that was supposed to be tin under my chin and glued each individual black rubber rivet on my face. Then they painted my lips black because painting my face silver made my mouth too red. Coloring my lips black made my gums and tongue duller. I couldn't breathe

Jack Haley, under contract to 20th Century-Fox, was loaned to MGM to make The Wizard of Oz. *"20th Century could lend me to any studio. It [making Oz] was the most horrendous job in the world, with those cumbersome uniforms and the hours of makeup, but I had no choice."*

through my face. None of us could. And Bert Lahr had it the worst of all."

"The only thing that was his," says Bert Lahr's makeup man, Charlie Schram, "was a bit of cheek and his eyes. On top of his head he wore that enormous fur wig, and his chin was covered with a fur beard. He wore mittens and, besides being a real lion skin, his suit was padded. It was like carrying a mattress around with you. He had to take his lion suit off completely after each shot, and he'd always be dripping wet. The poor man went through hell."

No matter how early he got to the studio, Lahr refused to sit in his makeup chair until exactly 6:30. He would stand silently beside the chair for ten or fifteen minutes, staring at himself in the mirror. "He dreaded it so," says Schram. Once his lion's nose and mouth were glued to his face, he could not open his own mouth wide enough to chew. His lunch was whatever he could sip through a straw. When he could stand the self-restraint of milkshakes and soup no longer, it meant an extra hour in the makeup chair after lunch to replace his broken prosthesis.

Lunch came at one o'clock. It is remembered by both Bolger and Haley—although for different reasons—as the high point of the day. "It meant I could take off my costume and lie down," says Haley. His costume was made of buckram, a coarse fabric used for binding books. The buckram was covered with leather that had been painted silver, and it was stiff as cardboard. "I couldn't lie down in that costume. I couldn't even sit in it. I could only lean against a reclining board, a tilted board that was originally built for actresses wearing crinoline gowns and lots of hoopskirts. You couldn't sit on the board, but you could lie back against it."

"I was up at four-thirty or five in the morning," says Ray Bolger. "And working. Working hard. By one p.m. that great big hole, that gnawing thing you call hunger, would be the most dominant thing; and Jack and I would order the menu. Wiener schnitzel with eggs, chocolate ice cream with cake. And we always started with Mr. Mayer's personal, private chicken soup. And Lahr would sit there and watch us and say, 'Look at you. I can't eat anything and you guys are eating up everything in the whole world. Besides, I had gas all night.' "

They ate together, the three of them, in the living room of a bungalow they shared. They were not allowed to eat in the commissary. They tried it once, dressed in bathrobes, their legs bare, their faces covered with rubber and fur and aluminum paste. They were told they looked disgusting. After that, one of them remembers, some sort of tacit arrangement was made with the studio. If they would eat in their dressing rooms, the studio would pay for lunch.

They got on well together—three ex-vaudeville performers who had made it to Broadway and then taken the train west. They knew each other, of course. Ray Bolger and Bert Lahr had even starred together a few years earlier in the E. Y. Harburg–Harold Arlen–Ira Gershwin revue *Life Begins at 8:40*. They would have tried to get along in any case, stuck as they were in each other's company six days a week for nearly six months. "We were schooled in vaudeville and we'd been all through the ropes," says Haley. "We had started down where it was rough and we'd struggled from the bottom right up to the top, and in the struggle we were conditioned. The fellow who gets it overnight and hasn't a chance to digest it, he's the fellow who gives the most trouble."

They told dirty jokes and played practical jokes and seemed all in all as solid a triumvirate as the characters they played linked arm in arm on their journey down the Yellow Brick Road. But there were, beneath the surface, subtleties in their relationship.

"I went along with them and acted funny with them, but I was actually a loner," says Bolger. "They had a common bond. They were more alike. I read different books. I listened to different music. In my library I have the Harvard Classics, the *Book of Knowledge*, Rabelais, De Maupassant, Boccaccio, Balzac. I have Russian dictionaries, French dictionaries, German grammars. And I've been a solo star on Broadway, I mean without sharing the bill with *any-body*."

Jack Haley and Ray Bolger were raised within a few miles of each other in the Irish Catholic ghettos of Boston. In 1976, living within four blocks of each other in their half-million-dollar houses in Beverly Hills, they remained acquaintances who smiled and nodded each Sunday morning across the aisles of the Church of the

Good Shepherd. It was Bert Lahr, the German-Jewish immigrant's son from New York City's Yorkville, who became Haley's "best friend." Not at first sight, of course. Definitely not at first sight. "I met Bert in 1922 or '23. I was doing a girl act in small-time vaudeville. And a man on the bill asked me if I'd like to be the juvenile in a summer-run show. And I was so green I didn't know what a summer run was. I was making 50 dollars a week, and they offered me 60 dollars a week to do this summer burlesque show in New York. And at the first rehearsal I felt terribly diffident and scared to death. I was just out of my teens. I had just started in show business. And Frankie Hunter, the top banana, came over and introduced himself to me. And Bert Lahr came over. No introduction. No handshake. He just asked, 'Have you ever been in burlesque before?' I said, 'No, I haven't'; and Lahr turned to Frankie Hunter and said, 'We'll put sand in his greasepaint.' I still don't know what the hell he meant. I never asked him, so I'll never know. The only thing I knew was that I hated the bastard. I could have stabbed him to death there. I was emotional, young, scared of my surroundings. It was my first day at rehearsal. And this son of a bitch was going to ruin it. He was going to fix me, put sand on my face. I loathed him. It turned out he became my best friend. Strange."

There are levels of poverty. Ray Bolger remembers a nice street "in rather a nice part of Boston. We were poor because of what happened to us, because of my father's illness. But I finished high school. I had to work in the afternoon, but I went to school in the morning and I finished high school." The poverty felt by Bert Lahr and Jack Haley was closer to the bone. In neither one did the ache of it ever completely go away. "Sometimes I used to look at my mother and think, 'My God, what'll happen to us if anything happens to her?'" says Haley. "Because she was our strength. She scrubbed floors to feed us well and clothe us well and keep us going. My father died when I was six months old, and she scrubbed floors to raise two children, and she inculcated me with the importance of money. 'Where do you think the money comes from? That it grows on trees?' All the clichés, she had them. I still can't stand waste or food left on a plate. No matter what I accumulate, there's always that deep fear she put in me years ago."

Lahr's childhood added emotional deprivation to physical privation. For Lahr, according to his son, there were only "three memories of family affection—a bag of candy, a five-dollar sailor suit with an extra pair of pants, and a trip with his father to the Schwartz Um Adler, a German theater on Third Avenue." Lahr remembered his childhood as a wasteland of empty Christmas stockings, school failure, birthdays without presents, culminating in his own early transformation into a petty thief.

The friendship between Jack Haley and Bert Lahr started during that fourteen weeks in the summer-run burlesque show. "Who knows how friendships are formed?" asks Jack Haley more than fifty years later. "Why does Jackie Gleason, so much younger than me, select me as a friend? Why did Jack Benny and I, so close when we were young, drift away? Vaudeville friendships were temporary. You played a whole week with someone, went out to dinner with him every night. Then you never saw him again. But that didn't happen to Bert and me. Bert was horrible onstage. He needed all the laughter, all the applause. Offstage, he was a decent person, a fair person, an honest person, and a generous person."

If at some deep level the relationship between Haley and Lahr made Ray Bolger an outsider, its only outward manifestation was in the kinds of jokes the three men played on each other. "Hey, do you want to have some fun?" Lahr would ask Haley. The fun would consist of dangling in front of Bolger a verbal bait that his personality would not allow him to refuse—Bolger always found it necessary to be verbal top dog. So Haley would invent some outrageous experience for himself or Lahr. "Bert used to be a boxer," Haley would say. "He was really good, had a belly on him like a washboard." Or, "One time when I was playing Minneapolis, we were snowed in the theater for two days. Had to burn the seats to keep from freezing to death." Bolger would jump at the bait. "*I* was a boxer once," he would say. Or, "I nearly froze to death in '26." He would elaborate on his eleven fights or the night he nearly froze to death in Albany. Half the time Bolger was not aware that he was being jibed at. Of the rest, he shrugs off his embarrassment. "Haley says I lie a lot, and it's probably true. An Irishman would rather have a good story than a dull conversation."

Twice he paid Lahr back. Lahr had bought five acres of land in a Beverly Hills canyon. On it, years later, he built a house with a swimming pool, a bar, an electric gate, and an orchard of avocado trees. It was the first house that Lahr had ever owned. But he eventually sold it because of the bafflement and frustration he felt in Hollywood. "He got tired of playing the star's best friend," says his widow, Mildred Lahr. "Often he was making more money than the star, but his parts were so meaningless." So he sold the house and the five acres to Betty Grable and moved back to New York. "He went back to Broadway feeling that he had been a failure in Hollywood," says his son. "But, in the long run, the fact that he could get no parts with the range, the material, or the quality of *Oz* lengthened his career by sending him back to New York and the higher-quality entertainments of the classical repertoire as well as musical comedy."

When Lahr was making *The Wizard of Oz*, the house had not yet been built. Driving down Sunset Boulevard in a rainstorm, Bolger saw a pile of dirt that had been washed down from the canyons. "I saw all that mud. It was so obvious—a gag that really had to be done." Bolger had a friend call Lahr and tell him to hurry and get a truck to pick up the dirt that had been washed down to Sunset Boulevard from his property. "And Lahr bought the joke," Bolger says. "He tried to hire a truck." Bolger's second attempt at revenge was more extensive. It came at lunchtime. He would order the most tempting things on the menu "just to annoy Lahr." Sipping his soup, Lahr would watch Bolger eat. Victory came on the days Lahr would push his soup aside and reach for the menu.

What is curious is how closely the three men resembled the characters they had been chosen to play. The Scarecrow, lacking both brains and a heart, had chosen to hunger for a brain. Bolger was the clever one. His Christmas gift to Judy Garland was a collector's copy of Edgar Allan Poe's "The Raven." He filled the studio behind his Beverly Hills house with three centuries of books and took a course in phonetics at Columbia University. The distance he felt from the Tin Woodman and the Cowardly Lion was, as much as anything, intellectual distance.

The Tin Woodman, having once had both brains and a heart, had chosen to yearn for another heart. Jack Haley's career was never so splendid as the career of Bolger or of Lahr. He did not possess the sort of dedication that kept Bolger dancing at least an hour a day at the age of seventy. And if he lacked Bolger's shrewdness at choosing roles for himself, he also lacked Bert Lahr's obsession. What Haley had in abundance was a strong Catholic sense of morality and sin that made him, quite humbly and without arrogance, his brother's keeper. "There's a great sweetness about Jack," says Margaret Hamilton. "He did a job with the Tin Woodman that's never gotten the acclaim that it should. He was inside that armor, and it was only his eyes and his personality that made the Tin Woodman so endearing. He was so perfect for that person who wanted a heart. I believed him thoroughly. I always believed that a heart was the most important thing to Jack." Haley became a Knight of Malta, honored by the Pope for his philanthropy. He served as vice-president of the American Guild of Variety Artists, as president of The Friars. He even created the Jack Haley Foundation to donate money to "whatever suits my whim or feeling." As the Tin Woodman, Haley would receive from Frank Morgan a testimonial certifying his kind heart. Haley's own house is filled with such testimonials.

It is the word "anxiety" that attaches itself like flypaper to Bert Lahr. "He brought to his Cowardly Lion that neurotic anxiety people who pursue perfection always bring," says Yip Harburg. "Lahr had it to a stronger degree than most people I've met." The depths of Lahr's anxiety is clear in a story Jack Haley tells. "It was the opening night of *DuBarry Was a Lady*. With Ethel Merman. 'She's got the whole show,' he had told his agent. 'I've got nothing.' And all through the rehearsals his agent had kept saying, 'You're going to be great in this show, Bert.' And now comes opening night and it's over and he's a success. And his agent, Louis Shurr, burst into the room. 'Didn't I tell ya? Didn't I tell ya?' And Bert looked up and said, 'Yeah, but what about next season?' "

Lahr was, if not a hypochondriac, incessantly at odds with his body. He had "gas." He had "insomnia." His stomach felt "sick." He would watch Jack Haley, encased in his silver armor and silver spats, fall asleep on his reclining board between takes and he would swell with rage. "I couldn't sleep last night, and that bastard can sleep on a meat hook." In whatever show he would twist a button on his costume until it came off. Then he would stick it in his pocket and start on the next one. The grotesque Cowardly Lion's costume was a double frustration because it lacked buttons. He tried, without much psychic success, to twist his whiskers and his tail.

Jack Haley, easier to please than either of his co-stars, was physically exhausted most of the time but emotionally at peace. The exhaustion came from *The Wizard of Oz* combined with his weekly radio show. He slept so well each afternoon on his tilted board because he worked from 9 p.m. to midnight with his writers for his Thursday-evening variety show sponsored by Wonder Bread. The emotional peace came from his wife, his two young children, the contract with 20th Century-Fox that seemed to guarantee financial security. He made $3,000 a week but had to give the studio back $1,000 in order to be allowed to do the radio show. Ray Bolger, although more ambitious, was also calm. He had fought to play the Scarecrow and won. Emotionally, 1938 was a bad year for Lahr, who, however funny he might be in front of the cameras, was a melancholy man. His wife had been institutionalized for over seven years. During that time, Lahr had spent nearly $250,000 to cure her, but no cure was possible. For the previous six years, Lahr had been in love with another woman. And she with him. "Mildred Schroeder," wrote their son,* "gave Lahr what no other woman had ever offered him—her complete devotion. . . . She did not stop to analyze him or understand his complexities. But faced with an emotional rapport she could not deny, Mildred accepted Lahr—his genius and his obsession." Mildred Schroeder Lahr puts it more matter-of-factly. "Bert was a real gentleman," she says. "He was bashful of people. He was so outgoing on stage, but inwardly he was a reserved person. Unlike many actors, he was a *real* gentleman, a very kind person."

In 1936, Mildred Schroeder had married another man when the years of waiting for Lahr—seemingly without hope of marriage—proved too difficult. Ten months later, her husband sued Lahr as a "love thief." Mildred was divorced in October 1937. In 1938 she was with Lahr in California. But in 1938 he seemed no closer to an annulment of his first marriage than he had been two years earlier. As

* John Lahr, *Notes on a Cowardly Lion* (New York: Alfred A. Knopf, 1969).

Lahr danced down the Yellow Brick Road arm in arm with Haley, Bolger, and Judy Garland, he was terrified that Mildred might not wait the seemingly endless years until he was free.*

Abrasive as their horseplay sometimes was, Haley, Bolger, and Lahr at least had company in their misery. Margaret Hamilton was alone. Her isolation extended beyond the walls of MGM. Her marriage had ended in divorce less than a year earlier, and she lived with her three-year-old son and his nurse. At the studio, she played her scenes alone or with Judy Garland and the Winged Monkeys. The most she saw of Dorothy's companions was a smile or a wave at 7 a.m., when she climbed into a makeup chair for her two hours of makeup. Her rubber pieces consisted of a false nose, a jutting chin, and a horribly ugly wart with large black hairs protruding from it. After the rubber was glued on, her eyebrows were built up and thickened; and her entire face, her arms, and her hands were covered with green paint. Once her hands were coated, she was almost as hampered as Lahr was by his lion's head and Haley by his buckram.

"From the time I got my makeup on, I was immobilized," says Margaret Hamilton. "If I touched my costume, it would be streaked with green. I couldn't do anything for myself, and that included the amenities in the bathroom. Naturally, I had to visit that emporium at some time or other during the day and I needed a great deal of help from the little girl the studio had assigned me as a sort of maid— holding up my skirt and that sort of thing."† Eventually, Margaret Hamilton's skin acquired a green tinge, something she became aware of five or six weeks before the picture was finished. "A friend of mine said, 'Do you feel all right? You look so odd.' I said, 'I feel fine. What do you mean?' And she said, 'You look kind of green.' I said, 'Oh,

---

* Lahr's annulment was finally filed on February 8, 1940. He and Mildred Schroeder were married three days later.

† Bolger, too, had trouble going to the bathroom. "Because of the straw. They sewed straw into my sleeves and my boots, and then they stuffed straw in the belly and the legs and the shoulders. If I opened up my costume, all the straw fell out, and then they had to put it back so it matched the way it had looked in the last shot. I didn't even take my costume off for lunch most of the time, because it was such a mess to put on again."

don't be ridiculous. I *am* green in the daytime, but I take it off at night.' But I went and looked in the mirror and she was quite right. I suppose the stuff gradually sort of sunk into my skin. It must have been months before my face was really normal again."

Lunch for Margaret Hamilton was a peanut-butter sandwich wrapped in wax paper so that she did not ingest too much of the green-tinted paint containing copper. Her maid brought her a cup of coffee and held her stalk of celery as she bit at it. She did not know Haley, Bolger, or Lahr, and the picture's schedule gave her little chance to make their acquaintance. Later, in summer stock, she worked intimately with Bolger, and, in television, with Lahr. During *The Wizard of Oz*, she was merely aware of "Lahr's extreme, terrible nervousness," and she would watch rather wistfully "his asides to the gentlemen players that sent them off into peals of laughter, those jokes that they didn't want ladies to hear." She did know Frank Morgan, having played the maid to his master in several films; and she looked forward to seeing him. But they were never once on the set the same day.

She ate her sandwich in the canvas tent MGM had given her as a dressing room. "I always thought they got me mixed up with the actual Witch," she says. "They must have thought that witches didn't have very nice dressing rooms, because mine was simply awful. It was a square of canvas, and the floor had some sort of dirty-looking rug on it, and there was one chair and a card table with a light over it." Once or twice when Billie Burke was not on the set, Margaret Hamilton finished off her lunch by standing inside Miss Burke's dressing room with its pink satin walls and pink chaise-longue "and the little fur rug next to the chaise-longue which she could step onto when she was through taking her rest." Margaret Hamilton thought the dressing room "enchanting" but did not begrudge it to Billie Burke. Miss Burke, after all, had been Florenz Ziegfeld's wife, while she was simply a featured player with a relatively small part—although, thank goodness, not another *maid's* part—in *The Wizard of Oz*. That the picture might make her famous was rarely in her thoughts. Her total time on the screen was only twelve minutes. So it was unimaginable that in 1974, while touring *A Little Night Music* in San Francisco, the young actors and actresses from *Grease* would hang around her stage door waiting for her—to give her flowers and a gold medallion, to take her to dinner, to talk for hours about *The Wizard of Oz*. And, of course—although the picture was always something more than "just another film"—it didn't make her really famous for more than twenty years, not until it started appearing regularly on television in the late fifties.

Frank Morgan didn't join *The Wizard of Oz* until the Emerald City replaced the Haunted Forest on Stage 27 in mid-January. He brought with him every morning a small black suitcase containing a miniature bar. He was circumspect in his drinking: the suitcase stayed in his dressing room, and he never blew his lines. "He was a very, very professional player," Margaret Hamilton remembers. "He always knew his lines and he was always ready. But he did like his drink. The second or third picture I made with him was *By Your Leave* at RKO. And the first day arrived and I was sitting on the set and Frank came along. And I said, 'How are you?' And he said, 'I'm really rotten. I need some hair of the dog, but you can't get it on this lot.' He was under contract to MGM and was just being loaned out to RKO. And I said, 'I bet you can.' And he said, 'I understand you can't.' He looked so miserable. I said, 'Do you want me to go and ask somebody?' So I went to the assistant director and said, 'Frank's got a little problem out there. He'd like to have a drink, but he doesn't think it's permissible.' And the assistant director said, 'Oh, hell, what does he want?' And so he got his drink. It just tickled me to pieces because he was important and I was just starting out, and all he had to say was 'Let's have a little snifter.' But he was so pleased and so appreciative. He was very lovable, very sweet, very considerate, one of the nicest people I ever knew."

Morgan was, says Ray Bolger, "a divine man." Whatever needs alcohol served for him remained private. No matter how many times he retreated to the black briefcase, he was never less than a gentleman, although when he attempted to stop drinking, he was often short-tempered and irritable. Morgan's wardrobe man, John B. Scura, remembers Victor Fleming asking Morgan to " 'get back on your champagne kick so we can live together.' He loved champagne. It was his favorite drink. And he would always give a bottle or two of champagne as a gift." Mary Mayer, the young girl assigned from the Publicity Department to *The Wizard of Oz*, was aware of Morgan's drinking only once. And only because it was pointed out to her. "He was standing in that guard box—it was when he was playing the soldier—singing a rather risqué song. And someone said it was lucky he had the guard box to stand in or he'd fall down."

The Wizard of Oz occupied little of Morgan's working time— less than a week as Professor Marvel, a few more weeks as the Wizard. And he did not live long enough for the television ritual of the film to make him famous. He died in his sleep in 1949, and none of his obituaries even mentioned the film.

Judy Garland died in her London apartment on June 22, 1969. All of her obituaries mentioned *The Wizard of Oz*. She had been singing "Over the Rainbow"—with, as Clifton Fadiman put it, the "universal, unanswerable query, 'Why can't I?' "—for over thirty years.

In the fall of 1938, she was sixteen years old. The other actors later remembered her as "enchanting," "cheery and bright and a joy to be around." She was, according to Margaret Hamilton, "one of the happiest people I'd ever seen." "Judy was as light-hearted a person as I ever met in my life," says Jack Haley. "She always wanted to hear something funny so she could laugh." Even screenwriter Noel Langley, who was hardly one to put a charitable interpretation on things, found Garland "absolutely enchanting. Her manners were perfect, far better than anyone else's there. She always called you Mister."

Yet, during the last year of her life, Garland appeared on the Jack Paar television show and spoke bitterly of the Munchkins as "drunks who got smashed every night." Her bitterness extended to Haley, Bolger, and Lahr—they had upstaged her, pushed her out of the way, shoved her into the background. Jack Haley, watching the Paar program, sat bewildered in front of his television set, whispering, "It's untrue. It's untrue." "How could you upstage anybody?" he asks. "For Christ's sake, we were linked arm in arm all the time."

Long before her death, Judy Garland found it necessary to invent and reinvent her past, shaping its facts to suit her needs and anxieties. "She lied a lot," according to people who knew her. The lies gave her the same kind of relief—although not nearly as much relief —as liquor and what she called her "happy pills."

"The experience of stardom when one is not old enough to deal with it," says psychoanalyst John Lindon, "causes a severe distortion not just of reality but of inner reality. For a child performer, there is almost a crippling of the normal developmental processes." Dr. Lindon—clinical professor of psychiatry at UCLA—practices in Los Angeles. Perhaps by accident of geography, his patient population is always laced with actors and actresses. Many of Lindon's patients "describe themselves as *dead* when they are not working. They say things like, 'I only come alive when I work.' 'I'm a hollow shell.' They see their ability to perform as a weapon they can use to control people, but it doesn't belong to them. They consider themselves marionettes. They themselves have nothing of value. The average psychoanalytic patient is afraid you will find out that he's 'bad' inside. What's characteristic of people who have been in the business of performing since childhood is the much greater dread than exists in other patients that I will find them 'empty.' "

A half-dozen psychiatrists would try to explain to Judy Garland that she was suffering from a severe disturbance of ego identity, that her life as Judy Garland was fantasy built precariously on fantasy, that she must come to terms with the Frances Gumm she had left behind. She would try to seduce each of them into giving her the same love and admiration and applause that she demanded from her other audiences. And she would lie to them as casually as she lied to everybody else.

"You would think," says Dr. Lindon, "that child actors would have an excessive, inflated idea of their own worth. In actuality, it is just the opposite. They feel they have no inner resources and suffer from a terrible lack of self-esteem. To grow up *normal*, we need the stability that comes from having a fairly well-known set of people to deal with who react in fairly predictable ways."

Dr. Lindon can "conceive" of a child star "growing up into a fairly normal adult," but only with a lot of luck and two extremely stable parents. Baby Frances Gumm's luck was all bad. Before she was six, she had twice almost died from sudden, inexplicable fevers. With the first infection, at the age of a year, she was hospitalized for three weeks. The isolation, the betrayal of those three weeks in the hospital were indelible. Nor did her parents provide stability. Frank Gumm was unable to rescue his daughter from the fantasies and ambitions of his wife; Ethel Gumm concentrated her enormous energy on making her youngest daughter a star. In that sense, Judy Garland was like a leaf held under a magnifying glass by someone who wants to set a fire.

Whether at the age of sixteen Judy Garland was really the simple, happy child Jack Haley and Ray Bolger and Margaret Hamilton remembered or whether she was already pretending is no longer relevant. As an adult, she had an extraordinary ability to bend herself into the roles that other people demanded she play. She was the most generous of friends, the most maternal of mothers, and—to men—the most helpless of children, the most coquettish of bed partners. At least, she might be those things for a while, until her lack of self-discipline, her inability to control her impulses, her need for instant gratification exploded the game or the friendship or the love affair. "She had charm such as I have never in my life been around," says Mary Ann Nyberg, who was the costume designer on several of her films. "She had an insatiable desire to please, to make you laugh, feel comfortable, feel totally equal with her. *Until* she got tired of you. Then it reversed exactly. Then she got exactly as mean as she had been charming, as determined to make you uncomfortable as she had tried to make you comfortable."

In November 1938, Judy Garland appeared to be a plump, sweet, likable, awkward, and rather unsophisticated young girl. It was Ray Bolger who knew her best later on, who appeared with her at the Sahara Hotel in Las Vegas during the last decade of her life when she would "stand in the wings, trembling, afraid to move. And we would have to half-hypnotize her with 'Judy, you're wonderful. You look great.' And we would give her a sip of wine and push her out onto the stage." But even Bolger, remembering the sixteen-year-old girl, can only say, "I can still see Judy standing there laughing at us. The three of us were ridiculous, absolutely ridiculous, in our costumes. And she would stand there and laugh."

The people who worked with Judy Garland on *The Wizard of Oz* have equally vivid memories of her ability as a performer. "Her acting instinct was impeccable," says Ray Bolger. "She was an instinctive artist," says Yip Harburg. "She could learn a song faster than anybody I've ever seen. She could sit down beside Harold [Arlen] on the piano bench while he played a song through and learn it right then." They—all of them—applied to the sixteen-year-old the ultimate adjective of approval: "Professional. She was completely professional."

The physical difficulties of working on the film were considerably less for Garland than they were for Lahr, Bolger, Haley, and Hamilton. Her costume was a loose-fitting gingham dress. Once George Cukor had scrubbed her face clean, she wore very little makeup. She suffered somewhat from the intense heat on the sets, but her only real physical obstacle was a binding cloth that held her breasts in. The corset was extremely uncomfortable, but she rarely complained. Nor did she ever complain of being "starved" by the studio. None of her co-stars was aware of any attempt by MGM to ration her food, although since she never ate with them, they may not have known if her diet was restricted. However, there is certainly ample evidence that, once *The Wizard of Oz* was finished and she was working in *Babes in Arms*, L. B. Mayer was personally concerned with keeping her on a diet.

The only serious conversation that anyone reported having had with her came in the spring of 1939. "I think Judy was asking me about my little boy," says Margaret Hamilton. "I don't remember her exact words, of course, but, in general, she said something about never doing 'many of the things that most little girls do.' I asked her what she meant, and she said, 'When I was little, I never had a birthday party, never really had a best friend, never belonged to a little girls' club.' I will never forget that because I remembered the endless clubs I had belonged to, all composed of the same three or four girls who lived on the same street. We'd have a club for this and someone would be president, and someone would be secretary, vice-president, treasurer. The four of us all had offices. Then we would dissolve that club and form another one and somebody else would be president. So I said, 'Why didn't you, dear?' And she said, 'Well, I was going on funny little trains to funny little towns. I didn't even play with dolls because I never had very much time. I do remember several times stopping at little towns on the train and pressing my nose against the window and seeing little girls pushing baby buggies with dolls in them. They seemed to be having fun, and that made me feel like I was missing something.' So I asked her what she did do, and she said, 'Well, I sang and danced. With my sisters and my mother. We were cute, and they thought that was one way to make money.' "

The point of the conversation was not Judy's reminiscences but the fact that she intended "to graduate with her Hollywood High School class. She even brought her dress for me to see. It was a very simple, sweet little white dress. I remember I read in the paper about the time the graduation would have occurred that MGM was sending Judy on a personal-appearance tour. And I thought, 'Oh, I wonder if she's going to miss her graduation.' Knowing MGM's concern for people, that didn't seem unlikely. So I called a friend of mine in the publicity department and I said, 'You'll probably think I'm crazy, but tell me something. Is Judy going to make her graduation?' And she said she didn't know anything about it."

Judy Garland did indeed graduate with her high-school class, but it was a different high school and a different year. She got her diploma in June 1940 at University High School. Nor had she missed out on all of "the things that most little girls do." She had had several birthday parties and at least one best friend, Ina Mary Ming.

On November 25, 1938, MGM announced that it had elevated Judy Garland and Hedy Lamarr to stardom. To solemnize the occasion, the studio gave Garland her own dressing room. It was wheeled onto Stage 27 encircled by a red ribbon fastened with a large red bow. The Munchkins and stunt doubles and stand-ins were all rounded up and sent to the stage to watch Judy cut the ribbon. "We all applauded and then we were allowed to walk into the dressing room and look around and then we were dismissed for lunch," says Betty Danko, Margaret Hamilton's stand-in and stunt double.

Betty Danko returned from lunch early. Judy Garland returned a moment later. "She went to the dressing room," says Danko, "but it was locked. She stood in the middle of the stage, and I could see tears coming into her eyes. I had never spoken to her directly before, but I asked her what was the matter and she said, 'I'm locked out of my dressing room.' I said, 'You mean you don't have the key?' She said, 'No,' and I said, 'Who has it?' And she said, 'I don't know.' And I remember feeling sick that they hadn't entrusted that girl with the key to her first great present."

It was an oversight, of course. Judy did, after all, get into the dressing room when the wardrobe woman who held the key returned from lunch. In any case, the dressing room was tangible evidence that she was a movie star.

Production #1060

THE MUNCHKINS

The midgets arrived at MGM in mid-November. There were 124 of them, and their presence was felt immediately.

"We had a hell of a time with those little guys," says Mervyn LeRoy. "They got into sex orgies at the hotel. We had to have police on every floor." "Very raunchy people," remembers screenwriter Noel Langley. "They raided the lot. The showgirls had to be escorted in bunches by armed guards." "They were drunks," recalled an aging Judy Garland. "They got smashed every night, and the police had to pick them up in butterfly nets." "The most deformed, unpleasant bunch of *adults* imaginable," writes Hugh Fordin in his book on Arthur Freed. "This unholy assemblage of pimps, hookers, and gamblers infested the Metro lot and all of the community."

The midgets who arrived at MGM in mid-November ranged in size from 2' 3" to 4' 8". With their high-pitched voices, their beardless faces, and their prematurely wrinkled skin, the little people were hardly ordinary. But the gulf between them and the big people who would feed them, dress them, dominate them, and pay them for the next nine weeks was far less than the big people imagined.

"Yes, ma'am," Hazel Resmondo says. "No, ma'am." She wears orange slacks and pours cream from an ornate yellow pitcher that looks as if it belongs to a little-girl's tea set. Hazel Resmondo is seventy-three years old, but her anxiety to please is that of an eight-year-old child. She is 4' 4" tall and weighs eighty pounds, nine more than she did when she played a Munchkin in *The Wizard of Oz*. She was thirty-four years old then, but she had never had a job. She had wanted to get a job once before, but her father had said, "What if Daddy's little girl gets sick?" He drove her to and from the studio every morning and every night. Even so, she was "scared to death to be away from home all day." She was thirty-six years old before she got married, and she wore a child's formal to her wedding. Now she is embarrassed to buy the little-girls' dresses she has worn all her life: "When you're older, your figure's different." She has, she admits, always been something of "a little girl" herself, first to her daddy, then to the "typical little midget man, very manly, very dignified," whom she married. Since his death a few years ago, she has lived alone in a bungalow court in Southern California. Much of what she is and owns—from the toy poodle to the two pink-and-green china ballet dancers with ruffled shades that serve as bedside lamps—seem a child's version of playing grownup. *The Wizard of Oz* was a central event in her life. She remembers that when she first walked onto the Munchkin set in her costume, she was so excited she cried.

Billy Curtis swaggers the length of a Hollywood cafeteria, carrying a cup of coffee from one table to another. The cafeteria—half a block from the magic intersection of Hollywood and Vine—has been his turf for the last twenty years. On days when there is no work for him in television, he can always find a friend at the Ontra Cafeteria. He is, he says, "a little man, a scale model of a tall man. Not deformed like a dwarf. Not with the high-pitched voice of the midget. If you only saw a photograph of me, you wouldn't believe I was a little person." He is 4′ 2″ tall, sixty-six years old, and he has been married twice—both times to full-sized women. "Little people are clannish," he says. "They live together. Psychologically, it's security for them. It's safer. I learned more from being in the adult world with the adult people—learning their ways, learning that they are liars and cheats."

Margaret Pellegrini waits outside an Arizona kindergarten. It is a longer step backward to 1938 for her than for the others, the ones who stayed in Hollywood. She was sixteen years old when she played a Sleepy Head in *The Wizard of Oz* ("Wake up, sleepy head / Rub your eyes / Get out of bed / Wake up, the Wicked Witch is dead"*). She is fifty-five now and has been married for thirty-one years "to a big person, an ex-prizefighter." Twenty of those years were spent in the Phoenix Sheriff's Department. Though retired now, she keeps busy: she is president of her lodge, and she is raising a five-year-old granddaughter. The days when she was nicknamed "Li'l Alabama" and "Popcorn" are long gone. What she remembers best about *The Wizard of Oz* is "the feeling of specialness. Someone was always there to brush my hair or fix my costume. For Christmas, Judy Garland gave all us little ones a big box of candy. We sat on the Yellow Brick Road and passed the box around. She also gave us autographed pictures. I still have mine. It says, 'To Li'l Alabam,

---

* Copyright © 1938, renewed 1966 Metro-Goldwyn-Mayer, Inc. Copyright © 1939, renewed 1967 Leo Feist, Inc. Rights throughout the world administered by Leo Feist, Inc.

Mervyn LeRoy, Judy Garland, and Victor Fleming with the Munchkins, most of whom were found for MGM by Leo Singer, manager of Singer's Midgets. Each morning at 6 a.m. they were made up in a large hall with thirty makeup chairs and mirrors arranged in a row. Each Munchkin moved from chair to chair as in an assembly line, emerging in full makeup from chair number 30.

Best Wishes, Judy Garland.' " Margaret Pellegrini stands in the Phoenix sun, remembering. The gates of the kindergarten open, and the present takes precedence. She holds out her hand to her granddaughter.

Nearly all of the midgets were hypopituitary dwarfs—men and women whose pituitary glands did not function properly. Deficient in growth hormone, they were in no way deformed. They were only miniature. They were neither pimps nor whores, although there were among them a few promiscuous women, a few sexually aggressive men.

Most of the men and a number of the women got drunk several

[190]

times during their nine weeks in Culver City. It was hard not to get drunk. Culver City was full of bars, and the bars were full of big people who bought the little people drinks with much the same spirit of adventure they might have felt in buying liquor for a pet chimpanzee. The ability to hold one's liquor depends to some extent on body weight. At fifty-six pounds, the average Munchkin was unequal to the five or six drinks pressed into his hands by the big people on adjoining bar stools. It was a rare night when the studio police did not have at least one midget to carry home.

The majority of the Munchkins were quartered at the Culver City Hotel, a shabby-genteel place on Main Street a mile or so from the studio. It was around the Culver City Hotel that the stories of depravity would hang thickest, as tangible as the mist dripping from the hotel eaves that long-ago Christmas season. There were, so the story goes, three prostitutes who moved into the hotel; and the lines for their services stretched down the block. "Everything you can imagine sexually was going on," says Mervyn LeRoy. "They had terrific fights over women," says John Lee Mahin. "I heard that knives were pulled. Midgets are evidently highly sexed or something."

Yet midgets are—most often—not oversexed but undersexed. "A reasonably large number of the hypopituitary people are sexually immature because they have multiple pituitary hormone disorders," says Dr. S. Douglas Frasier, a pediatric endocrinologist at the University of Southern California School of Medicine. "Probably fifty percent have isolated growth-hormone deficiency and fifty percent have additional pituitary disorders. Those people don't go through puberty spontaneously, don't get a low male voice or coarse facial hair."

Dr. John Money, professor of medical psychology and pediatrics at the Johns Hopkins University School of Medicine, also sees hypopituitary dwarfs differently from MGM folklore. "When hypopituitary people get angry, the anger tends to be turned into themselves. They get depressed or indulge themselves in a sort of childishness that's appropriate to their height but not to their age. And that very much relates to the fact that everybody else in the world infantilizes them. They go into a restaurant at the age of twelve, and the waitress says, 'Would the baby like a high chair to sit on?' And so then they do what, in the technical jargon, is called 'denial of illness.' They act as if they were as young as their height."

"The Munchkins were a pretty noisy bunch," remembers Yip Harburg. Why their employers misjudged their noise and quarrels and childish tantrums as depravity can only be guessed at. Perhaps it was that, being deviant in one way, they were automatically assumed to be deviant in all ways. One Munchkin did bite the leg of an MGM policeman who was barring his way. A few women did offer themselves to shocked stagehands and electricians. Several of the men carried knives and grandly brandished them with masculine oaths and all-encompassing threats. Memories are distorted because the activities of these few—biting policemen, carrying knives, soliciting business from men they faced at crotch level—were applied to all the Munchkins.

"Me being so young and alone," says Margaret Pellegrini, "they assigned me another little lady who was older for me to room with. She had been in show business before. And she was having problems with her ex-husband. He knocked on the door of our room and came in with a knife. We were sitting there writing out Christmas cards and letters back home. She was very religious, so she kind of talked to him. Talked him out of doing anything. Then we reported it and they moved us out of the Culver City Hotel to the Vine Manor, about two blocks away from Hollywood and Vine. He never bothered us after that. We didn't have any more trouble."

There was, in actuality, very little trouble. The Munchkins were timid more often than aggressive, shy more often than bold. Their preferred term for themselves was "little people," and they called the people who towered above them "big people," "adults," or "grownups." They identified as "grownups" even those big people who were younger than themselves.

Of all the grownups who worked with them on *The Wizard of Oz*, Ray Bolger probably defined them best. He had worked with midgets in vaudeville, had even been the object of a passionate crush from "a delicious-looking little woman named Olive and I had the time of my life running away from her." He had sat backstage in a dozen theaters trading tall stories with them. He did not find it

Dorothy's house has landed on the Wicked Witch of the East.
See Appendix A for an account of the auction of the ruby slippers,
thirty-two years after this scene was shot.

Glinda, the Good Witch of the North, and Dorothy confront
the Wicked Witch of the West in Munchkin City.

Top: Judy Garland and the others wait while the assistant cameraman positions the Lilly— a white card held within camera range at the end of each scene while three or four feet of extra film were shot. If the Lilly was white when the film was projected, the colors had not been distorted.

Middle: Glinda in Emerald City. An assistant cameraman (kneeling at left) adjusts the Lilly.

Below, from left: Margaret Hamilton, Judy Garland, and Billie Burke in Munchkin City as the Wicked Witch threatens Dorothy in order to get the ruby slippers. Note the Munchkins cowering on the floor.

*Top: The Wicked Witch
and her servant, Nikko
(and an assistant cameraman—
partially visible at right), in the
Tower Room of the Witch's castle.*

*Middle: The same scene with
Betty Danko, Margaret Hamilton's
stunt double, standing in while the
cameras were being adjusted.*

*Below: Frank Morgan in green
coachman's dress (for the Emerald
City sequences, four women worked
two weeks dyeing material green),
driving the carriage pulled
by the Horse of a Different Color.*

Above: Betty Danko being wired for the skywriting sequence. Heavy metal bolts secured the wires to her "flying" suit, made out of heavy canvas lined with sheep's wool.

Below: Judy Garland's stand-in, Bobbie Koshay, was in her mid-twenties. With her, Ray Bolger's stand-in and (center) Jack Haley's.

necessary to avert his eyes from their bodies or to deny the hungers trapped inside that small space. "A small person is looking at your belly button. In order to look at your face, he has to look up. He's like a small child looking up at a great big world. The little people were not accepted. They were segregated because of their size. They couldn't run as fast; they couldn't dance the same way you did. Dancing with one would be like dancing with your daughter who is five years old. They were considered not to be as bright as other people, even though some of them were terribly bright. So they figured that they were underdeveloped, that they were freaks. That made a kind of a sad world for them to live in, and yet they were brave people. They made out."

Most of the 124 Munchkins were acquired for MGM by Leo Singer, the proprietor of Singer's Midgets. Singer was a German Jew who found and trained his midgets as acrobats, singers, dancers, and wrestlers in Germany and Austria. "Singer didn't fool with American midgets," according to Henry Kramer, a 5′ 9″ man married to 4′ 1″ Dolly Kramer, "Queen of the Midgets." Between 1936 and 1952, the Kramers headed their own troupe of ten midgets. "American midgets were too independent for Singer," says Kramer, "and they wanted too much money." "Singer had a reputation for cheating his midgets," says Billy Curtis. "Some of those little guys didn't have the intelligence to know the value of money. And they were foreigners, too. Half of them couldn't speak English. Singer fed them and clothed them. And when they didn't work, Singer was still giving them a couple of bucks to spend. They thought that was great."

Arthur Freed first approached Singer in March, and Singer offered to supply not only midget people but also midget animals. The idea of midget animals was quickly dismissed, but in the summer of 1938 MGM hired Singer to supply the studio with Munchkins for *The Wizard of Oz*. He left his own troupe, which had dwindled to eighteen, in the custody of MGM and set out on a cross-country sweep.

He found Grace Williams in Minneapolis. Grace Williams had been for several years the only American midget in Singer's troupe.

She had left him in 1936 to form a troupe with her husband, Harvey Williams. For $600 a week, Singer offered to hire Harvey and Grace Williams and the nine other midgets who belonged to Harvey Williams and His Little People. Grace Williams had never had any trouble with Singer. "Mr. Singer was very good to his little people. We played the best theaters on the vaudeville circuit. We went to the Chicago World's Fair and the Cleveland Exposition. We were in Washington in 1926, and we had tea with the President, Calvin Coolidge. Mr. Singer taught his little people to dance and sing. He had private tutors to give them an education. He treated them fine and gave them beautiful hotel suites." Harvey Williams and His Little People signed a contract and set out for Hollywood in their jitney. The contract was for four weeks, but they worked nine weeks.

Harry Monty was performing in a Chicago nightclub when Singer dropped in and offered him $50 a week plus expenses. "I was working in a comedy-acrobatic-clown act with a partner," says Monty. "My partner refused to go, but another midget living in my roominghouse did come with me. Singer sent us train tickets and a money order for expenses. But when we got to California, he started to chisel a little bit, not paying us what he had promised. Eventually, MGM started paying the independent midgets so we would get what we were promised. They didn't want a lawsuit. For his gang, all those little people under real contract to him, they paid him a flat fee."

Many more than his original eighteen midgets were under contract to Singer. Hazel Resmondo had been walking along Hollywood Boulevard in the spring of 1938 when she "ran into some midgets. All of a sudden, even though I was so shy, I whirled around and asked them about a job. They took my name, and in the fall I got a telephone call. I was asked to come over to Mr. Singer's house. Mrs. Singer was so big. She had a long cigarette and a long cigarette-holder, and she was posing with her arm stretched out on her big mantel. And I felt so little, even though I'm one of the larger midgets. I call myself a *giant* midget, and they almost thought I was too big. Singer bid me in for peanuts. I got five dollars a day, thirty dollars a week. When I found out that some of the little people were getting fifty, even sixty dollars, I went up to him. He said, 'You just thank

God you have a job!' Mrs. Singer said, 'If you don't like it, you go home.' They scared me to death. I didn't know how to talk up for myself like I do today."

MGM had originally hoped for two hundred midgets. But Singer had difficulty finding even a hundred. Major Doyle, one of the best-known Ringling Brothers midgets, refused to deal with Singer—partly because of Singer's reputation, partly because little people who had remained independent tended to be hostile toward the big people who managed troupes of midgets. Major Doyle arranged directly with MGM casting director Billy Grady for his own employment. Henry Kramer was not as lucky. Kramer tried unsuccessfully to maneuver Singer into paying his wife, Dolly, extra money. When Singer refused, Kramer took his ten midgets directly to MGM and was told that Singer held the contract. Eventually, the two men bartered. Kramer helped bring in forty midgets. The midgets were paid $50 a week and expenses and Kramer was given a commission.

Singer also worked through studio scouts and actors' agents. "I was walking down Hollywood Boulevard," says Billy Curtis, "and some woman came up to me and said, 'You're an actor, aren't you?' I said, 'Yeah,' and she said, 'We need you. Get over to MGM and see Mervyn LeRoy or Arthur Freed.' " Billy Curtis gets himself a second cup of coffee and savors the memories of thirty-five years ago. "On my way I met this other guy, Tommy Cottonaro, and I said, 'Come on. I may have a job for you.' He said, 'I've never been in show business.' And I told him, 'I'm going to *put* you in show business.' I put him in show business, but he didn't stay. He's a bartender now in upstate New York."

Like Tommy Cottonaro, a number of other *Wizard of Oz* midgets were non-professionals. "I was sixteen and a half years old," says Margaret Pellegrini, "the same age as Judy Garland. I was a little Alabama girl, and I got a telegram from this agent in Hollywood. He said he needed little people for *The Wizard of Oz* and would I be interested? I don't know how he got my name except once I went to a fair in Memphis, Tennessee, and I met some little people and I gave them my name and address."

Like Harry Monty, Margaret Pellegrini was sent a train ticket. Nearly half of the midgets, however, were gathered in New York City and transported to the MGM studio in California by chartered bus. Jerry Maren was the youngest of the sixty midgets on the bus. "When I was thirteen, I began dancing lessons with my sister.* After that, during school vacations I did an act with my dancing teacher called Three Steps and a Hop. We played the New England circuit. Some MGM scouts saw me. They needed three little guys who could really sing and dance—as Lollipop Kids. I was the one with the candy, the one who gave the lollipop to Judy Garland. It was a fairy tale. I graduated from high school and there was a telegram from MGM to work on the picture—nearly a hundred dollars a week plus expenses. You couldn't write it.. You wouldn't believe it."

Jerry Maren was seventeen years old. "He was the cutest man I've ever seen in my life," says assistant dance director Dona Massin. "He was very good-looking. Even though he was a man, you just wanted to pick him up. He was always with some little girl who was almost as cute as he was." The little girl was Margaret Pellegrini. But nothing came of their relationship. "She was too young and I was too dumb," says Maren. At seventeen, Maren had never seen another midget before. "And all of a sudden I was on a bus with sixty of them. My reaction to that busload of midgets was to get just as excited as anyone else would who saw them. 'Look how funny he walks. Gee, do I do that?' I'd never compared because I had never had the opportunity."

The chartered bus pulled into Culver City on November 10, 1938, dropping a few of the midgets in front of the Adams Hotel, the rest at the Culver City Hotel. "We were so tired we just went to bed that evening," says Jerry Maren, "and the next morning there were bands playing and a big parade, and I said to another little fella, 'Boy, we must be something. They've got a special parade for us and everything.' Then I found out the parade was for Armistice Day. The next day they took pictures of a hundred midgets entering Metro-Goldwyn-Mayer, and my biggest thrill was going through the gate. I thought, 'God dang, can you imagine that? I'm a movie actor. I'm a movie star!' That's what I thought, walking through the gate of MGM."

---

* By coincidence, Maren's dancing teacher in Boston was the same man who had taught Ray Bolger seventeen years earlier.

□

It was not until the second week in December—a month after their arrival in Culver City—that the Munchkins stood in front of a camera. Their first four weeks at the studio were spent being measured for costumes, having molds made for false ears and pug noses, and being taught the intricacies of the dances they would perform to "Ding Dong! The Witch Is Dead," "We Welcome You to Munchkinland," and "You're Off to See the Wizard." It was part of Ken Darby's job to stand them in front of the playback machines on the stage and teach them to mouth the words to their songs. Although they had to learn the words in order to mouth them, they did not sing in the film.

Most of the midgets' time was spent in the huge dance-rehearsal hall. Thirty-two men and three women would have special business to do. The other fifty-eight men and thirty-one women would play assorted Munchkin townsmen and townswomen. Singer made sure that Mervyn LeRoy and Victor Fleming gave the eighteen midgets from his own troupe first chance at such roles as Mayor, Coroner, Town Crier, General, and Deaf Townsman with Ear Trumpet. Roles were also parceled out according to size and ability. In addition to his skill as a dancer, Jerry Maren was only 3′ 6″ tall—the height of an average five-year-old child. At 4′ 6″, Harry Monty towered over most of the other Munchkins. Tall as an average ten-year-old, he was an easy choice for a Munchkin soldier. (Neither Maren nor Monty is that height today. Monty, who was twenty-five years old in 1938, has grown another inch. Maren, who was seventeen, has grown nine inches. Hypopituitary dwarfs tend to go into puberty late and to grow slowly, quarter-inch by quarter-inch, until they are twenty-five or thirty years old.)

"They put us all in a big line," says Margaret Pellegrini, "and showed us a dance step. The ones who couldn't do it were taken out of the line. The rest of us got to follow Judy Garland to the borders of Munchkinland." It was Dona Massin, dance director Bobby Connolly's twenty-one-year-old assistant, who taught the Munchkins. She worked not only with the 124 midgets but also with the six or eight children who filled in the bare spots in the background during the Munchkin sequence. "I didn't teach them dances really," says Dona Massin. "Technically speaking, they did not do much dancing. Just little hopping things, cute little movements. There were no really difficult steps of any kind. When the good fairy tells them to 'Come out, come out, wherever you are,' it was just a matter of showing them how to sneak up behind her. That was more acting than dancing. For 'Ding Dong! The Witch Is Dead,' Mr. Connolly said, 'We've got to get some happy movements.' Then he remembered a can-can he had done in *The King and the Chorus Girl* for Mervyn LeRoy at Warner Brothers. So he told me to have them do that can-can but not to move their hips, just their hands and shoulders, a simple skipping, a happy movement because the Witch was dead."

Each morning a bus went the rounds of the hotels and motels in Culver City, collecting the midgets. In general, members of a midget troupe lived together. "They were like children," said Billy Curtis. "They'd take a house with two or three bedrooms and all live together with their big person. They'd all have their chores. To cook one night a week or wash the dishes. And the father was the big person. He'd say, 'You do this. You do that. Don't talk to nobody.' I disliked any man who handled midgets. I saw the dollar sign going into *his* pocket instead of into the kids' pockets."

Billy Curtis and Tommy Cottonaro shared an apartment in Hollywood and drove to the studio in the old Pontiac that Tommy had fitted with clutch and brake extensions so he could reach the pedals. "Of all the midgets," said Charlie Schram, a makeup man at MGM, "Billy Curtis was the handsomest and had the most style. He was flashily dressed and he smoked cigars. He was quite arrogant. He looked down on the others because he had had a degree of success in vaudeville." Curtis makes himself the hero of a dozen incidents. According to him, when Margaret Hamilton caught on fire, he jumped on her and put the fire out; and he used to help Judy Garland sneak out to meet David Rose at the roller-skating rink near his apartment. But Margaret Hamilton remembers every detail of her rescue, and no Munchkins were involved. And David Rose, who became Judy Garland's first husband, says that he did not even meet his wife until a year after she finished *The Wizard of Oz*.

□

The logistics of dealing with 124 midgets were formidable. The studio provided lunch in the commissary on Lot 2. A café on Motor Avenue about 1,500 feet north of the studio served them breakfast and dinner. No money changed hands, and any midget who preferred to go elsewhere had to pay for his own food. MGM's Makeup Department normally consisted of five or six makeup artists. Over forty extra men were hired for the film. "For that one picture, we trained a lot of kids who are doing makeup today," said Jack Young in 1976. "Because we couldn't find enough people with experience. We set up an assembly line in the basement of Rehearsal Hall 8. We hired office kids to carry trays with noses and cheeks for the Munchkins. They were like copy boys in a newspaper office. They would hand out noses, wigs, beards to whoever needed them. Little pug noses, little round apple cheeks. We had taken casts of every one of those midgets. They had to have new noses and cheeks every day. We would get three or four noses ahead and store them in boxes with the Munchkin's name on them. Just in case we ran into trouble. An apprentice might make a mistake in putting a cheek on and lose the edges. We'd have another cheek ready as a back-up."

It was cold in Rehearsal Hall 8 at 5:30 in the morning when the first makeup men would arrive to set out their black rectangular cases, to sharpen their eyebrow pencils to the right flat shovel point, to mix their spirit gum to the proper consistency. It was still cold when the midgets began to arrive at six. The makeup men called the huge cold hall the Bullpen. There were thirty or forty makeup chairs in a long row across the length of the otherwise empty hall and thirty or forty mirrors, one in front of each chair. Each man had his own station. The Munchkins moved from one chair to another, getting a cheek here, a bald skullcap with painted hair there. Since most of the midgets were too small to sit in the makeup chairs, boards were placed across the arms of the chairs, something like the boards used for small children in barber shops. The process of making up 124 Munchkins began at 6 a.m. By 8:30 a.m., all of them were ready to put on their costumes.

Their costumes, like the rest of the costumes in the film, had been designed by Adrian—MGM's No. 1 designer, the husband of Academy Award–winning actress Janet Gaynor, and the man who had

*Victor Fleming and Judy Garland with Munchkins Jack Glicken,
Charlie Becker, and Little Billy Rhodes.*

invented padded shoulders for Joan Crawford. The Munchkins' costumes were heavy with silk tassels, silver chain, wide buckles. Flowers were appliquéd everywhere—on gloves, on hats, on bodices, even on sleeves and capes. The huge vests and coats and jewelry were designed to make the Munchkins look even smaller. Because of the size and shape of the midgets and the intricacy of Adrian's designs, nothing could be bought. Each coat, vest, bodice, shoe, even each pair of stockings had to be made within the Wardrobe Department.

"The whole Munchkin number was made out of felt," says Vera Mordaunt, head of MGM's Dye Department in 1938. "Even their shoes and stockings were felt. Adrian wanted the midgets to wear striped stockings. So each pair of stockings had to be striped with wax or masking tape and then spray-dyed and left to dry before the wax or tape could be removed."

"The shoes were made in two pieces," says Marian Parker, who spent the ten years between 1933 and 1943 "at the sewing machine" before she "graduated one step and spent the next fifteen years in charge of the second floor of the Wardrobe Department, where they finished costumes and added accessories." The Munchkins were sent in one by one to have the felt shoes pinned together on their feet. "There was a side cut on each side with the seam in the back, and we sewed them together on a machine. The shoes had curlicue toes that were sewn on separately. Little turned-up cornucopias at the end of the toes."

Dressing the midgets was considerably easier than making their clothes. Sheila O'Brien, who served as wardrobe woman for the thirty-four Munchkin women, remembers that "I used to play a game with them. I used to have them all get their shoes and stockings on and step into their dresses. And then I'd say, 'All right, gang, line 'em up.' Because they liked to be treated like big people. Then I'd say, 'O.K., now the zips.' I just zipped the last one and then they zipped each other all the way up the line. That way it was big fun and not much trouble getting them dressed." At first, Sheila O'Brien felt "kind of squeamish about the midgets. But after I knew them, they were just like anybody else. Some of them were tough little gals who had been in circuses. One time I sewed one little woman's stockings together across the top, just for a gag. All the other little women were in on it. They were holding their hands over their mouths to keep from laughing and she let out a string of cuss words. 'Come here, Irish, you did this,' she said. And of course they all whooped and hollered and laughed, because I'm sure it's the first time anybody ever played a practical joke on them. Because so many times people don't see them as normal. That's why I think they dislike children so much. Because children gawk at them. They seemed not to have much patience with the kids in the film."

But even getting dressed had its own kind of embarrassment. "There was one fat, pot-bellied midget with flower pots coming out of his shoulders," says Betty Danko, Margaret Hamilton's stunt double. "It was a wet day outside. And the wardrobe man had that midget under one arm and another midget under his other arm. And he was crabbing. 'What am I, a wardrobe man or a nursemaid?' Because he had to take them to the bathroom and unlace their costumes and then lace them back up again when they were through."

After a few weeks, attendants were hired to help the midgets on and off the studio toilets. "It was the first time I'd ever had anybody help me go to the bathroom," says Margaret Pellegrini shyly. "But the costumes were so unhandy." The attendants were hired after one of the midgets fell into the toilet and could not get out. "Forty-five minutes later, they found him," says Billy Curtis. "They had to clean him off like he was a baby."

For a few of the men, there were even worse humiliations. "I dressed the children," says Marie Rose, "up on the third floor. And this one boy kept being shy and embarrassed. And I kept saying, 'I have to see if these pants fit. Don't you be shy because I have a boy older than you at home.' He looked to be about nine years old, but when I got his pants off, lo and behold if I didn't find out I was dressing a midget. All of a sudden, I realize this is a thirty-year-old man I'm dressing. I'll never forget it if I live to be a thousand."

Most of the technicians who worked on *The Wizard of Oz* remember the midgets with a certain amount of affection. "They were such cute little things." "They were such little toys." "They were like little dolls." The tone of voice is gentle, reminiscent of the tone in which one might praise a clever dog. Mervyn LeRoy remembers that he hired only "little people who were little and cute and looked perfect." His memory is validated by the surviving Munchkins, most of whom insist that there were no deformed dwarfs among them. But many of the big people who worked on the film do have clear memories of such dwarfs. The makeup men in particular remember a group of male Munchkins who had peach fuzz all over their faces. "To get the prosthetic pieces off them was like pulling a Band-Aid off of hair," says Howard Smit, who was "a very young assistant assistant" on *The Wizard of Oz*. "They were in agony. We'd soak the prosthesis in a mixture of oils to break the glue, and it was still agony." The makeup men almost unanimously agree that the dwarfs with facial hair were both deformed and nasty. "They were tough little guys to work on," says Jack Young. "Different from the little midgets who were delightful, cute—like little dolls." Yet the dwarfs with facial hair were not deformed; they were primordial dwarfs, miniature but not lacking in either confidence or sexuality. And it was their psychological toughness that probably caused the makeup men to see them as deformed.

It is hard for hypopituitary dwarfs, who look like children most of their lives, to force the adult world to take them seriously. In general, the Munchkins did function successfully in that world.

Harry Monty never went back to Chicago. "MGM offered me a good deal, sixteen weeks doubling Johnny Sheffield in *Tarzan Finds a Son*. After that I didn't have to go back. All the studios found out I was an acrobat and could do stunts. They called me Hollywood's Midget Stunt Man, and I got lots of jobs doubling children. I was even under contract at MGM and did all of the stunts for Margaret O'Brien."

Grace Williams had "fifty-four different ventures" in movies, television, and commercials before she retired. Hazel Resmondo was one of many Munchkins who got jobs as stand-ins for child actors. Adult stand-ins for child stars circumvented all the troublesome rules and regulations the California Welfare Department applied so carefully to children.

Jerry Maren did as well as anyone in his large family and better than some. Maren's father had been a foreman at a Boston shoe factory, and two of his older brothers had gone to work at the factory. After *The Wizard of Oz*, Maren worked in two *Our Gang* comedies. But he really came into his own as the original Little Oscar for Oscar Mayer wieners. The advent of outlandish television commercials was a bonanza for all the ex-Munchkins. Harry Monty became the Irish Leprechaun in a series of McDonald's commercials, while other midgets performed as the Hamburglar, Mayor McCheese, and the Mayor's two helpers. Billy Curtis did his share of commercials but tried to stay "legitimate," acting in *Gunsmoke*, in *Little Cigars*, and with Danny Kaye in *The Court Jester*.

They still speak of themselves as "kids," as "little ones," as "children" in juxtaposition to a big, adult, grownup world. Yet the showing of *The Wizard of Oz* on television each year has made them all celebrities. "People see the picture on TV, and then the children come up to me and ask for my autograph," remarks Hazel Resmondo. "Every time I go to the bank," says Margaret Pellegrini, "someone comes up to me and asks, 'Were you in *The Wizard of Oz?*'"

| Production #1060 | 8. |

"BELOW THE LINE"

The infinite details that created the illusion, including . . .
the nearly 1,000 costumes designed by Adrian . . . the
creation of the Emerald City and 60 other sets by Cedric
Gibbons (executed by the 500 carpenters, 150 laborers,
and 20 scenic artists of the Construction Department) . . .
the curious intricacies of Technicolor

A total of 9,200 actors faced the camera in The Wizard of Oz, *450 worked on the set behind the cameras and 6,275 on all branches of production . . . a total of 3,210 costumes were designed and made, 8,428 separate makeups were sketched in color and applied to faces, 68 fantastic settings built . . . and as many as 350 huge lights were used on a single set, generating enough electricity to light 550 five-room homes with two 60-watt globes in each room.*

—from a 32-page press release sent out by MGM's
   publicity director, Howard Strickling, in 1939

None of Strickling's extravagant figures is true. There were barely 600 actors and they required fewer than 1,000 costumes. On the largest of the 60 sets,* 80 or 90 men worked behind the cameras and controlled the 150 arc lights. The number of makeups designed more or less matched the number of actors. And although a considerable group of MGM employees sewed, hammered, painted, typed, and played violins in the service of *The Wizard of Oz*, by no stretch of the imagination did their numbers reach 6,275.

"There were only three thousand employees *at* the studio," says Jack Martin Smith, sketch artist on *The Wizard of Oz*. Actually, there were 3,200 artisans, craftsmen, laborers, and technicians, including 500 carpenters, 15 plumbers, two dozen men in the blacksmith's shop, one dozen in the foundry, one barber, one shoeshine boy, and a man in charge of the lions on Lot 4. In addition, there were some 600 actors, producers, directors, writers and their secretaries, assistants, and retinues. By the summer of 1938, when "temporary complete" scripts for *The Wizard of Oz* were sent down to the Wardrobe, Makeup, Art, and Construction departments, most of those producers and directors and several of the more favored writers were no longer on the main studio lot. They had moved into the new, four-story Thalberg Building. (The producers had the corner suites; the writers and directors had the small offices in between.) The dazzling white building was psychologically and physically outside

* Producer Mervyn LeRoy's somewhat rounded figure.

the high walls of the studio, and the craftsmen tended to refer to it as "the White Lung."

The executives went home at night, but the studio itself was open twenty-four hours a day, six days a week. Whatever had to be cast, welded, sewn, carved, baked, painted, or molded out of steel, lead, wood, rubber, leather, glass, canvas, or plaster of Paris could be made in some MGM shop. "If you needed a chimpanzee tomorrow," says Smith, "it was sitting there. If you needed an alligator, it was there. If you needed a couple of lions, they were there. There were three or four men in the leather shop who did nothing but repair carriages and harness. Lot 5 was all carriages and buggies and rigs and harness, a storehouse where you could pick out a period hearse for your picture, or a Hungarian carriage, or a landau, a spring buggy, an army wagon, any kind of bridle or saddle. Whatever you wanted, whatever you needed, it was there. And if it wasn't already there, someone would make it for you. When you went home at night and left a working drawing on your desk, you had to be very sure it was complete. Because when you came back in the morning, the thing you had designed was sitting there waiting for you."

A somewhat envious Frank Capra once characterized MGM directors of the early thirties as the very best; MGM technicians were the cream of the crop, too. "When I came to the studio," says special-effects man Glenn Robinson, "a loaf of bread cost six cents; a gallon of gas cost six cents; and carpenters got three dollars a day when they could find a job. The studio was paying four dollars. We had highly skilled talent, the best electricians, plasterers, wood-carvers, pattern-makers." "We had available to us a tremendous number of top technical people," says Buddy Gillespie, who designed the special effects for *The Wizard of Oz*. "Naval architects and machinists and hydraulic engineers. They were all at MGM. And they were there year in and year out."

The studio's record books are filled with the names of men who clung to the studio as tenaciously as ivy, leaving only when they were forcibly detached from the walls in the aftermath of their sixty-fifth birthdays. "I've never worked anywhere else," says Lorey ["Easy"] Yzuel, who came to the studio in June 1934. "I was nineteen years old, and I got a job by hanging around the gate. There were always fifty or a hundred people out there hoping for work. When the labor foreman needed some men to strike a set, he'd go out and pick ten or fifteen."

At sixty-two, Yzuel is the head of the Construction Department. On his desk, a small ceramic figure holds a sign that reads:

Starting Time
8:00 a.m.

Morning Coffee Break
9–11:30 a.m.

Lunch Hour
11:30 a.m.–1:30 p.m.

Afternoon Coffee Break
2–4:30 p.m.

Quitting Hour
5:00 p.m.

"The feeling for doing a good job isn't here any more." He is not sure when it disappeared, that special feeling of working in a special place. Perhaps it left with L. B. Mayer in 1951 or drifted away with the stars and producers and directors whose contracts were severed in '54 and '55. Probably some wisp of it remained until it was dispersed finally and forever in January 1970, when the Construction Building was locked and most of the machinery sold and MGM went into the business of building a Las Vegas hotel. The Construction Department's doors are unlocked now, and the power saws are working; in 1975 MGM made seven movies. But nothing important is the same. There used to be, behind the Construction Department, a complete lumber yard better than any commercial yard, stacked with moldings and exotic hardwoods. In 1976, when lumber was needed, it was bought from a nearby commercial yard.

"The loyalty isn't here any more," says Yzuel. Working at the studio is just a job, with as little work to be done as possible. "They didn't baby you then. You worked hard. It was go, go, go all day long. But we had a kind of loyalty that's hard to explain." Yzuel thinks, although he isn't sure, "that the loyalty was on account of L. B. Mayer. Thalberg did the brainwork, but Mayer mingled with the people."

"There was an *aura* about Metro in those early years," says Jack Martin Smith. "Everyone who worked there was extremely excited. They were exhilarated and complimented just to be on salary." Smith, a 1934 graduate of the University of Southern California School of Architecture, had been the art director on three pictures at Universal. But when he came to MGM in 1937, he had to "start all over again. If you wanted to come to Metro, you started at the bottom." He was pushed one rung down the ladder to sketch artist, and it took him five years to work his way back up to art director.

William Horning was the art director on *The Wizard of Oz*: it was up to him to invent Oz. The Wardrobe Department, faced with a similar problem, chose to follow as closely as possible the illustrations drawn by W. W. Denslow for Baum's book. Jack Haley's Tin Woodman was designed with the same inverted funnel hat, the same line of rivets down his chest, as Denslow's Tin Woodman. The head of Ray Bolger's Scarecrow was tied to his body by a rope that almost exactly duplicated Denslow's drawing of the Scarecrow, and he wore on his head a copy of Denslow's broad-brimmed, pointed hat. In several cases where Denslow's drawings were not explicit, costume designer Adrian followed Baum's text. Billie Burke's Good Witch of the North was quite different from "the little old woman, her face covered with wrinkles" in Baum's book, but she wore the same white gown sprinkled with "little stars that glistened in the sun like diamonds." And Dorothy's dress, in book and movie, "was gingham, with checks of white and blue."

Horning had less help from Baum and Denslow. No Munchkin City is in the book, only scattered farmhouses and cornfields. There is a description of the Deadly Poppy Field but no illustration; there is neither picture nor description of the Witch's Castle. Horning was, at first glance, the wrong man to set down in such boundaryless terrain. "It was difficult for him to handle things imaginatively," according to Randall Duell, formerly an art director at MGM. Most of the twenty MGM art directors, the five or six sketch artists, and the thirty draftsmen were licensed architects or had had some architectural training. Many of them had drifted into the studio because

From left: Malcolm Brown, first assistant director Al Shoenberg,
Victor Fleming, art director William Horning, and Mervyn LeRoy.
Bill Horning had to invent the Emerald City, the Deadly Poppy Field, and
the Witch's Castle, while the Wardrobe Department could follow
the W. W. Denslow illustrations for the costumes of the Tin Woodman,
the Scarecrow, and Dorothy.

they were interested in blending architecture with fine arts. Horning, a graduate of the University of California School of Architecture,
did everything in a straight, hard, architectural way. He was, says
Jack Martin Smith, "extremely practical, ferociously intelligent, and
hard as nails." It was the lunchtime game among the art directors to
try to ask Horning a question he couldn't answer. "We'd say, 'Hey,
Bill, how do those refrigerators work that have a gas element in
them?' And he'd take out a pencil and make a sketch that explained
the whole thing. You couldn't stump him."

Horning got to the studio at 9 a.m. and stayed until midnight.
And his assistants, no matter how early they got to the studio in the
morning, stayed with him. "Everything had to be done perfectly,

and you had to stay all night until it was," says Duell. "He was Jekyll and Hyde, a soft man away from the studio and hell to work for."

Oddly, Horning's lack of imagination was not a handicap. "The film was all details," says Duell. "Bill was a perfectionist. He *liked* details. He actually enjoyed working out all of the picture's complications."

Horning, as always, began his work by methodically reading the script—one of the Ryerson-Woolf-Langley "temporary complete" scripts—and breaking it down into the number of sets required, at the same time making an educated guess at the cost of each set. It had already been decided that the entire picture would be shot "under roof," within the studio sound stages. The camera would dictate how much of each set needed to be built. "We always just build the pieces the audience will see," says Smith. "You had to figure out how far they were from the Emerald City when they first saw it, in order to know how much to build." Some of what appeared to be sets would not be real buildings at all. The exterior of the Emerald City would be a matte painting—a color painting on a four-foot-wide piece of black cardboard. The cardboard painting would be photographed and then blended into the film taken of the characters staring through the Deadly Poppy Field to something in the distance. According to the script, the full shot of the Witch's Castle "silhouetted against the sky on the peak of the mountain" would be done in miniature. The aerial view of the Castle's "four towers, joined by narrow battlements and a wild mountain river flowing past one side" would also have to be done in miniature. (The Witch's Castle ended up as another matte painting.) The Witch's Tower Room would be photographed from enough angles to require a full room, but it would be necessary to build only a small section of the hallway outside the room. Building the door of the Tower Room for the Tin Woodman to chop down, the stairs leading up to the room, the Drawbridge, and the Inner Courtyard would also be required.

The Art Department's responsibilities did not end with designing buildings. Horning would have to create the Emerald City, and he would also have to design the Witch's hourglass, the Haunted Forest, and several apple trees that could use their branches to pick off apples and throw them at Dorothy. An acre and a half of poppies had to be created and some way arranged to wire the poppies to the floor of Stage 29. Details were piled on details—measurements accurate to the quarter-inch and solemn conferences on how to turn six white horses respectively green, blue, orange, red, yellow, and violet. (To paint the horses would be unacceptable, both to the ASPCA and to the animals. Food coloring was tried, but the colors were not subtle enough. The final decision was to sponge the horses down with Jell-O powder, a decision complicated by the fact that the horses invariably managed to lick off most of the Jell-O between shots.)

Among Horning's strengths, says Duell, was "a fantastic ability to absorb things. He would know more about a script after one reading than I would after three." Horning's first tentative ideas were turned into "thumbnail sketches" by Jack Martin Smith. "Ordinarily," says Smith, "you could go to a book or a town and say, 'I'm going to do this type of architecture.' For *Meet Me in St. Louis*, I had oil paintings, steel engravings, and carpentry books. So I could more or less copy a house that would have been there, in St. Louis, in 1900. But all of Oz had to be imagined and created."

Munchkinland was easiest. "You had something working for you. Doors are only this high because the houses are for midgets. Windows are only this high. Flower boxes have to be low enough for midgets to water them. Then we put grass roofs on the houses and shaped them like mushrooms, and that was Munchkinland." In contrast, sketch after sketch of the Emerald City was rejected—either by Horning or by the head of the Art Department, Cedric Gibbons.

Gibbons shared the screen credit and the Academy Award nomination on *The Wizard of Oz* with Horning—the credit read: "Art Director: Cedric Gibbons. Associate: William A. Horning." Gibbons shared screen credit on all MGM films, a fact that enabled him to win eleven Academy Awards between 1929 and 1956. But Gibbons and Horning did not win for *The Wizard of Oz*. The film lost—predictably—to *Gone With the Wind*.*

Gibbons had been at the studio since before it officially ex-

---

* In the field of Art Direction, MGM has won fifteen Academy Awards, second only to 20th Century-Fox's sixteen. The other studios lag far behind.

isted. He didn't leave it until he was terminally ill and too frail to work any longer. According to Jack Martin Smith, he was "an aloof man but very kind. He would never embarrass you in public." "He never threw out what you had done," says Randall Duell, "even if it was a half-baked idea. He worked constructively from it." A handsome man, he wore expensive tweeds and expensive shoes which he polished liberally with Meltonian cream. "He was impeccable," says Smith, "and he had an impeccable wardrobe. The finest of everything, and he always wore a maroon tie." Not *a* maroon tie, says his widow, Hazel Ross. "*The* maroon tie. Cedric wore the same maroon tie for months and months until it got dirty. Then he threw it away and bought another. He was so meticulous that he never dropped a spot of gravy on the tie. Rouben Mamoulian refused to believe Cedric always wore the same tie, so Cedric tore off a corner. Months later, he took the tie off and showed the torn edge to Mamoulian."

It was Gibbons who solved the problem of the Emerald City. There was a central research library at MGM where a writer or pro-

Dorothy's bedroom at home in Kansas. Many of the set stills such as this were sent out by MGM and printed in architectural magazines, home-decorating magazines, and in Sunday rotogravure sections.

ducer could find out the appropriate number of stars in a United States flag flying over an Arizona fort in 1877 or the proper form of address among Mandarin Chinese. (More often than not, the producer would insert the information into some preposterous film about soldiers and Indians or star-crossed lovers.) The Art Department had its own more specialized research department. Somewhere in the clutter of books and magazines on sculpture, architecture, abstract design, and painting, Gibbons found the Emerald City. "He found

A tree trunk is reserved for the Haunted Forest in the scene dock, a storage area. Opposite: a set still of the completed Haunted Forest.

a tiny, a really minuscule photograph of a sketch that had been done in Germany pre–World War I," says Smith. "We looked at the sketch—it actually looked like test tubes upside down—and it crystallized our ideas." (There was a small illustration of the Emerald City by Denslow, but the Art Department found his concept—a group of rather Moorish-looking domes topped by emeralds and interspersed with a few pencil-thin spires also topped by emeralds—too ordinary. However, the matte painting which was background for the renovation sequence looks somewhat like Denslow's drawing.) "We all thought the German sketch was right because it wasn't detailed. It didn't look like Rheims Cathedral. It didn't look like the Pyramids. It didn't look like King Tut's Tomb. It looked like some strange thing we had never seen before."

Once a design for a set had been approved by Horning, Gibbons, and producer Mervyn LeRoy, Smith and the draftsmen produced a detailed working drawing on the scale of quarter-inch to the foot. The working drawing was passed along to the Construction Department.

Nearly 1,000 of the studio's 3,200 craftsmen, laborers, and technicians were lumped together in Construction. The building looked like an enormous greenhouse. Built before sophisticated artificial light, it had a roof composed of hundreds of ten-by-fourteen-inch panes of glass. On the 110-foot-long main floor, the carpenters could partially construct sets before moving them to the sound stages to finish. There was also a sewing room forty feet by sixty where huge backdrops were stitched together by the grips. The building was "immaculately clean"—the men who worked there remember that "The whole lot was immaculately clean then."

The Construction Department encompassed the studio's 500

Below: The Witch's Tower Room. Opposite: The entrance hall to the Witch's Castle. The Tower Room was going to be shot from all angles, so the entire room had to be built, but only this section of the entrance hall was designed and constructed.

carpenters, 150 laborers, 15 plumbers, and 50 plasterers; the 20 scenic artists who painted the muslin backdrops; and the ordinary house-painters who painted the sets. The rule of thumb was simple: if you helped to build, decorate, or tear down the sets, you belonged in Construction, a fact which left Construction crowded with esoteric specialties. The Nursery was in Construction, a unit that was inappropriately named since the nurserymen were much more likely to dress a set with artificial bushes and flowers than real ones; and most of their time was spent wiring artificial leaves or blossoms onto real tree stumps. It was the nurserymen who would wire the artificial poppies to Stage 29.

The Prop Shop was in Construction, too. The men in the Prop Shop were responsible for building the monsters devised by Special Effects. They made the talking apple trees out of chicken wire and foam rubber, with liquid latex added to the chicken-wire frames layer by layer. They hung the finished trees from the grids on piano wire. Then some of them climbed inside the structures they had made to act as the animated souls of the trees. Prop Shop men were in great demand in 1938. "We made $1.41 an hour," says Billy H. Scott, who, for nearly a week, sewed plastic leaves a foot in diameter onto the Deadly Poppies' wire stems, using thin fishline. It was "a tremendous amount of money for those days. The average good mechanic only made $1.00 an hour. And most of us worked two jobs. I worked from six in the morning to noon at Paramount and from two to eight p.m. at MGM."

Before any drawing was sent out, it was scrutinized and signed by Gibbons. Since there were up to a dozen features in production at any one time, this meant a perennial line of art directors sitting outside Gibbons' office with their plans in their laps. When *The Wizard of Oz*—Production #1060—started shooting in October 1938, there were nine other MGM pictures before the cameras: *The Shining Hour* (#1063), starring Joan Crawford and Robert Young; *Out West with the Hardys* (#1061); Mervyn LeRoy's *Dramatic School* (#1064), starring Luise Rainer and Paulette Goddard; Joseph Mankiewicz's version of *A Christmas Carol* (#1068); Hunt Stromberg's big, expensive production of *Idiot's Delight* (#1056), starring Norma Shearer and Clark Gable; LeRoy's *Stand Up and Fight* (#1065), with Wallace Beery and Robert Taylor; *Honolulu* (#1048), with Eleanor Powell and Robert Young; *Let Freedom Ring* (#1075), with Nelson Eddy and Virginia Bruce; and *The Ice Follies of 1939* (#1066). If none of those nine films presented the complications of *The Wizard of Oz*, they still represented well over three hundred sets that had to be built, painted, soundproofed, and dressed.

In addition to the blueprinted working drawings, Smith also drew a series of color sketches, three feet wide and two feet high, of the projected sets. (The proportions of those presentation sketches were in the same ratio as the standard screen of the time.) When Smith was finished with the color sketches, Gibbons rejected them.

"He decided we should do an ethereal kind of thing, not full color but subdued color. So I had to turn around and do all the sketches over again, draw all the sets twice. It was an enormous thing to have to do them over again."

It was not Smith's fault that his sketches were rejected. In

1898 there had been a few experiments with coloring film by hand, and D. W. Griffith had color-tinted some of *Birth of a Nation* in 1914. But the first feature film shot entirely in three-strip Technicolor—*Becky Sharp*—had been made only three years before *The Wizard of Oz*, in 1935. In 1936, 20th Century-Fox, Paramount, RKO, Warner Bros., and United Artists had each made one picture in color. In 1937 the studios had moved from five to twenty color films. Yet it was nearly ten years after *Becky Sharp* before the studios were fully comfortable with color. "Everybody knows how to handle color now," says Smith. "You have blatant color, muted color, funny-paper color, dignified easel paintings transferred into color. Not then, not at the beginning. Up until the end of the war, there were three staff people who were color advisers, who did nothing but attend to

Cross Road, Land of Oz. To make the hills in the background George Gibson (head of the Scenic Art Department and the man responsible for all of the painted backdrops in the film), working with twenty artists, used a piece of heavy white muslin 400 feet long and 35 feet high, which was divided into four-foot, six-foot, or ten-foot squares and painted with pigment and watered glue.

*When the backdrop was finished, the trick was to make
the painted cornfield look like a natural three-dimensional extension
of the set that had already been built.*

color. They would even pick wardrobe. When we used to suit up a hundred ballgowns for a scene, they would send back the costumes that didn't fit the color. And we used to have to make color mock-ups showing the samples of every paint to be used on the set, along with swatches of all the material that Wardrobe was going to use, and even the leaves from the artificial trees and bushes we made. That was quite an expensive thing to do. But we had to do it. Because you couldn't ever be quite sure how it would all look together. We don't do that any more. Because we know about color now."

The Kansas sequences of *The Wizard of Oz* were sepia-toned. They were shot in black and white; then the film was placed in a brown bath to take away the harshness of the black and white. The rest of the film was in color. And color was still an uncharted sea. Designing the Emerald City was, in a sense, easier than finding the proper paint for the Yellow Brick Road. At least it was less tedious. Finding a paint that would not make the Yellow Brick Road look green was Randall Duell's responsibility, and it took him nearly a week. "Color film wasn't perfected then," says Duell. "We had to do a lot of testing and experimenting with the film to get the colors to reproduce properly. We'd start filming a set a week or two before it was going to be used. We had to color-test each set not only for the paints on the set but for the background. Part of the Yellow Brick Road was a painted backing, a backdrop. If that backdrop wasn't painted and lit properly, it would *look* like a painted backdrop. For a while we talked about completely cartooning the background, stylizing it rather than making it realistic, a cartooned cornfield rather than a real one. Then they decided that they'd go the route of only stylizing the characters."

The painted backdrops were George Gibson's responsibility. Gibson was a Scotsman who had come to MGM unwillingly in 1934 but who would stay until his mandatory retirement in 1969. "I was

After the painted backdrop was put together with the constructed stage set, the audience was unable to guess that there was a twelve-foot light well between the backdrop and the far edge of the set.

working at Fox as a scenic artist and I thought Fox much the better place to work. More exciting. But I was laid off in November 1934, and MGM called the same night and I needed a job." Gibson's skepticism about MGM lasted nearly a year, until Cedric Gibbons gave him artistic license in painting the miniatures for the Norma Shearer–Leslie Howard *Romeo and Juliet*.

By 1938, Gibson was thirty-four and head of the Scenic Art Department. In September of that year, he led a dozen of his twenty artists onto Stage 26 to start work on *The Wizard of Oz*. Stage 26 was empty except for a piece of heavy white muslin four hundred feet long and thirty-five feet high. It took three weeks for Gibson and his men to turn the muslin into a cornfield. He worked from one of Jack Smith's muted-color presentation sketches that allowed him to visualize the four-hundred-foot backdrop in scale to the set. He also worked from a one-half-inch scale blueprint so he could see each section of the backing in relationship to the other sections.

"We always started with the oldest form of reproduction known to man: squares. Using charcoal, we divided the muslin into four-foot or six-foot or ten-foot squares. If the backing had a close relationship of things—for example, lots of trees—we would make the squares four-foot. If we were painting a big, sweeping landscape, there was no sense in four-foot squares, so we'd make them ten-foot. We started off by drawing a horizon line six feet from the floor of the stage. That would be Line A. We'd label the vertical lines 1, 2, 3, 4, 5, and the horizontal lines A, B, C, D, E. We worked from a scaffold I had designed. It had five levels and was twenty feet wide. Your perspective from a scaffold is very limited, so I always tried to have the bottom platform run along the horizon line."

The backdrops were painted by using the temperamental medium of pigment and well-watered glue. "The glue had to be kept warm, and it used to make the paint go bad after a few days. Too smelly to work with. Since it would take several weeks to paint a backing, we'd have to mix and throw out several batches of paint. Eventually, I developed a plastic binder in place of the glue. Today

Opposite top: The interior of the Emerald City. To the left is the Guardbox; the entrance to the Wizard's palace is to the rear. A decorative light wheel still sits on a crate. Opposite below: The Emerald City set, January 19, 1939.

*The Lion Forest. Since the speed for color film was so slow in 1939,
a great deal of hot light had to be used. Banks of lights lined
the floor of the stages and the catwalks above the actors.*

they use latex and acrylics. The acrylics don't have as great a range
of color shadings. They're not as sensitive as the paints we used. We
used to have black and white and eight values in between. Today,
people don't care about refinements. They think that if they have
black and white and two values in between, it's enough."

After a few days, Gibson's cornfield looked like an immense
abstract painting: there was a four-hundred-foot-wide strip of blue
sky atop a four-hundred-foot strip of bluish-grey sky atop a four-
hundred-foot strip of greyish middle distance atop a four-hundred-
foot strip of yellow foreground. "You always started with sky area,
land area, middle distance, foreground, and only three or four values
of color. Then you started pulling things to a smaller area. Middle
distance became hills. The hills had ravines. The ravines had rocks."

The painted cornfield would be an extension of the real cornfield to be built on Stage 26. There was always a twelve-foot light well between the edge of a set and the painted backdrop. The trick came in making the viewer's eye leap the twelve-foot gulf and see the first row of painted corn as a continuation of the three-dimensional corn in the foreground. "Many times we'd make the first painted corn or the first painted tree or the first painted house over-size," says Gibson. "To trick the eye. For Munchkinland, we painted half a dozen cutouts—flat pieces of scenery we shaped like houses. The first cutouts were a little larger than the last real houses on the set. Then the cutouts kept getting smaller and smaller, to give the stage depth, to indicate a larger town."

The meeting of Dorothy and the Scarecrow in the cornfield was the first sequence filmed by Victor Fleming. When Fleming was finished with the scene, the Construction Department's grips tore down about three hundred feet of the carefully painted backdrop. "Since the action on that set moved from left to right," says Gibson, "we saved the last seventy or eighty feet on the far right. We moved that backdrop to the far left of the stage to give us a lead-in to the next scene—to the apple trees where Dorothy meets the Tin Wood-man and the forest where she meets the Lion. Then the grips sewed together and hung three hundred feet of new muslin and we started to paint an apple orchard and a forest on it. Munchkinland was easier for us. That was Stage 27. We hung the muslin in units a hundred feet wide by forty feet tall. When they were through shooting one section of the set, we'd take that hundred-foot piece down and hang it somewhere else. We used the same backings for several scenes."

It is not exactly accurate to say that George Gibson stayed at MGM from 1934 until his retirement thirty-five years later. He spent the years between 1942 and 1945 in the South Pacific, using his MGM specialty in a somewhat different way: to map the terrain of islands like Tarawa and Kwajalein for the Marine Corps. When the time came—the Friday of his sixty-fifth birthday—Gibson was ready to quit: "I'd had enough of the business by that time. I was ready to start painting seriously."

It was latex and acrylics and Anscocolor, Metrocolor, Warnercolor, De Luxe Colour by the time Gibson left MGM in 1969. Thirty-one years earlier, there was only Technicolor, and it was cumbersome and unpredictable. "There was no method of color motion-picture photography. We had to design something that would work," says Fred Detmers of what Technicolor did in the 1930's. Detmers was a Technicolor cameraman in 1938, Supervisor of Timing* at his retirement thirty-seven years later. "In 1938, there was no film that would record color. The negatives were black-and-white negatives and you filtered the light. You used a colored gelatin between the object and the film, which would cause one strip of film to record the green aspect, one the blue aspect, and one the red aspect. There were two mechanisms, two movements in the camera Technicolor designed. One mechanism had one film in it. The other had two pieces of film face to face with the emulsion sides together. Between those two apertures was a prism block, a glass prism which had a mirror between two blocks. It was a cube with a diagonal cemented interface that had a mirror in it that reflected part of the light to the aperture that had two films in it."

Those cameras were invented by Technicolor and controlled by them. When a studio wanted to make a color film, Technicolor supplied the cameras, a Color Director, and color consultants who were placed on the studio's payroll (at a cost of $108,000 for *A Star Is Born* in 1937 and $128,000 for *The Garden of Allah* in 1936). Technicolor cameras were scheduled months, sometimes years, in advance. Without an available camera, there could be no movie, so studios reserved cameras long before projects were ready to face them. The Technicolor Camera Department Schedule for March 10, 1938, shows MGM penciled in for three 1938 color films: Production #1, Stromberg, to start in May; Production #2, LeRoy, to start July 24; and Production #3, Hyman, to start in late October. By the Camera Department Schedule of August 15, 1938, Production #2 had turned into *The Wizard of Oz* and exchanged starting dates with Production #3.

---

* "Timer" was the name given to the men who were responsible for deciding the amount of exposure time for each color in the answer (master) print of a film. The job was a crucial and delicate one, since there was often a different exposure time for each color in each separate scene of a film.

A standard Technicolor contract of the late thirties required the studio to pay Technicolor $90 per week for each camera furnished and "to pay to Technicolor the cost of all repairs to said camera made necessary by accident or cause other than ordinary wear and tear." The contract also required a studio to "use the services of, and to consult with, a Color Director to be supplied by Technicolor." Technicolor was paid a flat $125 per week for each picture the Color Director supervised, despite the fact that the same Color Director was servicing several studios at the same time.

The Color Director on *The Wizard of Oz* was Henri Jaffa, who was later, in 1943, loaned to Cedric Gibbons by Technicolor and remained on loan to MGM for eleven years, until 1954, a year after MGM built its own color laboratory.

"I didn't make a motion-picture salary," says Jaffa bitterly. "All the people I worked with were making $1,000 to $3,000 a week. Since I worked as a consultant, my advice was advisory. I had to use great tact and diplomacy, and I hated all the behinds I had to kiss."

Each day in 1938, Jaffa made the rounds of Paramount, Warner Bros., 20th Century-Fox, and MGM. He had an assistant in each studio to take care of the minor problems. The major ones were his, although he, too, had to share credit. The screen credits on *The Wizard of Oz* would read: "Technicolor Color Director: Natalie Kalmus; Associate: Henri Jaffa." Mrs. Kalmus, head of Technicolor's color control, was the ex-wife of Technicolor president Herbert Kalmus. As part of her 1921 divorce settlement, she received a credit on every Technicolor picture. "Mrs. Kalmus came out to *The Wizard of Oz* one day," according to Jaffa. "She'd appear at odd intervals on my pictures and ride the camera boom and take it all over. Mervyn LeRoy just said, 'Look Natalie, we're not having any trouble on this film, so why don't you go to the set around the corner?' "*

Jaffa's only problem on *The Wizard of Oz* was with costume designer Adrian. In general, the studio art departments and wardrobe departments barely tolerated the Technicolor personnel. "Adrian made a scene about the costumes for the Munchkins. He wanted

---

* Mrs. Kalmus's appearance on the set must have been brief indeed. Correspondence at Technicolor indicates that she was in California for only two weeks during the entire six months *The Wizard of Oz* was being filmed.

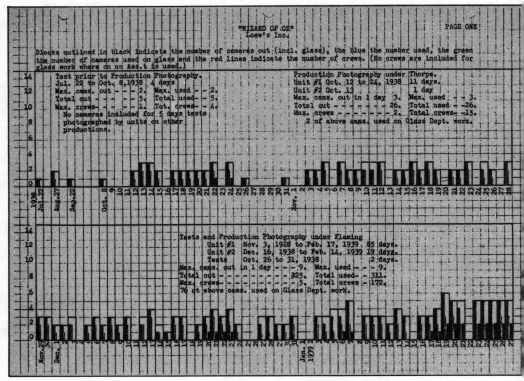

Technicolor's camera records for The Wizard of Oz. *In 1939, Technicolor controlled the only cameras that could produce color film. When a studio wanted to make a movie in color, the cameras had to be reserved months in advance; Technicolor leased the cameras and supplied a Color Director and color consultants, who were put on the studio's payroll.*

colors that wouldn't work. We had to be very careful with color then. For example, we couldn't shoot pure white. We had to use ecru or beige to give the illusion of white. And the whole color scheme of Jeanette MacDonald's pictures was cued to the peculiar color of her wigs." In the quarrel with Adrian, Jaffa was the victor because—and only because—Gibbons interceded for him with the executives on the third floor of the Thalberg Building. "Cedric Gibbons was an autocrat," says Jaffa. "He never called me Henri and I never called him Cedric. He wasn't married to Dolores Del Rio with a leopard and a tennis court for nothing. But he respected me. He thought my judgment about the costumes was right, and he talked to Eddie Mannix. Despite Adrian's willfulness and stubbornness and the fact that he had the big office, Mannix sided with me."

Henri Jaffa had his name on more than three hundred pictures. But in 1976 he did not have a color television set in his small Beverly Hills apartment. "I don't want one. I don't want to watch all of those pictures I used to work on." Of all the pictures on which he worked, there are two whose use of color most satisfies him, *Gone With the Wind* and *The Wizard of Oz*. But there are two color pictures he likes even better, pictures he had nothing to do with: *Black Narcissus* and *Gate of Hell*. "In color photography, you print for the face, and everything else should fall into balance. *Gate of Hell* was able to be perfect because the actors wore white rice makeup and so there was no face to print for."

Technicolor supplied the studios with more than a Color Director. In the thirties, Technicolor was unwilling to allow its cameras out of its hands. "We would bring the cameras to the studios at 7:30 a.m.," says Henry Imus, a color technician (equivalent to a second cameraman) on *The Wizard of Oz*. "We would shoot H&D tests and density tests and be ready for photography by 8." After work, Imus would take the cameras to the Technicolor plant where each night every camera was taken apart and lubricated and its plates and lenses cleaned.

A studio had the option of selecting a Technicolor First Cameraman (at $250 per week), a Second Cameraman (at $125 per week), or an Assistant Cameraman (at $62.50); but it had to select and pay for at least one of those technicians. For *The Wizard of Oz*, MGM hired only a Second Cameraman and an Assistant. The studio preferred to entrust the picture to its own cinematographer, Harold Rosson. Hal Rosson had a solid body of work behind him, including Leslie Howard's *Scarlet Pimpernel*, and the early color film *The Garden of Allah*, but he was best known as the ex-husband of Jean Harlow. Rosson, sixteen years older than Harlow, had been the object of the twenty-two-year-old Harlow's passionate but brief attentions shortly after the suicide of her second husband, Paul Bern.

Rosson was a short, dapper, pleasant man. He had started in the movies in 1912; even so, his brother Dick had beaten him by three years. Of Rosson's three sisters and two brothers, Queenie was a silent movie star; Helene, the heroine of early Westerns; Gladys, the secretary of Cecil B. DeMille; Dick, the second-unit director of complicated animal scenes; and Arthur, the director of several Douglas Fairbanks movies. There was a family joke that the sun never set on the Rossons, since one of them was always in some outlandish place making some movie.

Rosson's brother Arthur was the first husband of Victor Fleming's wife, a fact which disturbed Fleming's relationship with Hal Rosson not in the slightest. When Fleming took over *The Wizard of Oz* in November 1938, he was relieved to find that Rosson was his cameraman. Rosson had been the cinematographer on *Red Dust*, *Bombshell*, and *Test Pilot* for Fleming, and Fleming trusted him.

"Making *The Wizard of Oz* was complicated and troublesome," says Rosson. At eighty-two, he is a plump, cherubic man with a bristly white mustache. He suffered a physical collapse during the December 1970 fire at Malibu that devoured the house of his neighbor Angela Lansbury but left his own intact. Walking through the ruins of his swimming pool, his citrus-and-avocado orchard, his greenhouses, and his guest house, he began to choke and tremble. His sister swooped in from the East. In the spring, after four months of convalescence, she took him back with her to spend his winters in Palm Beach and his summers on Long Island. There are no family members in the movie business now, but Hal Rosson still remembers. "Six months earlier, *The Wizard of Oz* would have been more complicated, more troublesome, and tremendously more costly. Technicolor came out with a new film that was speeded up. That means that it could be used with less light. Even so, we had to use every light we could get our hands on. Because of the huge vistas in *Wizard*, the heavy scenery, the heavy colors, so much darkness."

"There was research going on all the time, trying to increase the exposure index of the film either by changes in manufacture or by changes in the processing," says Technicolor's Fred Detmers. "At that time, the film was manufactured by Eastman Kodak, and there was a significant change in 1938, a film that needed less light. But it was still a tremendous amount of light that was needed on those big sets."

The labor and equipment cost for lighting Warner Bros.' *Ad-*

ventures of Robin Hood (1937) was $68,500; the cost for *Gone With the Wind*, $134,490. To light *The Wizard of Oz* cost nearly $100,000 more than lighting *Gone With the Wind*. The estimated lighting cost of *The Wizard of Oz* if the picture had been shot in black and white was $86,206—the actual cost was $226,307.

Banks of lights lined the floor of the stages and the catwalks above the actors. Hot light. "Brutally hot," says Rosson. You could, they used to say, fry an egg on top of a bald actor's head when enough arc lights were turned on. And Rosson had never worked with so much light. Ten years later, color film was speeded up enough to use incandescent light. Cold light. Already, in 1938, you could use cold light with black-and-white film. In black-and-white photography, arc light was only used to get sharp shadows. "I used to feel so sorry for the poor Lion," remembers Rosson. "I used to pity him so much, in that costume with that hot light beating down on him."

Bolger, Haley, Garland, and Lahr in the Poppy Field, as a technician (partially visible at right) adjusts the Lilly (for an explanation of the Lilly see page 232).

Rosson's day began at 7 a.m. and ended at midnight. "When I left the studio at night, I would go to the Technicolor lab in Hollywood and stay there while the film was being developed. They would run the tests first and then we'd see how close they came to what I was trying to get." Test strips were taken at the end of each scene; the actors would stay in position for another three or four feet of film while a man darted into the scene, holding a three-sided white card called the Lilly. "The Lilly was a 6 by 9 inch card," says Henry Imus. "The Lilly boy would hold one side flat to the camera while the wing on each side was bent back 45 degrees. In those days, we had to have very particular lighting. The Lilly enabled the lab to see if we were using the proper front light and the proper key light or if we were trying to cheat a little." Rosson would look at the test strips, then order the main film to be processed lighter or darker, with more emphasis on the blue or less emphasis on the yellow. "We don't run test strips now," says Detmers, "because we know a lot more about processing color film. And the printing is much simpler, so if you do want to make an adjustment, you haven't wasted so much money and time. In 1938, the printing was so expensive that if you had to do it over, you wasted an awful lot of money."

The actual photography was even more difficult than the processing. "The costume of the Tin Man was so shiny that as he would turn, he'd throw a million reflections," says Rosson. "If the reflection hit the lens of the camera, we'd have no scene. We'd have to stop and find out what part of the costume was causing the reflection and dampen it down. The Witch was black and green. We had to try to keep her in front of a dark grey background. The sequins on the ruby slippers also caused a reflection, so we had to avoid any light shining on them which would project the reflection into the camera. We usually used one camera on a film. There were some scenes in *Wizard* where we used nine cameras. Because the sets were so large. One camera was back getting the whole scene. The other cameras would be hidden in bushes or potted plants. Those cameras would take in a small area. So we could take all the close-ups at the same time as the master shot in the crowd scenes. That was my concept."

It is difficult for Rosson to remember exactly whose concept it was to keep the main camera constantly moving. Perhaps his. Perhaps Fleming's. Perhaps a joint decision. "We mounted the camera on the end of a boom, and we constantly kept the boom moving. The camera was almost never still. We called it floating. Moving the camera aided the photography of those huge sets. By having the camera constantly changing its position from an object, we changed the depth on every object on the screen and gave them roundness. I've worked on thousands of pictures, but this was the only one where the camera was never still."

At one time or another, *The Wizard of Oz* utilized Stages 14, 15, 25, 26, 27, and the newly built 29. As the shooting company moved from sound stage to sound stage—from the cornfield and apple orchard of Stage 26 to the Munchkinland of Stage 27 and back again for the Witch's Haunted Forest—the carpenters and scenic artists stayed a frantic week ahead of them. With a new picture scheduled to roll off the assembly line every Monday, including Labor Day and Yom Kippur, there was no way of getting further ahead. As soon as the shooting company left a stage, the grips swarmed on to pull down the muslin backdrops and tear apart the set so that the carpenters could start building whatever came next. After the carpenters came Henry Greutert. Greutert, head of the Sculpture Department, was another of the MGM craftsmen who arrived at the studio at 8 a.m. and left at midnight. When he left the studio, it did not mean that his department had shut down for the night. "In those days the studio worked around the clock. I had eighty men in the department, twenty on each six-hour shift.* All the architectural details on a set were made by us. Moldings. Niches. Columns. Anything in plaster. We put the style and the period and the character in."

It was Greutert and his sculptors who built the trees of the Haunted Forest and the vulture that sat on top of one of them. Greutert stayed at MGM for thirty-eight years. He was laid off in February 1970 when his department was closed down. Six years later, he had not been back to MGM once. "Why should I go back?

---

* In order to increase the number of jobs available, the National Labor Relations Board had requested all factories to cut their shifts to six hours.

The Munchkin costumes, created by Adrian, were designed with huge vests and wide buckles to make the midgets seem even smaller than they were.

They didn't want me any more." Luckily, within six months of his leaving the studio he "fell into another job" for which those thirty-eight years at MGM had well prepared him. "The J. Paul Getty Museum. I worked on it for the next three years, making spiral columns, caps, moldings, and vaulted ceilings."

When a set was torn down, anything that could be salvaged was picked up and stored for use in some other picture. The concrete, tar, brick, and wood debris was swept onto trucks and taken across Overland Avenue to MGM's Lot 2. "For a long time, we were hard put to know where to put that debris," says Jack Martin Smith. "Then someone suggested that we dump the trash on Lot 2 and sooner or later we would have a hill. So we did, and pretty soon we had a hill. We made the French street out of it, and Gene Kelly and Leslie Caron used it for *An American in Paris.*"

The Wardrobe Department was not as frugal. Dresses routinely cost $500 to $1,500. It was protocol to design even the simplest of nightgowns or bathrobes for one of the studio's stars, no matter how destitute or impoverished the character that the star was playing. During the summer, the Wardrobe Department had broken down the script of *The Wizard of Oz* into the number and kinds of costumes required by each character and had assigned a tentative cost to each costume.* It was obvious from the beginning that almost every costume would have to be made within the department. Except for a few farm clothes and a coat for Professor Marvel, nothing was found in stock or purchased. The purchases included an apron for Aunt Em. "Fleming didn't like the apron," says John Lee Mahin. "It didn't look right to him. Then he saw the price tag. Twenty-five dollars. 'For Christ's sake,' he said to an assistant director, 'here's a dollar. Go down to the five-and-ten-cent store and buy a decent apron.'"

Not until the costumes for the 124 Munchkins had been finished in early December was the Wardrobe Department able to begin on the costumes for the 300 inhabitants of the Emerald City. For the three scenes in the Emerald City, including the "PRINCIPALS TRIUMPHAL RETURN AFTER KILLING WITCH," they would need to dress:

  1 MAN TO LEAD TRIUMPHAL PROCESSION ON FOOT
  2 CITY GUARDS TO FOLLOW LEADER IN PROCESSION
  1 BAND LEADER
 12 MEN IN THE BAND
  8 GIRLS TO THROW FLOWERS
  5 CITY GUARDS TO MARCH ON THE RIGHT OF THE CARRIAGE
  5 CITY GUARDS TO MARCH ON THE LEFT OF THE CARRIAGE
 20 MEN SHOP KEEPERS
 10 STREET VENDORS—MEN
 25 TOWNSMEN GENTLEMEN
 20 SHOP KEEPERS WIVES
 25 WOMEN WIVES OF THE GENTLEMEN
 25 GIRLS 18 TO 25 YEARS
 41 WOMEN ASSORTED TOWNSWOMEN
100 ASSORTED TOWNSMEN†

---

* The author's mother, Rose Meltzer, did this job on virtually every MGM picture, including *The Wizard of Oz*, between 1937 and 1951.

† From the Wardrobe Department's "Temporary list of people requiring costumes" of July 12, 1938.

The Emerald City had a different kind of complexity from the sequence in Munchkinland. The two basic problems the Wardrobe Department had faced in dressing the Munchkins were the sizes and shapes of the midgets and the extraordinary number of flowers, tassels, bells, bows, and ribbons that Adrian had designed to be attached to their felt costumes. In the Emerald City, all the costumes had to be green.

"Green shoes, green stockings, green dresses, green coats," says Vera Mordaunt. "We could buy some of the material, but we had to dye the rest. We dyed all the stockings. You can't get emerald green in cotton hose. Emerald green can only be done successfully on silk materials or on wool. And you couldn't buy green shoes, so we had to dye all the shoes."

On the second floor of the Wardrobe Department there was a metal spray-dying room with a galvanized interior for flammable materials; a long room with long tables where big pieces of material could be stretched; and a third room with a huge vat for water-

Judy Garland and the Lullabye League ballerinas being positioned by the assistant color cameraman for a color test.

A close-up of Frank Morgan as the Coachman, driving the Horse of a Different Color in the Emerald City.

dying. "I had four girls and I kept them all busy because we had so much to dye for that picture. When one of the big numbers had to be ready, we'd go in to work at seven in the morning and work until eight or ten or twelve o'clock at night."

For Vera Mordaunt, the most boring job was dying the shoes. "You have to tape the soles out, stuff the insides of each pair. And there were *boxes* of shoes! Satin shoes, dance shoes, things that had been used in other pictures and were left over. I had this new girl and I thought, 'Well, she's new, so *she* can do it.' I brought her the spray gun and showed her how to mix the dye. She worked along and along on that thing, and about two days later somebody said, 'Aren't you getting bored to death with those shoes?' She looked up so surprised and said, 'I was just thinking how wonderful it was. To be doing this and getting paid for it!'"

If the studio itself could be considered one enormous assembly line for the manufacture of motion pictures, the Wardrobe Department was its own kind of assembly line. "We had a manufacturing organization of a hundred and seventy-eight people," says John B. Scura, who spent forty-one years there.

The artistic head of those 178 people was Gilbert Adrian. Few people knew his Christian name. The screen credit always read: "Costumes by Adrian." Adrian dressed himself as well as he dressed his studio's stars. He wore the English cut, his trousers tapered to the back of his heel, with wide bottoms and no cuffs. And his jackets had the same wide shoulders he designed for Joan Crawford. Like Cedric Gibbons, his only MGM rival in sartorial splendor, he was a tall man built to wear clothes well. Around his throat he displayed a silk Italian scarf used as a cravat—tied as an ascot inside his open-throated Barrymore shirt. "He was a loner, not a friendly sort of person, but a genius," says Scura. "He would sit in a meeting with a producer with his sketch pad and create. Most of the costume designers simply open a book of the period and copy. Adrian never even used sketch artists. Very few of our designers today do their own sketching. I don't think they have the talent. But when Adrian made a sketch, no producer or director dared to change it."

The main wardrobe was housed in a three-story building, although there were auxiliary wardrobes sprinkled around the lot. The first floor contained the tailor shop, the offices, and what is still known as the Adrian Fitting Room, although Adrian died in 1959 and left the studio long before that. On the second floor were the Dye Department, the milliners and beaders, and the seamstresses for the female stars and featured players. The Modern Men's Wardrobe occupied the third floor. Even the seamstresses were specialists: some had a flair for bodices and others had a flair for skirts. "My job on *The Wizard of Oz* was Judy Garland's sleeves," says Marian Parker. "We had five or six of those gingham dresses, and Judy was constantly pulling the sleeves out in the back. My job was to get in early in the morning and replace the sleeves on the dresses that had been used the day before. I went to Metro in '33, a very green kid who had to hang on by her teeth. I sewed from '33 to '43. My first ten years at the studio were as a meek, frightened child who started out not doing the sleeves right because she was making them both for the same arm."

Marian Parker eventually graduated to accessories; John B. Scura eventually became head of the Wardrobe Department. But on *The Wizard of Oz*, Scura simply handled the costumes for Frank Morgan, Jack Haley, Bert Lahr, Ray Bolger, and Charley Grapewin. That assignment included making sure that the men had fresh underwear daily. All but Grapewin wore long johns, standard underwear for costume pictures. Grapewin wore the underwear that was standard for Westerns, two-piece balbriggan underwear with five buttons on the side. It was felt that balbriggan underwear added character to the clothes worn over it.

Also in the Wardrobe Department in 1938 was Vera Mordaunt's mother—the night lady, who came to work at 4 p.m. and got the clothes ready for the Malone Studio Service's truck. The truck came every night at 7 p.m. and collected the dresses that would have to be cleaned and pressed and back at the studio by 7 a.m. for the next day's shooting. The costumes of the stars were rarely sent to Malone Studio Service. All those beaded chiffons with pasteboard jewels were hand-cleaned at night by Marie Wharton, who spent forty years at that job. Every second or third night during the shooting of *The Wizard of Oz*, she would hand-sponge the Tin Man's leather-coated buckram and the Scarecrow's pants.

It was in Mrs. Cluett's Beading Department that Judy Garland's ruby slippers were made.

"The sequins were on a very fine chiffon," remembers Marian Parker, "and the beaders were working frantically with their little needles pushing all those red sequins onto the shoes. They had hoped to get by with just spraying a leather shoe red, but that didn't work."

"They tested many shoes," says Vera Mordaunt. "The first thing, they painted some shoes with a kind of shiny patent-leather paint. They must have tried five or six ways to make the shoes. I think the final shoes were satin. They were definitely some kind of cloth. The chiffon with the sequins was formed in the shape of a shoe and then sewed onto the cloth shoe."

Marian Parker remembers the sequins themselves as being glued onto the chiffon rather than sewn. She also recalls one of Mrs.

Opposite: The Witch and two of her Winged Monkeys. Above: Ray Bolger, Buddy Ebsen (before he was replaced by Jack Haley), and Bert Lahr disguised as the Witch's soldiers (Winkies) in order to rescue Dorothy from the Witch's Castle.

Cluett's beaders getting an ugly case of athlete's foot on her hands from working on the ruby slippers. But it was a long time ago and the case of athlete's foot might have occurred on a different picture.

What definitely did occur on *The Wizard of Oz*—perhaps the most astonishing thing that did occur—was dismissed as a publicity stunt. Yet it is vouched for by Hal Rosson and his niece Helene Bowman and by Mary Mayer, who served briefly as unit publicist on the picture. "For Professor Marvel's coat," says Mary Mayer, "they wanted grandeur gone to seed. A nice-looking coat but very tattered. So the Wardrobe Department went down to an old second-hand store on Main Street and bought a whole rack of coats. And Frank Morgan and the wardrobe man and Victor Fleming got together and chose one. It was kind of a Prince Albert coat. It was black broadcloth and it had a velvet collar, but the nap was all worn off the velvet." Helene Bowman recalls the coat as "ratty with age, a Prince Albert jacket with a green look."

The coat fitted Morgan and had the right look of shabby gentility, and one hot afternoon Frank Morgan turned out the pocket. Inside was the name "L. Frank Baum."

"We wired the tailor in Chicago," says Mary Mayer, "and sent pictures. And the tailor sent back a notarized letter saying that the coat had been made for Frank Baum. Baum's widow identified the coat, too, and after the picture was finished we presented it to her. But I could never get anyone to believe the story."

The story was published once—as an example of the lies press agents are willing to tell in order to get a story into print.

| Production #1060 | 9. |

SPECIAL EFFECTS

The art of melting a witch and stirring up a tornado

It cost MGM $8,000 to design, build, and photograph a tornado that didn't work. The failure of that first tornado—a thirty-five-foot rubber cone shaped like a wind sock—was hardly unexpected. The field of special visual effects was full of problems for which no solutions had yet been invented. A. Arnold (Buddy) Gillespie simply tore down the rubber tornado and tried again.

Gillespie had never made a tornado before. He had, however, made an earthquake two years earlier for *San Francisco*, and he won an Academy Award in 1947 for his second earthquake (in *Green Dolphin Street*). Like Cedric Gibbons, Buddy Gillespie had come to the studio before it was a corporate entity. Although he was retired forty-one years later, he has not really left the studio behind him. "I went to MGM before it was born. It's been eleven years since I left and I still go out there practically every day. I'm a frustrated architect, and I have designed many houses that will never be built, and I write poetry. But mostly I go out to the studio and answer questions and try to solve problems, and there isn't a day that three or four or five people don't come in to chew the fat and ask some questions. I went over to Universal when they were making *Earthquake*. They asked and I said for a free lunch I'd tell them all I knew about earthquakes. So I had four or five free lunches and then the last day I felt guilty and bought lunch for everyone."

Basically, what Gillespie knew about tornados in 1938 was that "we couldn't go to Kansas and wait for a tornado to come down and pick up a house." Everything beyond that was an experiment. "You don't quite know how to go about it, so you begin to think and wonder. I was a pilot for many years and had an airplane of my own. And the wind sock they had in airports in the old days to show the direction of the wind has a shape a little bit like a tornado and the wind blows through it. I started from that. We cast a cone out of thin rubber. We were going to whirl the rubber cone and rotate it. But tornados are called twisters and the rubber cone didn't twist. So that was rather an expensive thing down the drain. We finally wound up by building a sort of giant wind sock out of muslin." The giant thirty-five-foot muslin tornado was—technically—a miniature.

There are six categories of special visual effects—full-scale mechanical effects; miniatures; rear-projection process background;

mimeo'd

"Wizard of Oz"
"Effects"

1. Kansas Farm.
    A. Cyclone approaching Kansas Farm.
    B.   "   " Hitting Farm.
    C.   "   " Lifting Farm House into air
    D. Key of Cyclone approaching for cellar
        Door cut
    E. Farm House whirling around in Cyclone
2. Dorothys Bedroom up in Cyclone - Objects Passing.
    A. Floating By - Crate of Chickens
    B.   "   " - Old Lady in Rocking Chair.
    C.   "   " - Cow
    D.   "   " - Row Boat Two Men
    E.   "   " - Farm Hand and Cow
    F.   "   " - Miss Gulch and Walter
    G. Transformation of Miss Gulch and
        Walter.- on Tandem.
3. Cyclone Leaving Farm House in air and passing on.
4. Farm House Falling - Blocking out Camera
5. Munchkinland
    A. Dorothy opening Door seeing Munchkinland
    B. Dorothy Black and White Against color
        Background

    C. Good Witch: Bubble Appears - approaches
        - Pausing - Bursts and Reveals The
        Good Witch:
    D. Good Witch Changes Dorothy's Appearance
        From Black and White to Color.

An early list of special effects that were to take place during the
cyclone sequence. Note: In this list, Dorothy is in black and white (5B)
until the Good Witch changes her to color (5D).

optical effects; matte painting; and three-dimensional animation—
and five of them were used in *The Wizard of Oz*. Only three-dimensional animation—a giant ape stripping the clothes off the live actress
in the palm of his hand—had no place in the picture. "The earthquake sequences in *San Francisco* and *Green Dolphin Street* were
full-scale mechanical effects," says Gillespie. "We had actual people
in the earthquake, with breakaway walls and ceilings that collapsed
and a floor that wiggled. There were full-scale effects in *The Wizard
of Oz*—the Poppy Field and some of the flying monkeys. But the
tornado was a miniature. We built a miniature set—Dorothy's house
in the foreground, the barn, the fence—scaled at three quarters of
an inch to the foot. The miniature house was probably not more
than three feet tall and the cornfields three inches high."

The tornado was the most difficult and the most costly of the
film's special effects. The bottom of the muslin tornado disappeared
into a slot in the floor of Stage 14. The top was connected to a gantry
constructed by Consolidated Steel and suspended from the top of
the stage. The gantry cost more than $12,000, and it was built spe-
cifically for Buddy Gillespie's tornado. No one questioned the price.
If L. B. Mayer was hardly extravagant, he had a healthy respect for
the high cost of magic, a respect echoed by his subordinates. Eight
years later, Gillespie asked for $10,000 to build an atomic bomb. "We
had to do the atom bomb over Hiroshima with no knowledge of how
to do it. For *The Beginning or the End*, not a particularly good picture. I went to Cedric Gibbons and said, 'I need $10,000 to start
doing the atom bomb.' Gibbons said, 'What are you going to do with
the money?' I said, 'I haven't the slightest idea, but I have to start
somewhere.' So Gibbons called Joe Cohn, the production manager,
and said, 'Buddy wants $10,000 to start on the atom bomb.' And
Joe, of course, wanted to know what for. And Gibbons said, 'Buddy
doesn't have the slightest idea what he's going to do with it. He just
wants ten thousand bucks.' And I got the money. Uncle Louie
Mayer's idea of running a studio was to get the best help he could.
We had the top actors, the top actresses, the top heads of departments. We were the top studio, and we had the top people. There
were good special-effects men at the other studios, but the other
studios were frugal. If a picture didn't come up to snuff, MGM was

willing to spend $200,000 or $300,000 or $500,000 to make it better. The other studios didn't do that. And you could always tell."

The gantry was a movable steel structure of the kind used in warehouses to lift heavy weights. It moved horizontally down the length of Stage 14. Beneath and attached to it was a small car that could zigzag back and forth. The top of the muslin tornado was attached to the top of the gantry's car; the car was started at the far end of the stage from the slot in the stage floor that anchored the tornado's bottom. "You couldn't see the slot," says Gillespie. "It was covered over with a type of rubber dentists use, so that muslin wouldn't flap over. A rod came up through the slot to carry the bottom part of the tornado. The top area of the tornado could be at the right of the stage and the bottom area at the left, and then we could reverse it; and the muslin sort of squirmed around as it progressed toward us."

The first muslin tornado squirmed too violently. The rubber tornado hadn't twisted at all, but "that big muslin sock whipped and tore loose at the bottom," says Jack McMaster. McMaster had been hired off the street behind the studio as a laborer in 1935, but in three years he had worked his way up to the Prop Shop. "We had to double-lace the cyclone with music wire so it would hold together when we spun it. I was small, so they put me inside the cyclone. The men who were lacing the wire would poke their needles inside the muslin, and I would poke them back out again. It was pretty uncomfortable when we reached the narrow part."

To heighten the illusion of a cyclone, fuller's earth and compressed air were fed into the tornado from the bottom with air hoses, fed into a "dustpan"—a funnel-shaped pan twelve inches in diameter. "That was to create the dust cloud, the big disturbance that comes when a tornado goes along the ground disturbing things," says Gillespie. Fuller's earth was also fed into the top of the muslin wind sock. "The muslin was sufficiently porous so that a little of the fuller's earth sifted through, giving a kind of blur or softness to the material. That helped to keep it from looking like an artificial hard surface."

Four or five feet in front of the cameras that photographed the tornado were two panels of glass on which chunks of cotton had been pasted. The eight-by-four-foot panels moved in opposite directions and masked the car, the gantry, and the top of the muslin tornado from the cameras. The cotton was blended with a bit of grey paint to form the "dark and ominous sky" required by the script. Also helping to give the illusion of a stormy sky were dense clouds of yellowish-black smoke. It was Hal Millar, another Prop Shop man on the catwalks above the gantry, who made the smoke. "In those days," says Millar, "we had no respirators. You simply stayed up there breathing the stuff for as long as you could stand it. For days after we photographed the tornado, I was coughing up carbon and sulfur, thick black-and-yellow mucus."

"You couldn't do today the things that we did then," says Franklin Milton. "The Health Department wouldn't let you." It was Milton who made steam come out of the Tin Woodman's funnel hat by using talcum powder and compressed air, and who baked the latex-sponge talking apple trees for fourteen hours in plastic molds in the Prop Shop's slow ovens. Milton also made the breakaway glass through which the Cowardly Lion plunged in his escape from the Wizard's Throne Room. "We heated resin and poured it on a pool of mercury. Then we cooled the mercury down. Mercury! There was almost no ventilation. Now I wonder, 'How did I get through all those nights?' "

The forty men in the Prop Shop were Gillespie's tools. Except at MGM, studio special-visual-effects departments were autonomous. At MGM, Special Effects was a part of the Art Department, and Gillespie was under the titular control of Cedric Gibbons. In actuality, Gibbons gave Gillespie "practically complete autonomy." Gillespie had gotten his first job in the movies in 1922 by "jokingly" asking for one. "I had met Colin Tate, Cecil B. DeMille's assistant director, in the army in France during World War I. When I came to California, the first thing I did was go out and watch him make a movie, and I jokingly asked him if they had a job. Tate said, 'Well, are you an architectural draftsman?' I said, 'Of course,' not being one although I had gone to the Art Students League in New York. They needed someone for two weeks. I stayed eight months. I got 25 dollars a week, and the work was seven days a week and fourteen to sixteen to eighteen hours a day. My mother was very upset about

The model of the Gale farmhouse that was used in the cyclone sequence was three feet tall. First the house was photographed falling onto a floor painted to look like the sky. Then, to give the impression of the cyclone picking up the house, the film was run backward.

it. But I thought, 'I'm not paying any fee at all, there's no tuition, and it's like going to school.' Which, as I look back on it, was pretty smart of me, because what did I need money for then?" Early in 1923, Gillespie left DeMille for the Goldwyn Studios and $65 a week. That was over a year before the Goldwyn Studios became MGM.

Once the tornado had been photographed, the laboratory trickery that formed a considerable portion of special effects began. The film was processed so that it could be used as a background for the live actors. On all their trips to Western dude ranches and European cities, Andy Hardy and his family never moved a step away from Stage 14. In some of the Hardy pictures, nearly 40 percent of the film was rear-projection process: a projector was placed behind a translucent screen and previously shot film was projected onto the screen while the live actors were placed in front of it. In the case of *The Wizard of Oz*, the wind machines were turned on and Dorothy raced the film of the cyclone home.

The inside of the tornado—as seen by Dorothy when her house is whirling in mid-air—was a muslin-covered drum thirty-five feet in diameter. "It was just another hunk of muslin," says Gillespie, "with stripes painted on it and a little dust inside. The camera was in there and we whirled the camera around and around. That gave us our background—as though we were on the inside of a tornado that was whirling. We could have rotated the drum itself and left the camera stationary, but that would have been more complicated. It was easier to turn the camera around to give us progression. Then, onto that film of the inside of the tornado we double-printed all the things Dorothy saw through her window—the crate of chickens, the men in the rowboat, the old lady in the rocking chair, the school-teacher on her bicycle. We took pictures of, say, the rowboat with the two men in it against a neutral background and then double-printed it onto the film of the inside of the tornado. And that film, in turn, became a process background which was projected on a translucent screen; and we photographed Dorothy looking through her window at the rowboat."

If the tornado was complicated to create and equally compli-cated to execute, there was nothing—theoretically—very difficult about making the Witch's Winged Monkeys fly. The difficulties came in the execution. The miniature monkeys, many of them only six inches high, were hung from the gantry's car on strands of music wire one thousandth of an inch in diameter. As the gantry moved down the stage, the monkeys appeared to be flying. "What was difficult," says Gillespie, "was the tremendous amount of rigging. There were about eleven hundred wires, four wires on each monkey. We needed so many wires because we had to make the monkeys' wings go up and down. The monkeys were cast out of rubber. Inside each monkey there was a little lightweight metal armature with hinges to the wings so that the wings would be sufficiently flexible.* It was tough to do because of the numbers of wires. If one wire

_____

* Jack McMaster remembers the smaller monkeys as being solid rubber. "I would take a scissors and nip their wings so the wings could be moved up and down."

Most of the Witch's Winged Monkeys were six inches high, cast out of rubber, and were hung by piano wire, one-thousandth of an inch thick (four strands per monkey), from a movable steel structure.

broke in the middle of a scene and the monkey would go half-cocked, we'd have to do a retake." "One morning we came in and one of the main wires was down," says Jack McMaster, "and the whole mess was on the ground."

There were also real people dressed in monkey costumes, about a dozen of them, suspended on wire somewhat thicker than the wire that held the miniature monkeys. "Underneath their monkey suits were small battery-driven electric motors adapted from windshield-wiper motors," says Franklin Milton, who helped to wire the costumes. "The motors made their wings go up and down." The "small, thin men" for whom the Special Effects Department had asked the casting office flew on wires approximately the diameter of the lead in a No. 2 lead pencil. "We always came as close to the margin of safety as we could," says Gillespie. "So close that sometimes we'd have a net or mattresses underneath in case the wire should break. Which, occasionally, it would do."

The small, thin men were paid $20 for swooping down on Dorothy, the Tin Woodman, the Scarecrow, and the Cowardly Lion. When the stunt didn't photograph properly, they were hoisted up and flown again. Then a third time. "The men figured that now they've got sixty dollars," says Jack Haley. "But the studio says, no, they're hired as actors at twenty dollars a day. Finally, one of them left a note on the assistant director's chair that they're not going up again until this is all straightened out. And so some guy came from the Screen Actors Guild and it was the most ludicrous thing you've ever seen in your life. All those monkeys standing on chairs and shouting at him. I think the studio made some sort of settlement, gave them a little added money. But the monkeys were right. The studio was trying to make believe they were playing a part. But it wasn't a part. It was a stunt."

To photograph the Deadly Poppy Field, Gillespie had to design his own camera dolly. "The lens of the camera had to be very low, right down among the poppies. That's what they wanted, so we had to find a way to do it. We always had to find a way to do what they wanted. We designed a special track. We built an underslung dolly. Instead of wheels, we had half-tubings to form the track right down on the floor. Then we had a half-round—another tubing the next size bigger—for the runners that went on the camera dolly. When that was greased and oiled, you could slide this thing along very smoothly. It was the first dolly of its kind. We laid it out, designed it, built it. And they used our track for many years afterward."

Unlike the tornado and the monkeys and the Poppy Field, some of the most effective moments in the picture were child's play for Gillespie, kindergarten exercises. The melting of the Witch was accomplished by having Margaret Hamilton stand on top of a hydraulic elevator in the floor of the stage. Her costume was fastened to the floor, and dry ice was attached to the inside of her cloak. The elevator, with Hamilton standing on it, was lowered; the dry-ice vapors gave the illusion of melting; and nothing was left on the stage but the costume. "That was," says Gillespie, "a very, very simple thing to do."

*The simple optical trick that produced the images in the Witch's
crystal ball is described below.*

The Witch's crystal ball was equally simple, "an obvious way
to do it. The crystal ball was a great big glass bowl, not solid
although it looked solid. We used a process projector and we projected into the ball from the side with a mirror on a forty-five degree
angle. Then the picture hit the mirror and came up on a translucent
screen. It was a very small translucent screen with the hollow ball
placed on top of it." When the live characters looked into the ball,
they saw the film that was being projected onto the screen.

For the eerie effect of the disembodied head floating in the thick
mist of the Wizard of Oz's Throne Room, not even a translucent
screen was necessary. Of the three standard ways of filling a set with
vapor, it was easiest to use smoke, but smoke had one severe disadvantage. "Pretty soon," says Gillespie, "your whole stage was full
of smoke. So we only used smoke when we absolutely had to." Dry
ice placed in hot water would also make vapor, as would piped-in

steam. Since the set of the Throne Room was too large for dry ice to work effectively, Gillespie used steam, provided by a boiler outside the stage. The steam was then carried onto the stage by a pipe, which had a wide nozzle to keep the steam from coming out in one narrow column. The steam rose and formed a large cloud. Directly onto the steam cloud was projected the huge head conjured up by the Wizard. Since steam is opaque, rear-process photography could not be used. Instead, a regular projection machine was placed behind the movie camera: at the appropriate moment, it threw a picture on the steam exactly as one might use a living-room wall to show a home movie.

The enormous ball in which Billie Burke appeared and disappeared was even simpler—purely an optical effect. "We used a silver ball about seven or eight inches in diameter, a beautiful silver ball just like a Christmas-tree ornament, only bigger. We didn't move the ball at all. We photographed the ball against a neutral

The Wicked Witch is melting with the help of an elevator and dry ice.

background and moved the camera *to* it. So it appeared to get bigger and bigger and bigger. We had plotted out what course the ball was supposed to take through the sky and where it was to land. That was all pre-planned. Then we had the cameraman shoot the Munchkinland set under our direction with tied-down cameras so that there was no movement to the camera at all. Now we had two pieces of film: the original set and the shot of the silver ball. Instead of matte-printing that into the original set, which would have made it seem a solid ball, we double-printed it—put one piece of film over the other—so that it was transparent. Then, still with the same tied-down camera, we put Billie Burke in the proper spot and filmed her. Then we lap-dissolved the ball out and Billie Burke was there—a very simple little optical effect."

Matte painting, which Gillespie chose not to use for the silver bubble, was used for the exterior of the Emerald City and to add the river and cliffs to the Witch's Castle. "If you want to show something—say, St. Patrick's Cathedral or a ten-story building—and you don't have the money to do it," explains Gillespie, "all you have to do is build the aisle of St. Patrick's or build up to the third story of your building. Then you can have a person walk down the aisle or hang out the second-story window and you photograph them with a stationary camera, a camera that's tied down. The top of the cathedral or the upper part of the building is painted. Then the painting is photographed, and the pieces of film are put together." All of the studios except MGM made their matte paintings with oil paints on white cardboard or on glass. MGM's matte paintings were always done with crayon pastels on black cardboard. The ones for *The Wizard of Oz* were four feet wide, although matte paintings varied from a minimum of sixteen to a maximum of forty-eight inches. At its simplest, matte painting was a double exposure. A 1940 report of Technicolor's Special Effects Department subcommittee describes the use of multiple rather than double exposures in *The Wizard of Oz*: "An example of multiple exposures handled by the painting matte method is seen in *The Wizard of Oz* when a second exposure, the river and cliffs, [was] added to the drawbridge photographed on the set, and a third exposure, the sparkle of moonlight, was added to the river. In the same subject, the colored blinking columns of Emerald City were also added by a third exposure."

"I had a glass tank six foot square," says Jack McMaster, who designed and executed the skywriting sequence of *The Wizard of Oz.* "The bottom of the tank was glass. The sides were wood. The tank was only three inches deep; and the bottom was covered with an inch and a half of water mixed with calla oil. That was supposed to be the sky. The camera was beneath the tank, shooting up. The water and oil mixture was opaque, so it hid me. The miniature Witch who did the skywriting was three eighths of an inch high, and the broom she was riding was a hypodermic needle. I filled the hypo-

A photograph of a matte painting of the road leading from the Gale farm, Kansas. The matte backgrounds were done with pastels on black cardboard (see page 255) and, to save money, were used instead of building an entire set. Note the word "color" (the Kansas scenes were placed in a sepia bath to give them a brown tone) scrawled on the unpainted area in front of which the set was built.

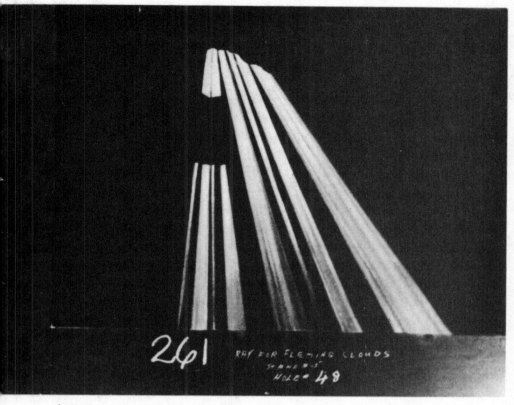

A matte painting for the inserted shot of sun rays used in the "Over the Rainbow" number. To the effects department, Oz was Fleming's picture whether he was directly involved in Kansas or not, hence the note on bottom.

dermic with a combination of canned milk and nigrosine dye.* I wrote SURRENDER DOROTHY OR DIE upside down and backward in the fluid in the tank, using the needle in place of a pen. I practiced for two months before I did it. My hand wasn't in the tank, but the Witch and the broom needle were. The skywriting seemed to come out of the tail of the Witch's broom. To give the writing the appearance of smoke that was drifting, I had a fifty-gallon drum of water feeding into the tank. I had tinted the water the same milky color as the liquid in the glass tank. The water current was a stream—like an air stream—blowing the letters apart."

* The idea of using nigrosine dye came from a Tarzan picture made a few years earlier. Bags of nigrosine dye were attached to a mechanical crocodile's throat and turned the water red when Johnny Weissmuller's knife pierced them.

□

By the 1970's it was all considerably more complicated. The job that chance and brazen self-confidence had given to Buddy Gillespie a half-century ago had been codified. Making wind, rain, snow, sleet, fire, fog, smoke, steam, cobwebs, waves, waterfalls, and a storm at sea were Special Effects and could be handled only by someone with the proper union authorization. To have a union card stamped SPECIAL EFFECTS required an apprenticeship as a propmaker; several more years in the Prop Shop; 1,200 hours of spare time spent as assistant to a special-effects man; and the passing of a written examination.

Hal Millar came to the studio in April 1929. He was seventeen years old and his father had just died. He had an uncle on the night shift, and the job in the Prop Shop was his legacy. Just as the sons and son-in-laws and nephews of the studio's producers and executives filled the studio's white-collar jobs to such an extent that MGM was at one time derisively called The Sons of the Pioneers, so the men in the Wardrobe Department and the Prop Shop took care of their own. Millar tries to explain the way it was then: "It was not uncommon to come in Monday to go to work and not get home all week. We would sleep in corners of stages or up on the catwalks. The night I was married I had worked sixty-eight hours straight. There was so much production the studio had to stay open twenty-four hours a day. Every day the shooting schedule covered three sheets of legal-size paper. We felt a competition with the other studios. They made good pictures. We worked for MGM. We made better ones."

In 1934, from fifty to three hundred men waited outside the gates each day—laborers and grips on Overland Avenue, carpenters and painters on Culver Boulevard. Glenn Robinson's father was head of the night crew. "He would telephone home when there was going to be a job. I'd get dressed and go to the studio and wait out there on the street." Robinson's first job lasted a week. His second was as a helper in the Blacksmith Shop. Finally, like Easy Yzuel, he was hired permanently.

It was a six-day week, and production manager Joe Cohn didn't see any reason why companies should stop shooting before midnight Saturday night because they could sleep late on Sunday. Yet . . .

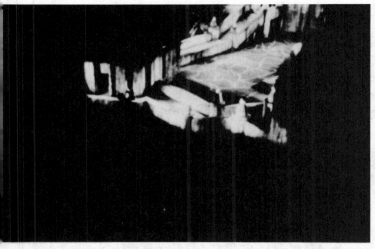

THE WITCH'S CASTLE

The part of the Castle walls on which Dorothy is captured by the Witch was constructed as a set.

The matte painting was filmed separately.

The matte painting and the set put together on the same piece of film. (This is a test shot.)

INTER-OFFICE COMMUNICATION

To_____ Mr. Chic

Subject_____ Status of uncompleted Newcombe Shots for Prod. 1060.

From_____ Warren Newcombe _____ Date April 4, 1939.

Return to Newcombe

Following is a list of shots that have not been completed for the "Wizard of Oz". The status of each is listed below.

1. Newcombe Shot - Emerald City - as seen by principles from hill in Poppy Field. (All over painting)

Expect to deliver completed
Take to cutter

When the Takes have been shot on the below listed Poppy Field, that painting will be completed as an all over painting for this shot.

2. Newcombe Shot - Four principles going towards Emerald City after leaving Poppy Field. Sc.#118-L.

A screen test of this shot was shown to Mr. Le Roy today and O.Ked by him. We are starting to shoot Takes this afternoon.

3. Newcombe Shot - Gates to Emerald City as four principles enter to gates. Scene #129-A.

This shot has been O.Ked by Mr. Le Roy. Shooting of the Takes now in progress.

4. Newcombe Shot - High Shot - Procession - Emerald City.
5. Newcombe Shot - Low Shot - Procession - Emerald City.
Scene #236-A. There is only one set up for above two Procession Shots, and should be listed as only one shot.

This shot has been O.Ked by Mr. Le Roy. Shooting of Take now in progress.

6. Newcombe Shot - Emerald City - Long Shot - Bubble's approach. Scene #256-A.
Expect to receive 5 ft. test from Technicolor Lab tomorrow. If O.Ked., will start shooting Takes.

7. Newcombe Shot - Long Shot - Emerald City - with balloon stationary. Scene #243-A.
When the above Emerald City Shot-Scene #256-A, has been O.Ked., will start producing this shot. Same painting to be used for each shot.

8. Newcombe Shot - Long Shot - Establishing Witch's Castle without the principles. (All over painting)

Expect a Test-Take from the Technicolor Lab tomorrow, and if O.Ked, this shot will be completed.

Memo from Warren Newcombe about matte shots (called Newcombe shots because he drew them) not yet completed as of April 4, 1939.

"We used to enjoy it. We used to have a lot of fun," says Robinson. "We worked and worked and worked very hard," says Gillespie. "Today they say, 'If they don't pay me, I'm not going to stay three minutes overtime.' We never questioned staying until midnight."

That MGM of 1938 is beyond retrieving but not beyond recall. Once, after L. B. Mayer had left and Dore Schary was head of the studio, Gillespie told all the executives that he wouldn't be able to make *The Wizard of Oz* if it were to be made that day. "If I told you guys, 'We need Consolidated Steel to build a big steel structure that travels the full length of the stage with a car underneath it,' you'd say, 'Oh, Buddy, we can't afford that. You'll have to figure some other way to make a tornado.' But I don't believe I'd be able to figure out some other way. I tried all the ways I could think of. There might be another way, but I wasn't smart enough to do it."

ACCIDENTS

Buddy Ebsen was the first casualty.

Nine days after *The Wizard of Oz* started production on October 12, 1938, Ebsen was in Good Samaritan Hospital under an oxygen tent. His skin was bright blue; his breathing was labored; and his lungs felt as though someone had coated them with glue.

August and September had been good months for Ebsen. There had been the luxury of nearly four weeks of rehearsal, something not available either on his low-budget MGM films or during his four loanouts to 20th Century-Fox. By October 12, all of his songs had been pre-recorded. The wardrobe and makeup tests were also finished—much to Ebsen's relief. "I was a guinea pig. They didn't know how to simulate the Tin Man's garments, so I found myself doing tests with clothes made of real tin and clothes made of silver paper and clothes made out of cardboard covered with silver cloth. The makeup was just as bad. Try this. Try that. In the end, they glued a cap on my head and covered it and glued on a rubber nose and rubber chin and then covered the whole thing with clown white and then powdered aluminum dust onto my face and head."

Ebsen took a deep breath when the tests were over. Two weeks later, he could hardly manage to breathe at all. "One night, after dinner, I took a breath and nothing happened. They got an ambulance and had me down to Good Samaritan for a couple of weeks. My lungs were coated with that aluminum dust they had been powdering on my face."

Ebsen's memories of his first week in the hospital are full of indignant telephone calls from MGM. "It seemed they couldn't understand that an actor could get sick. They were furious. Mervyn LeRoy kept calling the hospital and saying, 'He can't be in bed. He's due on the set.' And Jack Dawn called me to tell me I couldn't possibly be sick because he had used 'aluminum dust—*pure* aluminum dust' on my face."

Dawn's seemingly bizarre insistence that Ebsen couldn't have been poisoned by such dust was accurate according to the medical knowledge of the thirties. In 1938, pure aluminum dust was considered harmless and was given to miners to breathe in order to protect their lungs from silicosis. There is actually a specific disease caused by the inhalation of very small particles of aluminum, but its onset and symptoms are different from those experienced by Ebsen. What Ebsen suffered was either an allergic reaction to the aluminum or a chemical effect from fumes from some substance mixed into the aluminum. Since Dawn insisted that he had used only "pure aluminum dust," Ebsen's two weeks in the hospital were probably the result of an allergic reaction.

Eventually, Mervyn LeRoy got tired of calling the hospital and hired Jack Haley for the role of the Tin Woodman. Haley was not asked if he wanted to play the part. Under contract to 20th Century-Fox, he was simply told that he had been loaned to MGM. "The type of contract I had, I had to respond to their commands. I had no choice. I was under contract, and they could lend me to any studio. It was the most awful work, the most horrendous job in the world with those cumbersome uniforms and the hours of makeup, but I had no choice."

Haley was not told what had happened to Ebsen. He assumed that Ebsen had been fired, but he didn't ask. And there was no grapevine to tell him. If Ebsen had found himself unable to breathe during working hours, his illness would have been visible to cast and crew. When he didn't show up for work one morning, it was considered polite not to ask questions. During the first few weeks of shooting actors often disappeared and were replaced by others. And this cast had already been subjected to a tongue-lashing from LeRoy. The coincidence of director Richard Thorpe being fired a few days later made it seem obvious that Ebsen had also been fired.

Haley managed to avoid most of the wardrobe, makeup, and acting tests. Ebsen's buckram costume was simply shortened to fit him, and Ebsen's makeup—with one important modification—was layered onto his face. On November 8 he recorded the Tin Woodman's solo, "If I Only Had a Heart." He had little trouble learning the simple dances—the only difficulty came in learning how to slip into the metal runners in the stage floor which would keep him from falling when he leaned forward and sideways during the dance that accompanied his song. Although he had no choice about coming to MGM, Haley felt "a certain amount of flattery that MGM, a new studio, wanted me," and a certain nervousness that "I'd be another Buddy Ebsen and they'd have to let me go and have someone else come in. I kept feeling that my first scene was a way to check me out thoroughly. After that, I knew I was home free."

After his two weeks in the hospital, Buddy Ebsen recuperated for a month at the Coronado Hotel in San Diego. He thought briefly about suing the studio, but "you didn't just lightly sue MGM, because it was a power. And there was a certain cohesion between the moguls. They all used to play poker together on Saturday nights and decide who were the good actors and who were the bad." Perhaps if he had had severe aftereffects, Ebsen would have taken the chance. But at the end of six weeks, he seemed well enough; it would be years before he became aware of his tendency to bronchitis.

The one change that was made in the Tin Woodman's makeup after Jack Haley inherited the role was the method of applying aluminum. It was not brushed on as a powder but was made into a paste and painted on. Haley had no trouble with his lungs. He did, however, suffer a severe infection in his right eye from the aluminum paste. He was off work for four days, but the doctors managed to stop the infection before it damaged his sight.

The next two accidents occurred the week before Christmas.

Betty Danko was Margaret Hamilton's stand-in and stunt double. "We were the Wicked Witch of the West," Betty Danko says. "I wore the same horrible costume, the same horrible green makeup. I wouldn't even eat lunch with the other stand-ins because the wart and the chin were so hideous. I ate my lunch in the little wardrobe dressing room, and the only bright spot of the day was when they had blueberry pie in the commissary and Bobbie Koshay, Judy Garland's stand-in, would bring me back a piece."

As a stand-in, Betty Danko made $11 a day. On the days when there was some stunt for her to perform, her salary was $35. She was twenty-eight years old, frail and ethereal-looking, slender, with small bones. She had come to California in 1927, six months after her graduation from high school. She had planned to work for a year to get enough money for her tuition at a New Jersey chiropractic school, but some of the family had settled in Los Angeles, and their enthusiasm for the land of eternal sunshine had convinced Betty

Danko's father to sell his house and eight lots in Elizabeth, New Jersey, and move his family west. Her first week in Los Angeles, Betty Danko was approached in a five-and-ten-cent store by a woman who asked if she would like to see a motion picture being made. "I said, 'Not particularly.' She said she knew where they were going to shoot some outdoor scenes that night but she had to have someone to go with her. I went home and told my mother and sister, and they said, 'Go because you might get in the movies.' I said I didn't want to be in the movies. But I went. There were a lot of cowboys dashing around on horses. And a man came over and looked at me and said, 'Do you work in pictures?' And I was about to say, 'No,' when the other woman said, 'We both do.' Still looking at me, ignoring her completely, he said, 'When we get through with this Western, we're going to do a series of six college films. I think you'd make a good college type. If you leave your number, I'll telephone you when we're ready to go.' I had had it drilled into me to look out for Hollywood wolves, but I didn't want to make a fuss then. So I thought, 'When he calls me and tries to make a date, I'll just say I'm busy.' But some weeks later the phone rang and there was this voice, and he said, 'I want to give you your call for tomorrow.' And I thought, 'What a stupid man. Why does he call me today and tell me he's going to call me tomorrow?' So I said, 'All right,' and I hung up. Then the phone rang again, and he said, 'I guess we were cut off. I want to give you your call for work tomorrow.' They had a girls' basketball team in the picture, and they found out I was athletic. I had played right forward in school, and I had medals for high jumping. I did several of their college two-reelers. Then somebody said, 'Go to Hal Roach's. They could use somebody that's as active as you.' So I did. But the movies still meant nothing to me. Even Laurel and Hardy, when I worked with them, meant nothing. I just wrote it down in my records as a job."

In eleven years as a stunt double, Betty Danko had been hurt seriously only once: a mountain lion had bitten her on the left leg, just above the ankle, when she was doubling Patsy Kelly in a Hal Roach comedy. After they finally pried the lion loose, the leg required thirteen stitches and was permanently scarred, although it was not permanently damaged.

Betty Danko's first accident on *The Wizard of Oz* left her with nothing more than a sore back. She was standing in an eight-foot-deep pit underneath Stage 27 waiting to be catapulted to the floor of the stage. It was Betty Danko, not Margaret Hamilton, who would be making the Wicked Witch's first entrance into Munchkinland. The top of the pit was covered by a thin piece of aluminum painted to look like the Yellow Brick Road. The aluminum would be jerked away by an invisible wire, and she would spring, rather like a jack-in-the-box, into the scene. Smudge pots and long smoke tubes would produce enough fire and red smoke to keep the audience from being aware of the trickery.

During the last rehearsal, dance director Bobby Connolly fell through the pit's aluminum roof and landed on Betty Danko's shoulders. He had been showing the Munchkins how to avoid the metal pitfall for the seventh or perhaps the tenth time when he slipped. Connolly, a kind, polite, balding Irishman who always wore a coat, suit, and tie, was mortified. He chewed furiously on his cigar —his usual gesture of nervousness—while he was being pulled out. After Connolly had been dusted off, the smashed piece of metal on top of Betty Danko's head was removed, her Witch's hat repaired, a new piece of metal inserted in the floor, and the scene photographed without further trouble. Afterward, Bobbie Koshay found her a chiropractor—there was always one available to the executives at MGM. "That relieved me a little bit. But for a while I could hardly drive. I couldn't lift my arm up. But stunt people often work when we're hurt. Sometimes it gets to the point where you're working in a fight sequence and Chick'll say, 'Watch out for Billy's wrist,' and you'll know it's all taped up. They don't talk about it. They just get it bound up and put a jacket over it. Because, otherwise, the insurance company will think you're too fragile. And I'm pretty rugged, despite my appearance, despite the fact that people think I'm frail."

It was Betty Danko's first accident that made the assistant director so cautious a few days later. Danko had arrived in Munchkinland—her back to the camera—as the Wicked Witch of the West.

But Margaret Hamilton would have to depart for herself. The script required that she finish her last speech at the moment of her departure into the same fire and red smoke that had accompanied her appearance:

> WITCH (*falling back with a snarl*):   Very well—I'll wait my time—
> (*to Dorothy*)
> —and as for you, my fine lady, it's true, I can't attend to you here and now as I'd like to; but just try to keep out of my way, that's all—just try! I'll get you, my pretty, and your little dog too!
> (*With a burst of laughter, she whirls around on her heel and vanishes in a burst of red smoke and a clap of thunder.*)

Betty Danko was asked to make sure that Margaret Hamilton could do the shot without getting hurt. "They had replaced the catapult with an elevator. She would step on the elevator and then it would go down. I tested and found out it was pretty slow going down. The only thing I found that might be a little hard to take was the jog when you hit the bottom. So I simply told her to flex her knees to absorb what might be a little shock. Also, the pit was very narrow at the top. We had just enough room for our shoulders to come through. You had to make a clean entrance and you also had to go down cleanly or you'd catch your shoulder. I told her to be sure to hold her position so she wouldn't whack her shoulder."

"Mr. Fleming wanted it all done in one shot," says Margaret Hamilton. "I had to back away from the Good Fairy and land on this little piece of flooring on top of the elevator. I had this long cape that trailed on the floor and I had to keep from tripping on it while I walked backward; and I had to land exactly, because if one foot were over the space, I would probably have broken the leg when the elevator went down. So we practiced and practiced with me kicking the cape train behind me and my eyes fixed on an object they mounted on the camera for me. When it was absolutely straight in front of me, I knew I'd be standing in the right place. We practiced and we practiced until I got it so I could land exactly. Then I stood with Judy and the Good Fairy, Billie Burke, and watched the men practice making the smoke and fire and pulling three different wires so a piece of Yellow Brick Road would cover the hole after I disappeared. We were about forty feet away from the fire and Miss Burke shook her head and said, 'Oh, I'm not going to stand here.' And I said, 'Why not, Miss Burke?' And she said, 'Oh, my dear, it's much too hot.' And I thought, 'You're forty feet away, but I'm going to be right in the middle of it.'"

Despite Margaret Hamilton's misgivings, the first take went "like clockwork." Her last-minute instructions from Victor Fleming had been to pull her elbows in so she wouldn't break her arms in the narrow space at the top of the pit. She walked backward without tripping, landed perfectly, pulled in her elbows and hugged the broom close to her face, and disappeared in a puff of red smoke followed— a few seconds later—by flames. The pit was considerably wider at the bottom. There were a few chairs and two men who helped her off the elevator. "I rather thought there were two so that there would be one for each leg if I broke both legs." She climbed back to the stage to find Fleming, untypically, smiling: the shot had been perfect. He would, however, get another for insurance.

"But, unfortunately, there was a little thing called lunch. It was one o'clock and people had been there since seven. So we were all starved and everyone wanted to go to lunch. And you may be in the middle of something or not, it's just too bad. And when we got back, everybody was full of food and sleepy; and nothing went right."

In the second attempt, the smoke and fire started too late to disguise Margaret Hamilton's disappearance. In the third, the smoke started too early and the fire didn't come on at all. "We did it about four times with various and sundry mistakes. And then we got the full tilt of Mr. Fleming's impatience and anxiety. In no uncertain language, he told us to pull ourselves together and get the shot done. He said, 'There's no excuse for this. The minute she gets her foot on, I want—' And I said, 'Mr. Fleming, I want to get *both feet on*,' and he said, 'Yes, yes, of course, but I want this shot done right and done right now.'"

This time the smoke and the flames came quickly—too quickly.

Billie Burke, Judy Garland, Margaret Hamilton, and Munchkins getting ready to shoot for the fourth time the scene where the Wicked Witch of the West disappears. A moment later there was an unscheduled burst of flames.

"I felt warmth on my face, that's all. It's still unbelievable. There was a whole lot of running and hullabaloo and shouting, and my hat and my broom were on fire and I didn't know it."

The flames had jumped from the broomstraw, scalding her chin, the bridge of her nose, her right cheek, and the right side of her forehead. The eyelashes and eyebrow on her right eye had been burned off; her upper lip and eyelid were badly burned. But even when the broom was snatched away from her, she was aware only of a slight sensation of warmth.

"To my surprise, the broom was grabbed out of my hand. And then someone went bang, bang, bang, on my head, and off with the hat. I thought it was funny, such a hullabaloo, and I said, 'Well, everything was on time that time,' sort of laughing. And they thought I was hysterical. I wasn't hysterical. I didn't know anything had happened to me. I knew that apparently the hat and the broom were on fire, but I wasn't alarmed about that. I thought I was perfectly safe."

Margaret Hamilton found out how wrong she was a few moments later when she looked down at her right hand. From the wrist to the fingernails, there was no skin on the hand. It was as though someone had taken the top of her hand and peeled it like an orange.

The pain began soon enough. It would have been another matter if she had not been wearing green makeup: makeup man Jack Young would have gently blotted off the greasepaint and Dr. Jones, the MGM doctor, would have covered the burns with salve. But green makeup was toxic.

"Because of the copper oxide," says Young. "There are only two colors you have to worry about: gold and green. Gold is a sealer. It closes up the pores. And green is toxic because it's made with copper. Every night when I was taking off the Witch's makeup, I would make sure that her face was thoroughly clean. Spotlessly clean. Because you don't take chances with green. So, when she was burned, I knew that I didn't want to take any chances. I knew that makeup had to be cleaned off."

It was usual to use acetone to take off the makeup. This time Young used alcohol, "for the antiseptic value."

"I stood it as long as I could. And then I said, 'I'm going to have to scream.'"

Young continued to rub. And Margaret Hamilton did not scream. Screaming was not an appropriate activity for privately educated Midwestern gentlewomen. She sat, very politely, until it was over. "But I'll never, as long as I live, have anything that took my breath away like that pain."

When it was over, Dr. Jones layered her face with salve. "Butescin Pictrate, I think. She just plastered this stuff on in great globs and bound me up. What I looked like was a mummy. I had two slits left for my eyes; my two nostrils were open; and there was a slit for my mouth. A friend who was staying with me at the time came over and got me. That was always amazing to me, that the studio didn't send me home in a limousine. But they didn't. My friend came over

A scene from the Renovation sequence (cut from the final version) in which Dorothy and the others triumphantly return to the Emerald City carrying the broomstick of the Wicked Witch.

The Witch's Flying Monkeys. Note the Lilly in the foreground.

Top: The four-foot-wide, crayon-pastel-matte painting of the corridor leading to the Wizard's Throne Room. The blacked-out area in the middle was constructed as a set (above, with the principals) on which the action was filmed. In the middle of the blacked-out area at top: samples of the colors appearing in the matte painting that had to be matched in the set.

Opposite, top: The constructed set of the end of the Poppy Field and a part of the Yellow Brick Road. The blacked-out area was a matte painting (not shown here) of the Emerald City.

Opposite: The result when both pieces of film were put together.

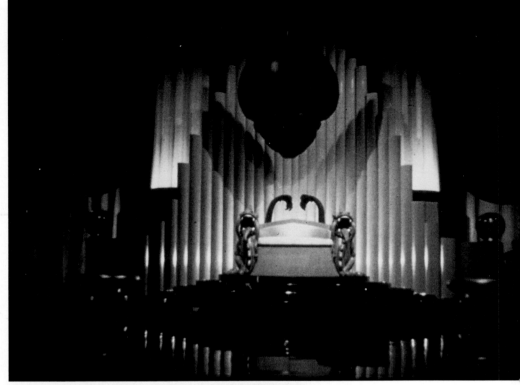

Above: A test shot of the interior of the Wizard's Throne Room. At far right a studio policeman and a carpenter wander by.

Left: The Wizard's disembodied head.

and got me, and the next day somebody drove my car home from the studio."

She had the presence of mind to make two phone calls before she left the studio: the first to her doctor, the second to her housekeeper. "I didn't want my son to see me. Hamilton* was only three years old, and I knew he'd be terribly frightened. So I told her to keep him in his room and to tell him that I was going to work late and would kiss him good night after he was asleep and would see him in the morning."

It was 4 p.m. on December 23, 1938, when she left the studio. She didn't return for six weeks.

When the doctor arrived, she was sitting up in her bedroom. He insisted that she go to bed—she refused. He said quite firmly that she was probably in shock, put her in bed, and waited until another friend—who was a nurse—arrived to take care of her. He told her he would be back the next morning to take a look at what was underneath the bandages.

"Dr. Stan was there the next morning removing the bandages when the telephone rang. Alice answered it and I heard her say, 'I don't know. . . . I don't really know. . . . No . . . well . . . no.' Well, finally she came in and said, 'It's the studio, Marg. They want to know how soon you can come back to work.' Dr. Stan said, 'I'll take that!' With a goodly temper, he roared, 'I don't want you calling up here again. She'll come back to work when I get good and ready, not one second before. Furthermore, if she doesn't sue you, she is a fool. This is absolute negligence. There's no reason for this to happen. If she has any sense at all, she'll sue you for every cent you've got. Now I want no more calling up and no more inquiring about it. When she's ready to come back, I will call you!' That was the end of that. But I'm sure that they were hoping *I* would answer. Because had they said to me, 'How are you?' I would have said, 'Oh, fine. I'm all right.' Because you don't lay it on and say how horribly you're feeling. I often think that if I had talked to them and had later decided to sue them, they would have brought that conversation up. 'She was not in any kind of pain. She said she was

* Hamilton Meserve.

fine.' Of course, they didn't have tape recorders in those days, but they certainly had stenographers. And I have often wondered if there was a stenographer listening in. I knew that my disappearance was the last time they would need me for six weeks. So why did they call?"

She decided not to sue "for the very simple reason that I wanted to work again. And I knew very well that if I sued, I would never work again in any studio."

One day in January she picked up the morning paper to discover that Billie Burke had sprained her ankle. "The studio never mentioned my accident, never. But when Billie Burke sprained her ankle, they had an ambulance come and there were pictures of her being carried out. And I was very much amused."

Margaret Hamilton returned to work on February 10. She was not scheduled to work until Saturday, February 11, but the studio asked her to come in a day early to discuss the broomstick ride she would be taking the next day. It is more likely that they wanted to take a look at her face. "My face was all right. I could put makeup on it. But not the hand. All the nerves in my hand were still exposed. Instead of makeup on my hands, I was going to wear green gloves. The skin wasn't thick enough for makeup. I went over to Mr. Fleming and he said, 'How's your hand?' I said, 'Well, it's coming.' He said, 'Let me see it.' So I—very gingerly and very carefully— took the glove off. And he took a good firm hold of it and said, 'That looks fine.' And I almost fainted, the pain was that terrific. I said, 'Mr. Fleming, you're touching all my nerves and a very, very thin layer of skin.' He was terribly sorry. And then he said, 'Well, anyway, we have the film on your disappearance, and it was a great shot.' "

The agenda for February 11 was simple. Margaret Hamilton was to ride her broomstick in mid-air. The camera would focus on her laughing and screaming. She was sitting in the makeup chair at 7 a.m. when she was asked if she wanted her "regular costume" or her "fireproof costume."

"I said, 'I don't have a fireproof costume.' And this young production-assistant said, 'Yes, ma'am, you do.' And I said, 'I can tell you one thing. I don't want it!' "

Margaret Hamilton and Buddy Gillespie, the head of MGM's Special Effects Department, preparing for the skywriting sequence.

She asked to have Keith Weeks, the film's production manager, meet her in her dressing room. Word was sent back that he didn't have time. "So I sent a message back that he'd better come right away because 'Miss Hamilton's mad.' I didn't usually get mad about anything, so I thought that might have an effect. And it did. He said, 'I'm glad you're back.' And I said, 'It's nice to be back.' And he said, 'It's nice to have you back.' And I said, 'Now about what I'm supposed to be doing today . . .' He said, 'You're doing a very simple shot. It's the skywriting. You're sitting on the broom for the skywriting close-ups, and the smoke is coming out the end of the broom.' "

She was, she discovered, to sit on a steel saddle attached to her broomstick. The broomstick would be raised ten or fifteen feet in the air and suspended from the top of the stage by four wires. The saddle and a pipe underneath the saddle would be hidden by her costume. The wind machines would be turned on to simulate air currents. She would scream and cackle while smoke poured out of the pipe at the end of the broomstick.

"I said, 'What sort of fire do you anticipate?' Mr. Weeks said, 'We don't anticipate any fire.' And I said, 'Well, I have a fireproof costume, I understand.' And he said, 'We don't want to take any chances.' And I said, 'I can tell you one thing right now. You're not going to take any chances with me. You've had all the chances you're going to get with this girl.' "

The conversation continued for another ten futile minutes with Weeks insisting that the shot was perfectly safe and Margaret Hamilton asking why a fireproof costume was necessary for a perfectly safe shot. Well, Weeks admitted, he supposed that if you stuck tissue paper into the pipe, it might burn.

"I told him that he could just consider me tissue paper from then on. I said, 'I'm not doing this shot. And I'm not doing any other shot with any kind of fire whatsoever within twenty-five hundred feet.' "

Weeks said he was sorry she felt that way but of course he would have to inform Mr. Mayer of her refusal to cooperate. The threat backfired. "I said that if Mr. Mayer had been me, the studio would have the biggest suit of its life on its hands. I said, 'I'm not suing

Margaret Hamilton leaving the Witch's Castle for the Emerald City;
in the foreground, the constructed set; behind her, a matte painting.

you because I know enough about this business to know I won't work again if I do sue. But I won't go near fire again. You can terminate me if you like. I'll be glad to bow out of this picture right now. Practically anybody can do this part. Make her up and you'll never know whether you've got me or somebody else.' Then Mr. Fleming came and the special-effects man, Mr. Gillespie. They cajoled and teased and implied that I wasn't playing the game. I couldn't have cared less. I said, 'No, thank you, I've had all the fire I want at your hands. I have a little boy and I'm his sole support and I do not intend to do anything to jeopardize my life further.' "

She agreed to ride the broomstick for close-ups without the pipe connected. She was strapped to the saddle and the broomstick raised. The wind machine was turned on and the broomstick rocked back and forth. "I cackled and looked menacing and then the broomstick was lowered and I got off and got dressed and went home. When I was leaving, I saw my stunt double. And I said, 'Betty, are you going to do the shot?' And she said, 'Yes.' And I said, 'I wish you wouldn't because I think it's very tricky.' And she said, 'Well, I'm getting a lot of money for it.' And I said, 'Well, I hope it's worth it, dear.'"

Margaret Hamilton had been home for less than an hour when someone called from the set to tell her that Betty Danko was in the hospital.

Betty Danko's experience in February was almost an exact duplicate of Margaret Hamilton's experience in December. The first two takes, under the direction of Buddy Gillespie and his special-effects crew, worked perfectly. "But Fleming was the killer," Betty Danko says, still bitterly, thirty-eight years later. "We were the second unit. He was directing the other unit, Judy Garland, and he came over to watch. It was his fault that I was injured."

Betty Danko's cape was pinned down to hide the pipe. Fleming wanted the cape to blow in the wind from the wind machines. He told the special-effects crew to find a way to hide the pipe beneath Danko's body instead.

Betty Danko watched them remount the pipe beneath the steel bicycle-seat saddle. "I had a peculiar hunch when I saw them covering the pipe with asbestos. I jokingly said, 'Do you think I'm going to get a hot seat?' And they said, 'Well, this is just to be sure you *don't* get a hot seat.'"

A button was concealed on the broom on the side away from the camera. The first two times Betty Danko pressed the button, smoke had poured out of the broomstraws—the third time she pushed the button, the pipe exploded. "I felt as though my scalp was coming off. I guess that's because my hat and my black wig were torn loose. They found them, days later, at the top of the stage. The explosion blew me off the broomstick. I managed to grab it with both hands and throw my leg over it. I hung upside down while the men handling the wires lowered the broomstick to the floor and put me face down on the stage."

Betty Danko's left leg was bruised from thigh to knee, and the two-inch-deep wound that nearly circled the leg was full of bits of her costume. "While I lay there on the floor, waiting for the ambulance, the wardrobe woman came running in, and she said, 'What did you do with the hat? I have to turn it in, you know.' "

She was in the hospital eleven days. Her doctor told her that two Winged Monkeys had been in the same hospital a few weeks earlier: they had fallen, he said, when their wires broke. Margaret Hamilton came to visit twice. Bobbie Koshay came to visit, too. Bobbie told her that the studio had hired Eileen Goodwin to finish the broomstick ride. Bobbie had gone over to the set where Eileen was up on the wire and told her that "Just yesterday, that broomstick exploded with Betty and she's in the hospital." Then Eileen had gone right up to the man in charge and said, "I don't want any part of this!" And he had told her that they weren't using any explosives in the scene any more because they had gotten two good takes before the broomstick exploded.

Betty Danko's total earnings from *The Wizard of Oz* came to $790, not including the $35 she received for riding the broomstick.

A few years later, she worked on another picture with Victor Fleming. "I had a fight sequence to do, a Pier Six brawl in the middle of a dance hall. Fleming asked one of the stunt men who I was. And the stunt man said, 'You ought to know her. You were responsible for blowing her off the broomstick in *The Wizard of Oz*.' And a little later, I felt a draft on my leg and I looked down and it was Fleming. He was trying to get a look under my skirt to see my scars."

There was one other accident on *The Wizard of Oz*: one of the Witch's soldiers stepped on Terry, the Cairn terrier who played the part of Toto. It had taken the dog weeks to learn how to cope with the wind machines. Eventually, she had learned to duck behind the principals when the wind machines were turned on. Then, during the rehearsals of the scene where Toto is pursued by the soldiers, one of them jumped on top of her and sprained her foot.

"We had to find a double for Terry," said Carl Spitz shortly before his death in 1976. "I looked everywhere. Finally, I raced up to San Francisco and found one. I took $350 of my money to buy the dog. Later, I found that a quarter of a mile down from my place on

Riverside Drive was identically the dog like Toto, better than the $350 dog I had bought."

In a few weeks, Terry recovered and returned to the film. But the anxieties caused by her accident and "the scariness of this little dog surrounded by so many people and those wind machines" made Carl Spitz sick. "You would read the script and there was always a headache and how were you going to get that scene tomorrow?" One night he fainted, "for the first time in my life." His own doctor told Spitz to go to bed for a week, but someone was needed to work the dog, so the next morning he got out of bed and went back to the studio. Luckily, MGM's Dr. Jones prescribed just the right medicine —"a few drops" in a spoonful of sugar whenever he felt faint. His stomach held out until the picture was completed, but he was not sorry—definitely not sorry—when he was told that he could take his dog and go home.

Production #1060

AFTER OZ

On Thursday, March 16, 1939, principal photography was completed on *The Wizard of Oz*. It had taken three days more than five months, but the picture was "finished." Nearly six hundred people had appeared in the movie, but not many of them were around the last few days.

The three hundred extras in the Emerald City sequence had worked their four days, turned in their green dresses, picked up their $44 paychecks, and reported back to Central Casting. Betty Danko was home in bed. Buddy Ebsen was looking for a job. With the exception of Harry Monty, the Munchkins had departed from MGM and Culver City early in January. Monty was over on MGM's Lot 3 doubling for eight-year-old Johnny Sheffield in *Tarzan Finds a Son*.

Victor Fleming was a few miles away, directing *Gone With the Wind* for Selznick International. But he came back to MGM that night, as he did most nights, to work with Blanche Sewell, who was editing *The Wizard of Oz*. Margaret Hamilton had already gone home to her three-year-old son; Bert Lahr, to dinner with Jack Haley; Ray Bolger, to sleep.

The Kansas farmhouse set was struck the following day: laborers swept up the debris, and trucks carried the sweepings to Lot 2.

Blanche Sewell, the editor of The Wizard of Oz.

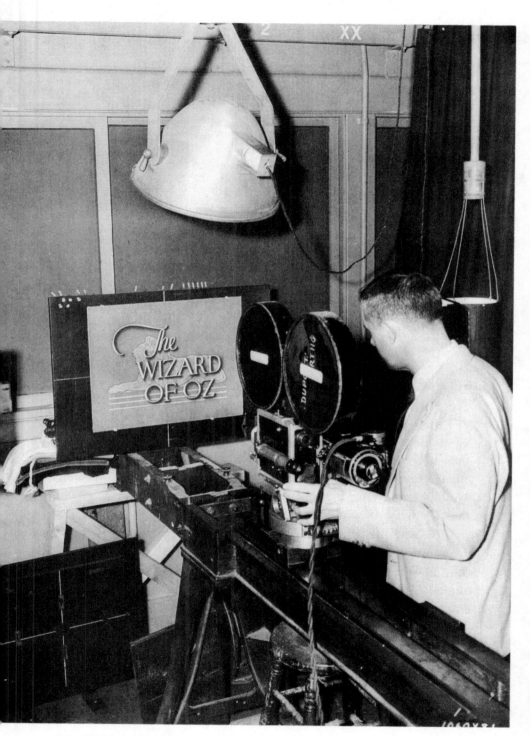

The MGM Optical Department:
the place where the titles were photographed.

The film lab at MGM.

Symbolic as the empty stage may have been, it hardly signified the end of work on the picture. There was sound-recording, editing, music-scoring, laboratory trickery to be completed before the film would be ready for its first preview in June. And there was, of course, the necessity of mounting a publicity campaign.

In May, Arthur Freed sent a memo to Mervyn LeRoy outlining ideas for exploiting the music in *The Wizard of Oz*. His thesis was that " 'We're Off to See the Wizard' ought to become a slogan, and one of the best ways of accomplishing this is through the free cooperation of the big radio programs." MGM was given a large assist in exploiting the music by the popularity of "Over the Rainbow." A week before the picture opened, "Over the Rainbow" was already No. 4 on the list of the ten largest sheet-music sellers, a list headed by "Beer Barrel Polka." The start of World War II was less than four weeks away.

"From the time a property was purchased, you began to publicize that property," says Eddie Lawrence, who was the unit publicist on most Clark Gable films in the late thirties and who became assistant head of the Publicity Department several years later. "We all sat down together—there must have been thirty key people in the department—and discussed a picture: what we were going to do for *Life* magazine, what we would try to do for *Collier's*, the *American*, the *Woman's Home Companion*, the *Saturday Evening Post*. 'Can we sell Judy Garland to *Life*?' 'What can we do with Bert Lahr?' You had tremendous print outlets then, before television. We'd try to get the picture into all the big newspapers—*The New York Times*, the *Kansas City Star*, the *Atlanta Constitution*—to give it advance prestige. Newspapers before the war had a tremendous amount of space available. We'd provide the material, sometimes even write articles, to fill that space. When I handled Greer Garson one year, she did thirty-two interviews for national magazines, including a *Time* cover."

The campaign to publicize *The Wizard of Oz* included drawings of Judy Garland and Frank Morgan making jelly with Certo in women's magazine advertisements ("Anybody can be a wizard at jelly-making"). It also included the fabrication that Mervyn LeRoy would operate a Wizard of Oz concession—the sets from Munchkinland peopled by the midgets—at the 1939 New York World's Fair. In addition, it was standard practice for the studio to provide theater owners with press books and exploitation books. *The Wizard of Oz* press book was replete with meretricious interviews and prepared reviews for the theater owner to hand to his local newspaper ("Audiences last night sat in rapture over the music and color, chuckled with glee over sparkling dialogue and lyrics . . ."). The exploitation book encouraged tie-ins with twenty-five different wholesalers of items ranging from Wizard of Oz wool dresses and handbags to dart games and underwear. The campaign was successful: on July 17, there were two full pages of color in *Life* magazine, accompanied by a short article on the difficulties of making the picture. In August and September, there were articles in *Good Housekeeping*, *Harper's Bazaar*, *Cosmopolitan*, *Liberty*, *Look*, *Pathfinder*, *St. Nicholas*, *Child Life*, *Motion Picture*, *Movie Life*, *Movie Mirror*, *Photoplay*, *Screen Book*, *Screenland*, *Screen Romances*, and most of the major news-

The West Coast premiere, August 15, 1939, at Grauman's Chinese Theater.
The day it opened, 2,800 children saw the movie.

papers. *The New York Times* actually published four articles on the movie between the time it started shooting in October 1938 and the day it opened in New York—August 17, 1939.

Accompanied by Mickey Rooney and Judy Garland onstage, the picture did extremely well that first week at Loew's Capitol Theater. Opening day broke the house record. According to the *Hollywood Reporter*, "The lines started to form at 5:30 in the morning and when the box office opened at eight there were 15,000 four abreast lined up around the corner almost to Eighth Avenue." By the end of the day, the picture had been seen by more than 37,000 people. There had been no stage shows at the Capitol for nearly five years, and the prospect of seeing Mickey Rooney and Judy Garland on-

At a preview of The Wizard of Oz. *The man on the left is holding the sound track of the film; the man on the right is holding the visual track. A composite print was not made until after all of the previews because it was easier to make editorial cuts and to resplice before the two tracks were put together.*

stage probably accounted for a considerable part of the first week's gross of $93,000.*

The picture also opened well in the thirty-two key cities surveyed by *Variety*, bringing in more money the first week than such recently successful MGM films as *Goodbye, Mr. Chips* and *Idiot's Delight*. But the picture didn't have firm enough legs to justify its cost. Part of the problem was the fact that nearly half of a typical audience for the picture consisted of children, who got in for reduced prices, so that even when the picture played to full houses, the theater made considerably less money than usual. Arthur Freed's *Babes in Arms*, which was released two months after *The Wizard of Oz*, cost $748,000 and grossed $3,335,000 for the studio. *The Wizard of Oz* cost $2,777,000 and grossed $3,017,000. When the costs of distribution, prints, and advertising were added to the cost of making *The Wizard of Oz*, it meant a loss to the studio of nearly a million dollars. The movie edged into the black during its first re-release in 1948–49, when it brought in another $1,500,000; but it did not really make money until it was leased to television. By the summer of 1998, theatrical distribution of *The Wizard of Oz* had brought MGM (and Ted Turner who bought the MGM library in 1986) $5,400,000. Weighted for inflation and translated into 1998 box office figures by Exhibitor Data Information, the movie had earned its owners the equivalent of $219,929,105 in film rental. Worldwide television sales exceeded $50 million. *The Wizard of Oz* had done even better in videocassette sales. By the movie's fiftieth anniversary in 1989, MGM had sold 850,000 videocassettes and earned $16.7 million. During the last decade, another 11 million videos were sold, worth $225 million. (In the tangled financial web that is Hollywood in 1998, most of those videocassette revenues have gone to Warner Bros. Warner acquired *The Wizard of Oz* in 1995 when Turner Broadcasting Company was merged into Time Warner.)

*   *   *

*That same August, *Stanley and Livingstone* brought in $58,478 during its first week at the Roxy; *Beau Geste* grossed $56,000 its first week at the Paramount; and *The Rains Came*—which would defeat *The Wizard of Oz* for the Academy Award in Special Effects—had a box-office gross of $86,000 the week it replaced *Stanley and Livingstone* at the Roxy.

This posed photograph of the cast and several similar shots were used extensively in magazine advertising the year the film was released.

The first sale to television came almost by accident. "I was vice-president of program development at CBS," said Robert Weitman in 1976. "Bob O'Brien, who was then executive vice-president of MGM, and I had worked together at Paramount Theaters and ABC. I went to O'Brien and asked if MGM would be interested in leasing *Gone With the Wind*. I had permission from my higher-ups, Bill Paley and Frank Stanton, to offer a million. MGM said no. I started thinking. Shortly thereafter, I met with Bob and broached the subject of *The Wizard of Oz*. Mostly because I thought it was timeless. Production-wise, costume-wise, it will never go out of style. I said, 'Look, you've got this picture that's lying fallow.' He said, 'What have you got in mind?' I said, 'Let's work out a deal.' "

The deal that was worked out entitled CBS to broadcast *The Wizard of Oz* twice, at $225,000 for each broadcast. "The agreement with CBS was signed August 2, 1956," said Frank Rosenfelt, the lawyer who assisted in the negotiations for MGM and became the studio's president seventeen years later. "It is my recollection that feature films were not being broadcast on a network basis in 1956 and *The Wizard of Oz* deal was unique in that regard. Additionally, the license fee of $225,000 for a single run was regarded as stupendous."

CBS also had options to broadcast *The Wizard of Oz* seven more times at $150,000 per run. Both the studio and the network expected that two or three showings would exhaust the film's potential—the other options were simply for insurance. The film was shown for the first time on November 3, 1956, from 9 to 11 p.m. Eastern Standard Time.* With a 33.9 rating and a 52.7 percent share of the audience, *The Wizard of Oz* did extremely well—but not as well as it did in 1959, 1964, and 1965. As of July 1975, *The Wizard of Oz* was in 11th place on the list of the highest-rated movies ever shown on network television.† (It was also in 12th place, 14th place, 16th place, 21st place, 23rd place, and 25th place.)

---

*According to Weitman, CBS received several thousand letters asking the network to rerun the film at an earlier time. The network responded by scheduling future broadcasts of the film from 6 to 8 p.m.

†The top movies were *Airport, Love Story, The Godfather Part I* (second half), *The Poseidon Adventure, True Grit, The Birds, Patton, The Bridge on the River Kwai, The Godfather Part I* (first half), and *Ben Hur.*

When MGM's contract with CBS ran out in 1967, the studio demanded more money. CBS refused, thinking the new price was too high, and NBC decided to make a bid. Says Don Durgin, who was NBC network president in 1967, "As so often happens when you're the rights-holder of something and they jack the price up on you, you hesitate. From an outsider's point of view, the shock of the price isn't as great if you never had the same thing for a lot less money. We were the outsiders, and we couldn't really understand why CBS was dropping it."

It cost NBC $650,000 per year to show *The Wizard of Oz* in 1968, 1969, and 1970, and $500,000 per year to show the film once each year between 1970 and 1976. When the NBC contract was up, CBS was the outsider and paid MGM $4 million ($800,000 per year) to televise the film five times between 1976 and 1980. CBS then offered $1 million a year from 1981 through 1985. On February 24, 1988, *The Wizard of Oz* created one of television's most extraordinary milestones when it played for the thirtieth time. The aggregate audience over all those years was more than one billion people, according to Arnold Becker, vice president of television research at CBS. Another decade has only sharpened the phenomenon. When CBS's contract ran out in August 1998, *The Wizard of Oz* had been shown on network television an unprecedented thirty-nine times. Because CBS had an exclusive contract, the movie had not yet been syndicated or shown on cable; those untapped revenues were waiting.

By the time the picture returned to CBS and was televised for the eighteenth time in the spring of 1977, *The Wizard of Oz* had long since become an American institution. Its characters were so recognizable that they could serve as shorthand in the marketplace. The Wizard of Avis played on the name. A Subaru commercial had a hopelessly lost driver meet Dorothy and the Tin Woodman. In *Crawdaddy*, a rock-music magazine, an advertisement for a record album showed ten fingers reaching for a pair of shoes. There is no identifying caption on the two-inch picture, and the wearer of the shoes is cut off at the knee. But the ruby slippers unquestionably belong to Judy Garland and the fingers to Margaret Hamilton.

In March of 1975, after a year of research, Marty Abrams of Mego Toy Co. decided to market dolls of Toto, the Scarecrow, the

Tin Woodman, the Cowardly Lion, the Wizard of Oz, the Wicked Witch, and a ruby-slippered Dorothy. "We did our research in nursery schools and day-care centers," says Abrams. "There was an eighty-percent recognition factor. That's incredible. For a toy to achieve that, it usually takes $900,000 of promotion. And every kid who recognized them loved them."

By 1998, Oz ornaments hung from the branches of most American Christmas trees. Wind chimes, beach towels, get well cards, mylar balloons, tapestries, teapots, clocks, and computer games proudly wore the movie's logo. A commemorative plate of Judy Garland as Dorothy that was sold by the tens of thousands in 1977 now sells to fanatic collectors of Oz memorabilia. The Yellow Brick Road in Chesterton, Indiana, is one of a number of stores dedicated to the MGM movie.

The prices paid for memorabilia from the movie have escalated almost unimaginably. The black wool Witch's hat, which sold for $450 at the MGM auction in 1970, was auctioned by Sotheby's in December 1988, for $33,000. In May 1998, Sotheby's auctioned the Cowardly Lion's Courage Medal for $29,000, $9,000 more than the auction house's highest estimate. Even a "possible" test dress for Judy Garland's stand-in brought more than $5,000 in 1997. And, at Christie's East, the pair of ruby slippers that Roberta Bauman won in a contest in 1939 sold for $165,000 in June 1988. It was, at that time, the highest price ever paid for a piece of movie memorabilia.

And then there are the attempts to create a new experience that duplicates the old one. In 1989, a $5 million stage show based on the script and music of the movie toured arenas in dozens of American and Canadian cities. Financed by Ralston Purina's Purina Dog Chow and Downey fabric softener, the show made no one forget the movie. In the spring of 1998, a different theatrical version of the MGM movie opened in New York's Madison Square Garden to full houses. With Mickey Rooney as the wizard and Eartha Kitt as the Wicked Witch, this *Wizard of Oz* was in the middle of a yearlong tour of North America.

The Wizard of Oz was equally serviceable as metaphorical shorthand. *Zardoz*, John Boorman's philosophical science-fiction film about a world of bored immortals who wish to be allowed to die, is named for the great stone head the immortals have set up as god of the mortals. The stone head, Zardoz, is a deliberate fraud, its name coined from wiZARD of OZ. Elton John entitled an album *Goodbye Yellow Brick Road*, and the cover picture showed John setting his foot upon a yellow brick road over which one bird was flying. During Watergate, a dozen or more newspapers and magazines used a cowardly lion and a counterfeit wizard as metaphors. TRB in *The New Republic* described Nixon as "the make-believe strong man Nixon, caught like the little ventriloquist from Kansas behind the throne in *The Wizard of Oz*." In one of the best cartoons, later reprinted by *Time*, Bill Sanders of the *Milwaukee Journal* showed a Cowardly Lion labeled House and a Tin Woodman labeled SENATE scanning public-opinion polls. At the end of a yellow brick road labeled IMPEACH-MENT stood—in place of the Emerald City—the White House. The cartoon was captioned, "Looking for courage and heart in the Land of Oz."

The half-life of the movie, its impact nearly four decades after they took off their costumes and went home, was perhaps most surprising to the men and women who were connected with it. In interviews in the 1970s Mervyn LeRoy and Ray Bolger credited the picture's longevity to "its simple philosophy: that there's no place like home, that everybody has a heart, everybody has a brain, everybody has a soul." Jack Haley, somewhat less sentimental, said, "It's like a toy. You get a new generation all the time because of television. The film didn't bowl anyone over when it first came out. It was never the big smashing hit that television made it."

It is accurate to say with Haley that the movie has become a part of the American cultural fabric because it is shown each year on television. It was, recalls Margaret Hamilton, only after the third or fourth repetition of the film on television "that all the fuss began. There were no repercussions the first time." It is, however, almost as accurate to say that the movie is repeated each year *because* it has become part of American culture. A simple addition of the Nielsen figures for each separate broadcast shows that the film reached an aggregate of 262,800,000 homes during its first seventeen years on television. No other movie in the top-rated twenty-five ever made the list the second time it was shown, much less the third, fourth, fifth, seventh, and eighth times.*

How firmly *The Wizard of Oz* had become part of the culture by the mid-seventies was most evident in the mass literature of television and comic strips. It was a rare situation comedy that had not at least once referred to a character as "the Wicked Witch of the West." When Garry Trudeau created an energy czar for his comic strip, *Doonesbury*, and sent a group of truck drivers dancing down the highway to Washington singing "We're off to see the Czar," it was because "the picture just surfaced in my mind. I guess the picture is that much with us."

Lyman Frank Baum was forty-three years old when he created Oz. In 1899, he wrote a book that he called "The Emerald City" and took the first rough draft to the George M. Hill Publishing Co. in Chicago. Baum had been inventing "The Emerald City" for at least a year before he put it down on paper, creating it as a bedtime story for his four sons.

By the age of forty-three, Baum had been a failure as actor, playwright, and axle-lubricant salesman, as owner of a five-and-ten-cent store and editor of a weekly newspaper. The failures never seemed to be *his* fault but came through thievery, mismanagement, or the lack of rain in the Dakota Territory. Although the publication of "The Emerald City" as *The Wonderful Wizard of Oz* in 1900 made Baum financially secure, in 1911 he had to file for bankruptcy.†

The Wonderful Wizard of Oz was an instant success. In the first two weeks, it sold out its first edition of 10,000 copies. Nearly 90,000 copies were sold during 1900 and 1901. In 1902, with Paul Tietjens composing the music, Baum turned *The Wizard of Oz* into a five-act children's operetta. Luckily, stage director Julian Mitchell insisted that Baum rewrite it as an extravagant musical comedy, which was extremely successful, mostly because of the performances of Fred Stone and David Montgomery as the Scarecrow and the Tin Wood-

---

*In its thirty-ninth airing, on May 8, 1998, the movie was still going strong. For the 1997–1998 season, it ranked thirty-first out of the 108 theatrical movies shown on the four television networks.

†For an account of Baum's life, see Appendix B.

man. According to Michael Patrick Hearn,* only *Floradora* and *The Merry Widow* were more successful as Broadway musicals during the first decade or two of the twentieth century. The book itself was never out of print. By 1956, when the copyright expired, 4,195,667 copies of the book had been sold. One can only guess at how many million more copies have been sold in regular, abridged, Golden, pop-up, and supermarket versions since then.† Baum had managed to do successfully what he had set out to do: write a modern fairy tale. And without intending it or knowing it, he had written a psychological fairy tale.

In his preface to *The Wonderful Wizard of Oz*, Baum said that his book had deliberately eliminated "all the horrible and bloodcurdling incident" of the standard fairy tale. His book, he wrote, "aspires to being a modernized fairy tale, in which the wonderment and joy are retained and the heart-aches and nightmares are left out." Yet most of a child's deepest fears can be found somewhere in the book—of being lost, abandoned, broken, of bad mothers and omnipotent fathers, of dreams seeming real. The Yellow Brick Road is the path through the chaos, the anchorage to reality like the river in *Huckleberry Finn*. The men who are broken in body (the Scarecrow, the Tin Woodman) are restored to wholeness, as is the one who is broken in spirit (the Cowardly Lion). The bad mother is killed, the all-powerful father cut to smaller size when he is discovered to be a humbug, and, in the end, reality and home are restored by the good-mother witch.‡

"Actually," says Justin Call, chairman of the Department of Child Psychiatry at the University of California at Irvine, "Baum

---

*The *Annotated Wizard of Oz* (New York: Clarkson N. Potter, 1973).

†There is even a society devoted to the land of Oz as it was mapped out in L. Frank Baum's fourteen books and revised, after his death, in twenty books by Ruth Plumly Thompson, three by John R. Neill, two by Jack Snow, and several by the Russians who have claimed Oz as their own. The International Wizard of Oz Club has 1,600 members. Club members from the western United States meet each summer at a Winkie Convention in Yosemite National Park. Those who live in the eastern United States share a Munchkin Convention held in New Jersey or Pennsylvania, and a national convention is held annually in Castle Park, Michigan.

‡Baum's psychological underpinnings are much more evident in the 1975 Broadway musical comedy *The Wiz* than in the movie. The Yellow Brick Road is animate in the play—portrayed by four dancers. The Cowardly Lion has his own psychoanalyst, an Owl. And both Baum's Witch and his Wizard are flexible enough to serve as archetypes of the black experience.

included the heartaches and nightmares. But he also provided a model for the mastery of those things, a way of working them through and out." *The Wizard of Oz* was published the same year as Freud's *Interpretation of Dreams*, and a number of psychiatrists and psychologists have used the Wizard as metaphor.

The seductive theme of *The Wizard of Oz* lies in the powerful Wizard who turns out to be powerless, that good man who is a bad wizard, and in Baum's other deception—the clever Scarecrow, the kind Woodman, and the brave Lion who search diligently for things they already possess.

Freud once said that a creative writer is playing with his own thoughts in the way a child plays with his toys. In certain books written for children, there are fragments of theme or character that connect the adult that is to the child that was. *Peter Pan, Charlotte's Web, The Tale of Peter Rabbit, The Wizard of Oz, The Wind in the Willows*, and *Winnie-the-Pooh* vary considerably in literary merit: *Peter Pan* is coy and sentimental; *Winnie-the-Pooh*, almost patronizing; *The Wind in the Willows*, exquisitely written. But the boy who refuses to grow up and the children who do not have Peter Pan's stubborn, arrogant confidence to defy the inevitable—time—captivate the adult as well as the child. Stories of a child playing with his stuffed animals are an equally strong lure. Beatrix Potter wrote any number of delicate and charming books, but it is the small, vulnerable Peter Rabbit escaping with his skin—although not with his clothes—from Mr. McGregor's garden, who makes us reexperience the terror of being smaller than everyone else. *The Wind in the Willows* would be an elegant book without Toad, but it would be considerably less read: it is his childishness, his self-centeredness, that compels us. And in *Charlotte's Web* it is the whole notion of death and birth that magnetizes us just as profoundly when we are adults. The same people who as children cried at Wilbur's loss (Charlotte's death), cry again as adults.

The appeal of MGM's 1939 movie version of *The Wizard of Oz* starts with the appeal of the book but does not end there. There is the same wizard who is a good man but a very bad wizard. There are the same straw man, tin man, and lion who refuse to believe in themselves until they are given outward signs of their cleverness, kindness, and courage. Added, however, is the classic fairy-tale witch, that sleek, malevolent force who had so much to do with the success of Walt Disney's *Snow White and the Seven Dwarfs* two years earlier. Baum's Wicked Witch of the West, desperately afraid of water and the dark, is wholly contained within two chapters of the book. Stronger and more terrible, she pervades the movie despite the fact that Margaret Hamilton appears on the screen for only twelve minutes. "The footage is very short," says Margaret Hamilton. "But the point is that she's constantly there because she's constantly a threat all the time. So that you're much more aware of her than I think anybody realizes."

The most horrifying moment in the movie comes when Dorothy, locked in the Witch's tower with the hourglass whose emptiness will signify her death, begs for help. Her anguish enables her to see, in the Witch's crystal ball, Aunt Em searching for her. But she cannot reach into the ball for Aunt Em's protection, nor can Aunt Em hear her. As she looks, Aunt Em's face dissolves into the face of the Witch, who mocks Dorothy's terror with, " 'Auntie Em, Auntie Em, come back!' I'll give you Auntie Em, my pretty!" To the very young child, the nurturing, milk-giving mother and the angry mother who abandons the child (even if only for an afternoon) are two separate people. In fairy tales, these Good and Bad Mothers are institutionalized into Fairy Godmother and Wicked Witch. (Note how often in fairy tales the child's real mother has died and been replaced by a stepmother.) In a heavy-handed psychoanalytic interpretation of the film,* psychiatrist Harvey Greenberg does make one valid point: "For a brief, nightmarish instant Em and the Witch have fused identities." As the Witch replaces Aunt Em in the crystal, the Good and Bad Mother are bound together. Greenberg adds that the scene "is particularly troubling to most children, no doubt because it captures so effectively our archaic terror of the mother's destructive potential."

The original reviews of the movie in 1939 paid little attention either to Margaret Hamilton or to the character of the Witch. But she was central to the children who saw the film. And the further

---

The Movies on Your Mind (New York: Saturday Review Press/E. P. Dutton, 1975).

the distance from which the film was viewed, the more pervasive she appeared to reviewers.

Small children meeting Margaret Hamilton hide behind their mothers' skirts and, if they can be coaxed out, scream at her that she was mean to take the dog. Older children *become* afraid. "Almost always they want me to laugh like the Witch," says Margaret Hamilton. "And sometimes when I go to schools, if we're in an auditorium, I'll do it. And there's always a funny reaction, like *Ye Gods, they wish they hadn't asked.* They're scared. They're really scared for a second. Even adolescents. I guess for a minute they get the feeling they got when they watched the picture. They like to hear it but they *don't* like to hear it. And then they go, 'Ohhhhhhhhhhhhhhhh.' And they'll talk, talk, talk, talk, talk, and it's hard to get them quiet again."

Sometimes the remembered laughter of the Witch even makes adults uncomfortable. "The picture made a terrible impression of some kind on them, sometimes a ghastly impression, but most of them got over it, I guess. Although some are still struggling with it. Because when I talk like the Witch and when I laugh, there is a hesitation, and then they clap. They're clapping at hearing the sound again."

There are some middle-aged adults who have only to close their eyes to hear the laughter of the Witch. In 1965, Carolina Caribbean Corporation built a ski resort on Beach Mountain in North Carolina. The top of Beach Mountain consisted of huge rock cliffs, caves, and loose boulders. Jack Pentes, a designer, was given the job of turning the area into a tourist attraction that would use the corporation's chair lifts, parking lots, and village during the summer. Because of the prevalence of the movie in his own private consciousness, Pentes chose to turn the top of the mountain into The Land of Oz. "I knew The Land of Oz was to be The Land of Oz the first time I set foot on the property. It was then and is now truly the one place in the world that was pre-ordained to be what it is. The first clue came from the twisted, gnarled trees that reminded me of the apple trees I had seen—first run—as an eight-year-old in 1939."

* * *

Dorothy's urgent desire to get home was a part of L. Frank Baum's book. (Understandably, since in the book, unlike the movie, the cyclone that picked her up was not fulfilling any wish on her part.) But the movie, by design, inscribed that theme with a hatchet. "Be it ever so humble, there's no place like home" was a truism and a moral lesson on which L. B. Mayer, Mervyn LeRoy, and Arthur Freed wholeheartedly agreed. World War II coincided with the release of the picture and gave that overly sentimentalized theme a resonance it would not otherwise have had. In England, particularly—where the movie was seen during the first year of the war— "Over the Rainbow" became a personification of some future peace. RAF pilots used "We're Off to See the Wizard" as theme music for their defense of London against the German Luftwaffe. Getting home again seemed an unattainable goal in 1940, and the British public's pleasure in Judy Garland for attaining it carried over a dozen years and was partly responsible for the idolatry with which she was greeted in her engagement at the London Palladium in 1951.

It has been suggested that part of the movie's appeal nearly forty years later lies in the fact that in it one sees Judy Garland restored. It is more likely the deeper revelation of seeing one's own innocence restored, the innocence that allows one to return home.

The men who reviewed the movie during its first re-release in 1949 seem to have reacted to it as a safe harbor. *Time*, which had been dubious in 1939 about the picture's merits, and began a 1949 review with: " 'The Wizard of Oz' (MGM), dusted off and reissued, proves that true wizardry, whether in books or on the screen, is ageless. In the magical land of Oz, nothing changes. . . . The whimsical gaiety, the lighthearted song and dance, the lavish Hollywood sets and costumes, are as fresh and beguiling today as they were ten years ago."

Even one of the screenwriters, Noel Langley, who had thought the film "lousy" and "unimaginative" when he first saw it in 1939, had changed his mind by 1949. Langley spent the last three years of the war in the Canadian Navy. "When the war was over and I went back to England, my cousin proudly took me to the cinema in Kingston because *The Wizard of Oz* was there. And, suddenly, I could see it objectively for the first time. And I thought, 'It's not a bad picture. Not a bad picture, you know.' "

It is *not* a bad picture: it is, in fact, quite a bit of fun to watch. But that does nothing to explain its lingering effect on men and women who first saw it as children. The men who reviewed and disliked the film in 1939 were adults. The consistently more favorable reviews the film received after 1949 were partly because most of the second and all of the third set of reviewers had first seen the film as children or adolescents. And the film speaks to children: it is the child who kills two witches and protects her two companions from a lion and returns home by her own magic after finding out that the wizard in whom she has placed her trust is actually weaker than herself. The child is stronger than the Bad Mother and takes on some of the responsibilities of the Good Mother in her nurturing of the maimed or incomplete men she meets along the Yellow Brick Road.

Because it is a Hollywood movie and not the product of one person's unconscious mind, *The Wizard of Oz* does not provide its viewers with a completely accurate, genuine map for the journey from passivity to activity, from dependence to independence, from childhood to maturity. (After all, the film had ten writers and four directors, and decisions were made because one way of doing things cost less than another way.) As art, the movie is flawed by its sentimentality, by its cheerful insistence that "east, west, home is best," and by the decision to void Dorothy's experience by making it into a dream. As art, it is salvaged by its musical score, by actors who manage to make a Scarecrow, a Tin Woodman, a Cowardly Lion, a Wicked Witch, and a fraudulent Wizard credible, and by Judy Garland's absolute sincerity. There is art in the moment when the Emerald City is first seen in the distance and more durable art when the film turns from black-and-white to color. But it is in the tangled subtext—beyond or beneath art—that the film has remained alive.

Adrian, Billie Burke, Arthur Freed, Clara Blandick, Charley Grapewin, Bill Horning, Cedric Gibbons, Bert Lahr, Frank Morgan, Florence Ryerson, Edgar Allan Woolf, Keith Weeks, Bobby Connolly, Jack Dawn, Victor Fleming, Carl Spitz, L. B. Mayer, and Judy Garland are dead. So, now, are Mervyn LeRoy, Jack Haley, and

Margaret Hamilton, and even the last of the companions who danced down the Yellow Brick Road, Ray Bolger. The MGM they shared is dead, too. That MGM is buried in a pit dug near the intersection of the San Diego and Golden State freeways. Between January 1970 and June 1971, the buildings were locked, the imitation Hepplewhite chairs and star wardrobe sold, and the contents of a thousand filing cabinets dumped into the pit. All the inessentials—music scores, production files, screen tests, photographs, test recordings of every MGM actor and actress—were disposed of under six feet of dirt. All that escaped, besides the scripts and a few financial records, were the movies—those ephemeral pieces of celluloid in their tin cans. Yet perhaps in the end the movies are less ephemeral than the men and women who made them. Nominated for Best Picture of 1939 were *Dark Victory; Gone With the Wind; Goodbye, Mr. Chips; Love Affair; Mr. Smith Goes to Washington; Ninotchka; Of Mice and Men; Stagecoach; Wuthering Heights*—and *The Wizard of Oz*.

APPENDIXES
NOTES ON SOURCES
INDEX

Production #1060

Judy Garland's ruby slippers were found, wrapped in a Turkish towel, in a bin in the basement of MGM's Wardrobe Department sometime during February or March of 1970.

"Very undramatic," says Dick Carroll, proprietor of a trendy Beverly Hills men's-clothing store. "A guy came up to me and said, Here are some shoes Judy Garland wore in *The Wizard of Oz*.'"

Although the towel had obviously been intended as protection, the shoes were covered with dust and cobwebs; in some places, sequins were missing. Despite the condition of the shoes, Carroll recognized "that here was an item that could be publicized, an item that had the history of MGM written all over it." He sent the shoes to Malone Studio Service, where each sequin was cleaned by hand. When the shoes were returned to him, he put them in a safe.

Carroll's concern with publicity is understandable. MGM was not exactly going out of business; but the new principal stockholder and vice-chairman of the board, Kirk Kerkorian, was interested in using MGM's resources to build the $125 million MGM Grand Hotel in Las Vegas. Lot 3 had been sold to a real-estate developer, and it was rumored that Lot 2, if the proper zoning variances could be acquired, would become a two-mile-long row of used-car dealers. Everything that could be sold was being sold, including the bougainvillea plants in the nursery on Lot 2. Carroll's father-in-law, auctioneer David Weisz, had purchased—for approximately $1,500,000—most of the props and costumes that had been used in MGM pictures during the preceding forty-six years. Even Weisz was not sure exactly what he had purchased, although when he bid he was guessing that the inventory would total around 300,000 items. Weisz intended to sell the 30,000 most interesting costumes, pieces of furniture, and oddments—including everything that could be authenticated as having belonged to a particular picture or star—at an eighteen-day auction in May 1970. Everything else was sold at a glorified junk sale a few months later. Mounting the auction cost him another million dollars.

Dick Carroll and his wife had volunteered to organize and authenticate what was to be referred to—in the auction's pink catalogue—as "Star Wardrobe." The minute he unwrapped the towel, he felt he was looking at "the single most important piece of clothing in the whole world." The slippers brought $15,000. The only other item to sell for that much was the sternwheeler Mississippi riverboat of *Showboat*, which was purchased by the Texas oil millionaire Lamar Hunt. And— out of 30,000 costumes, airplane propellers, fog machines, cut-crystal decanters, play swords, silver vegetable dishes, fake and real African artifacts, Conestoga wagons, decorated horse collars, Coromandel screens, and Louis XV chairs—newspapers and magazines focused most of their attention on "Judy Garland's ruby slippers."

During the preview week before the auction began on May 3, 1970, the sound stages were dressed with 3,000 items of furniture and clothing. Item: "MANTLE CLOCK, *French Boule, bronze with tortoise shell inlay, porcelain numerals 51″ high* (NINOTCHKA)." The clock would go, during the auction's first hour, for $3,750. Item: *"Pant suit, black moire, beaded (Helen Rose) worn by Lana Turner in* THE BAD AND THE BEAUTIFUL." The pant suit would be sold for $225 to bidder C-579.

"The only article we didn't identify," says Carroll, "was the red shoes. We put them in a glass case with a light shining on them. Hundreds of people crowded around the case. Some stayed there for fifteen minutes."

Whatever magic or mystery the ruby slippers held for the hundreds who surrounded the glass case, they held neither mystery nor magic for the participants in *The Wizard of Oz*. It is tempting to think of them all—the producer, the Tin Woodman, the Wicked Witch, the Scarecrow, the Munchkins—as survivors of an extraordinary common experience, as though they were snowbound for that long winter and are, forever after, secret sharers. But for each it was, after all, just another movie in a lifetime of movies. The only real friendship on the film, that of the Tin Woodman and the Cowardly Lion, was broken by Bert Lahr's death in 1967.

"My God," says Mervyn LeRoy, "I've made so many pictures." "My dear," says Margaret Hamilton, "all my scenes were with the monkeys. Years afterward, when I did a play with Ray Bolger, people said, 'Oh, how nice, such a lovely reunion.' Well, there was no reunion about it. The only real scene that I had with any of them other than Judy was the last scene when I set fire to the poor Scarecrow. People think you were all so clubby and you must have had a lot of laughs. And I say, 'Well, yes, but not as many as you might think.' "

The night the ruby slippers were auctioned for $15,000, Arthur Freed was home watching television. By May 1970, that ferociously ambitious man had grown old—he had arthritis and heart trouble, and he walked with a cane. When his wife asked him if he would like to go to the auction, he shook his head no. Nor did Mervyn LeRoy have any interest in the ruby slippers. "I was out at MGM the night before the auction opened. A big black-tie charity thing for the Motion Picture Relief Fund. It was cold and a devil of a night and I didn't have an overcoat, and my wife was walking around freezing. I saw a lot of the props I'd used and a lot of dresses Greer Garson was supposed to have worn in my pictures that she never wore. I didn't want to buy anything."

The film's songwriter, E. Y. Harburg was at his cottage on Martha's Vineyard that night, oblivious of the fact that there was an MGM auction. Harold Rosson thought briefly about buying the director's chair for his pal Victor Fleming, but he let the opportunity slip away. Ray Bolger would probably have seriously considered buying his own Scarecrow costume if he had not already owned it. Although MGM was notorious for keeping every hat, every handkerchief, every garter belt, during the last week of filming, someone from the Wardrobe Department had stopped Bolger and offered him the costume. In May 1970, he was still thin enough to fit into it, a fact of which he was quite proud. King Vidor, like Mervyn LeRoy, had been to the posh dinner party that preceded the auction. But his interest was so slight that he left Los Angeles the next day for his cattle ranch in Paso Robles. A few days later, his friend silent-screen star Colleen Moore surprised him with a gift of two lamps from his film *H. M. Pulham, Esq.*

Jack Haley and his wife were eating dinner at an expensive Italian restaurant at 8 p.m. when the shoes were auctioned. "I had no interest in purchasing the shoes or seeing them auctioned," says Haley. "It's like a guy who used to eat at a restaurant going out to buy the old pots and pans. MGM was just a place to work. It was just another studio, and I'm an actor."

Even if his Tin Man costume had been found, polished, and placed on the auction block, Haley would not have purchased it. "Those costumes were hell. You wanted to run away from them, not buy them. Where would I put it? Down in the basement? Hey, come on down, see my Tin Man suit! Acting was a job, and money was my prime motivation. I was brought up very poor. My mother brought up two children and inculcated them with the importance of money. 'Turn that light out in the bathroom if you're not using it.' 'Do you need all that butter on your bread?' "

The ruby slippers and Clark Gable's "good luck" trench coat were to be auctioned at 8 p.m. on Sunday, May 17. It was the only time that the auction would be stopped to allow the sale—out of sequence—of specific items. After the catalogues were printed, the Cowardly Lion's lion skin was unexpectedly found, and it was decided to add the lion skin to the special 8 p.m. sale.

By that night, the guessing was that the shoes might sell for as much as $8,000 or $9,000. Two or three prospective bidders had been identified. Debbie Reynolds, the only movie star who seemed to feel any deep pain at the MGM auction, had tried to buy the entire inventory as the nucleus of a Hollywood Hall of Fame, a museum of Hollywood artifacts. When her bid had not been high enough, she had borrowed $100,000 from a bank and was attempting to buy as many important items as she could as her "personal contribution" to a Hollywood museum.

[305]

Debbie Reynolds wanted the ruby slippers. So did Mayor Martin Lotz of Culver City. Lotz stood up the night of the auction and begged people not to bid against him so that—for "the little children" of Culver City—he could "try and save one object that to them is a symbol that represents everything that is pure and clean in a world of magic and make-believe." Mayor Lotz had raised a substantial amount of money in pledges and was reasonably confident he would get the shoes. The third clearly identified bidder was Carolina Caribbean Corporation, which saw in the MGM auction a way of authenticating its theme park, The Land of Oz. Harry C. Robbins, then president of Carolina Caribbean, authorized $25,000 for the purchase of furniture, props, and costumes from *The Wizard of Oz*.

The auctioning of the costumes started at 1 p.m. on May 17. By the time the auctioneers stopped for dinner at 5 p.m., Carolina Caribbean—which later acquired Dorothy's blue-and-white-checked gingham dress for $1,000—had picked up the Witch's dress for $350 and the wizard's suit for $650. The Witch's hat had gone for $450. (By comparison the hat Charles Laughton wore in *Mutiny on the Bounty* had been sold for $300, Fred Astaire's hobo hat from *Easter Parade* for $250.)

A few weeks earlier, Margaret Hamilton's agent had called and told her he was going to get someone to bid on the Witch's hat. "And I said, 'What for?' And he said, 'Wouldn't you like to have the hat?' And I said, 'No, I wouldn't care at all about having it. I don't know what in the world I would do with it, and it would just draw a lot of dust.' I once had someone write and ask if he could have the nose I wore in the picture. And I wrote back that it was impossible to sneak out of the studio with anything so valuable as a nose. Although I suppose that if I had said it would fill me with pleasure, MGM might have given me my nose."

When the shoes were auctioned, it was 10 p.m. in Houston, Texas, and Margaret Hamilton was onstage at the Alley Theater as Madame Arcati in Noel Coward's *Blithe Spirit*.

It took exactly forty-six seconds to auction the shoes. David Weisz auctioned them himself—the auctioneers he had hired were competent, but he wanted "to be sure it was under control." When Weisz climbed to the auctioneer's stand, there were 2,500 people packed onto Stage 27 or waiting in an amplified standby area. Stage 27 had been picked for the sale of "Star Wardrobe" because it was one of the largest at MGM. The fact that Judy Garland had started along the Yellow Brick Road on that stage was incidental, and it is doubtful whether anyone in the audience was aware of the fact. Yet, looking down, Weisz could feel "such emotion from the audience" that he would later identify the evening of May 17 as "the most exciting moment of the whole auction."

Weisz began by introducing Martin Lotz. Mayor Lotz had asked Weisz to give the red shoes to Culver City. Weisz had countered by offering to let Lotz try to persuade the audience not to bid against him.

Lotz's theme, rather fervently stated, was that "in a world where even our little children look with awe and sometimes, I'm afraid, with favor on the use of narcotics and mind-expanding drugs as a means of finding adventure," he was delighted to have gotten hundreds of letters "from little children" asking him to acquire the wholesome magic of the "ruby-red slippers." When he had finished, Lotz sat down to tepid applause.

"Now, what is your pleasure?" asked Weisz. "How much do I hear for the shoes? Start it out, somebody. There they are."

A slide projector flashed a picture of the shoes:

Shoes, red sequined "ruby" shoes (Adrian)—
Judy Garland, THE WIZARD OF OZ.

Lotz looked quickly over at Debbie Reynolds. He had had several arguments with her. "She wanted me not to bid against her. I told her not to bid against *me*."

The ground rules for the auction were standard ones: bidders, identified only by numbered cards, would raise their cards; floor men with hand-held microphones would relay the bids to Weisz. The first bidder raised his card.

"A thousand dollars to start it. One thousand dollars. Two. Two thousand dollars I'm bid for the shoes. Three. Three thousand dollars I'm bid for the shoes. Make it four. Three thousand dollars I'm bid for the shoes. Will you make it four? Four thousand. Five thousand dollars. Bid six. Six thousand dollars I'm bid for the shoes. Now make it seven. Six thousand dollars I'm bid for the shoes. Seven thousand dollars is bid. Now make it eight. Seven thousand dollars I'm bid. Will you make it eight? Who'll say eight? Seven thousand is . . . "

Martin Lotz's pledges totaled $7,500. The $7,000 bid was his first and last bid. At that, he did better than Debbie Reynolds, who was "prepared to go to $5,000" and never got a chance to bid at all. He had considered her his chief rival. Yet "it went over our heads so fast," says Lotz, "went by us so fast."

"Ten thousand dollars is bid for the shoes. Now make it eleven. Eleven thousand is bid. Now twelve. Eleven thousand dollars I'm bid. . . . "

The $11,000 bid was Carolina Caribbean. Lotz looked over at Debbie Reynolds sitting dejectedly on her folding chair. Now they were both simply spectators.

"Fifteen thousand dollars is bid. Will you make it twenty? Fifteen thousand dollars I'm bid for the shoes. Will you make it twenty? Fifteen thousand dollars I'm bid for the shoes. Now twenty. Seventeen-and-a-half for the shoes, seventeen-and-a-half, seventeen-and-a-half for them. Will you make it seventeen-and-a-half? Seventeen-and-a-half for the shoes? Do I hear it over there? Yes or no? Fifteen thousand now. Seventeen-and-a-half?"

Despite Carolina Caribbean's $25,000 budget, Harry Robbins had placed an arbitrary limit of $15,000 on the red shoes. A single item—even the most important one—from *The Wizard of Oz* would do his theme park no good. The unidentified bidder who had jumped from $11,000 to $15,000 no longer had any competition.

"Fifteen thousand dollars I'm bid once. . . . Fifteen thousand dollars I'm bid twice. . . . Fifteen thousand dollars I'm bid third and last call. . . . Are you all through? FAIR WARNING! And they are sold. The bidder's number, please!"

The bidder's number was P-890. It belonged to an emissary, a messenger, a thirty-five-year-old lawyer named Richard Wonder bidding for an anonymous client. Wonder was swallowed up by the reporters and photographers lying in wait for the purchaser of the ruby slippers. A month later, he walked into the barber shop where he had had his hair cut for nearly twenty years to find himself the butt of admiring jokes. There was his picture in a movie magazine, captioned "California millionaire buys ruby-red slippers."

Even as Wonder disappeared behind the flashbulbs, Weisz was no longer interested in the red shoes. "Fine. Let's move on. We've got a long way to go. Anybody want to make a talk about the trench coat?"

Clark Gable's trench coat was sold for $1,250, the Cowardly Lion's costume for $2,400. Then Weisz slipped away from the auctioneer's stand with, "Stan, do you want to take over before my car is towed away to the Culver City Police Department?" And Stan started his part of the evening with, "All right. Back to reality. Back to reality."

Any explanation of why the ruby slippers sold for $15,000 while the shoes Elizabeth Taylor wore to her wedding in *Father of the Bride* sold for $200 can only be a partial one. But there is at least a clue in the second auctioneer's "Back to reality. Back to reality." The reality of which he was speaking was, after all, the auctioning of red velvet robes, gold brocade capes, sand chiffon nightgowns, and ecru suits with soutache embroidery. Yet, among the merely unreal the ruby slippers were magical. The magic had something to do with Judy Garland's clouded death; it had more to do with the ritual appearance of *The Wizard of Oz* each year on television. But it probably had most to do with how visible the slippers are as a talisman—fiercely desirable but useful only to their possessor, capable of keeping one safe in the darkness of the outer world and of bringing one home again without pain or loss of innocence.

A controversy over the authenticity of the slippers began within forty-eight hours of their purchase.

"We must have had five or ten pairs of those shoes," says producer LeRoy, "and this guy thinks he got the original pair."

People trip and fall. Feet sweat. Beads break. On a movie set, there are always duplicates. Except for the Cowardly Lion's skin and the Tin Man's silver-painted buckram, there were at least three copies of every major costume for *The Wizard of Oz*. The costumes included three Witch's hats and five or six blue-and-white-checked dresses.

Judy Garland had worn size 4B shoes and the auctioned slippers were labeled 4B. Debbie Reynolds, who also wears a 4, insisted that the auctioned slippers were too big for her and thus must have belonged to Garland's stand-in. The stand-in, Bobbie Koshay, wore size 6; and a Mrs. Henry Bauman of Memphis, Tennessee, displayed a pair of "Judy Garland's red shoes"—size 6B—that she had won in a contest in 1939. What happened to every pair of the ruby slippers is not clear, but at least two pairs were stolen from the Wardrobe Department several years before the auction. Late in 1974, Debbie Reynolds was offered one of those stolen pairs for her museum—still unbuilt but tentatively scheduled to be a part of a project with Universal Studio and various Hollywood craft guilds.

What the purchaser of the $15,000 ruby slippers thought of all this is unrecorded, since he retained his anonymity. Wonder did not see or hear from him between 1970 and 1975. In 1975, Wonder managed to contact him to transmit a reporter's request to speak to him on the telephone without trying to penetrate his anonymity, but the request was turned down. So what he had done with the ruby slippers and whether he was still happy with his purchase remained a matter of conjecture.

It is hard for Julius Marini, M.D., a West Covina general practitioner, to say whether he is happy with his $2,400 purchase of the Cowardly Lion's African lion skin. Two months after the auction, Marini was offered $5,000 for the costume by a children's museum. "If I were a businessman, I probably would have jumped at it," he says. But Julius Marini found himself unable to sell the costume for the same reason he purchased it in the first place: "I saw *The Wizard of Oz* when I was down and out. I was eight years old; my father was ill, my mother depressed. The picture gave me a certain sort of lift. It told me what to do when things go wrong. And things were very wrong. It said you don't get things from someone else, you get them from within yourself."

Time destroys everything. Bert Lahr's lion costume has already outlasted the man who wore it. Each year, when the movie played on television, Lahr would sit at the writing desk in his bedroom playing solitaire. "He would glance up occasionally," says his son, "but it was not as pleasant an experience for him as it was for the rest of us sitting around the TV. His comic mechanism in the 1960's was a much more subtle, disciplined thing than it had been in the thirties. It made him sad to see how much *more* he could have done with the role." And yet there was one moment in the film with which Lahr was almost satisfied. His family could tell from the expression on his face that he was nearly happy when he watched himself sing, "If I Were King of the Forest."

The holes in the lion skin have been mended and the costume lined with leather. Now, its skins restored by a taxidermist, the costume is in cold storage like any other fur.

Jack Haley sits in the living room of his Beverly Hills house and looks at a photograph of himself and Victor Fleming taken on the set of *The Wizard of Oz*. Seventy-eight years old now, he is "amazed to see how young Fleming looks. At that time, he seemed so old to me." Yet something remains. "The other forty-nine pictures I made," Haley continues, "who ever heard of them? But when I'm dead and gone, *The Wizard of Oz* will be forever."

Lyman Frank Baum was born on May 15, 1856, in the Mohawk Valley in upstate
New York. He was the seventh of nine children, but—as was common in the mid-
nineteenth century—only two of his sisters and two of his brothers lived to
adulthood. Two children had died by the time Frank was born. His next-oldest
brother died when he was a month old. His youngest brother died before Frank was
eight. Frank himself is reputed to have been born with "a seriously defective heart."*
However, more than a century later, Justin Call, chairman of the Department of
Child Psychiatry at the University of California Medical School at Irvine, thought
the diagnosis questionable. "His parents probably thought he would die like his
brothers before him and were overstating to prepare themselves." If it was a heart
problem, it was certainly a selective one. It flared up when, at the age of twelve,
Baum was sent to a military academy, but it seems to have caused him no trouble
during his rugged years in the Dakota Territory.

Baum was a shy child. He was also a rich man's son: from the time he was
five years old, home was Rose Lawn, a fifteen-acre residential farm north of Syracuse. Rose Lawn was attached on the north to his father's eighty-acre dairy farm.
North of that was a 160-acre farm where his father raised grain and livestock.
L. Frank Baum's father, Benjamin, had started as a cooper. After watching his bar-
rels being used for oil storage, he had quickly gone into the oil business himself. He
was probably never quite as much an independent oil baron as the Baum/MacFall
book implies, since the family fortune was easily lost as an immediate consequence
of the accident which helped lead to his death when Frank was thirty-one. But he
was a wealthy man, well able to indulge the whims of his children.

Frank Baum was educated at home by tutors, except for two years at Peek-
skill Military Academy. As a young child, he was fascinated by chickens and would
sit for hours outside the fence of the chicken yard. (A yellow hen is the heroine of
his third Oz book.) When older, he was fascinated by books; he read the Vic-

* Frank Joslyn Baum and Russell P. MacFall, *To Please a Child* (Chicago:
Reilly & Lee, 1961). This book, on which Baum's oldest son collaborated, is the
source of the best and most detailed biographical information on Baum.

torian novelists popular at the time—Dickens and Thackeray—but his favorite book seems to have been *The Cloister and the Hearth* by Charles Reade. On a trip into Syracuse with his father when he was fourteen, he found himself in front of a print shop and spent an hour watching the owner operate an old-fashioned foot-treadle press. He demanded a press of his own, and his father bought him one.

In May 1871, at the time of his fifteenth birthday, he and his younger brother, Harry, began printing a monthly paper, most of the stories and poems in it written by Frank. Two years later, Baum and a friend, Thomas G. Alford, founded a more sophisticated monthly newspaper, *The Empire*. *The Empire* was published by Alford and edited by Baum until 1875, when Baum—at the age of nineteen—became both a chicken-breeder and an actor.

Fowl remained an intense interest all of Baum's life. He won prizes for developing and exhibiting new strains of Hamburg chickens, and in 1886, when he was thirty, he wrote a seventy-page pamphlet, *The Book of the Hamburgs*, on their care, mating, exhibiting, and judging. Twenty-five years after that, Baum was raising Rhode Island Reds in Hollywood for meat and eggs. In 1875, he combined his chicken-breeding with haunting the Syracuse theaters to find some traveling company of actors that would allow him to join them. According to the Baum/MacFall book, he was royally fleeced by a third-rate company which agreed to give him starring roles if he would provide several thousand dollars' worth of silk, velvet, and lace costumes. The costumes got plenty of stage experience, but Baum—under the name of George Brooks—rarely enjoyed even a talking part.

He went back to Syracuse to work as a salesman for one of his father's companies; tried acting again with somewhat more success at the Union Square Theater in New York City; worked on a weekly newspaper, *The New Era*, near his father's Pennsylvania oilfields; then managed a number of small-town theaters his father owned in Pennsylvania and upstate New York.

He was twenty-five years old when he decided to become a playwright. His first play, *The Maid of Arran*—based on a Scottish novel, *A Princess of Thule*—was a success. He toured the play north to Canada, west to Kansas, and twice to New York City for two successful one-week runs.

It is strange how often Baum's first attempts at anything were successful and his later ones disastrous. His other efforts at playwriting during the 1880's were failures. His first full-length book, *The Wonderful Wizard of Oz*, became one of the best-selling children's books of the twentieth century. His attempts to create different magic lands would meet with, at best, tepid interest on the part of readers. The first stage play he made from an Oz book, *The Wizard of Oz*, in 1902, played two full seasons on Broadway and toured for eight years. The stage plays he made out of his later Oz books were critical and financial failures. Even the first month of Baum's Bazaar, his five-and-ten-cent store in the Dakota Territory, was successful, although the store eventually failed.

It was at Christmas 1881 that Baum met Maud Gage, the meeting carefully engineered by Baum's oldest sister. (Maud Gage's grandfather was an Abolitionist who had used his house as a station on the Underground Railway. Maud's mother was the Matilda Joslyn Gage who had co-authored the four-volume *History of Woman Suffrage* with Susan B. Anthony and Elizabeth Cady Stanton. The fervor her father had expended on the abolition of slavery, Matilda Gage threw into the cause of women's suffrage.) Maud was the youngest and best-loved of Matilda Gage's four children. Maud lived her life without causes except the cause of raising four sons despite an often improvident husband. At the time she met twenty-five-year-old Frank Baum, she was twenty, a student at Cornell University, and as strong and strong-willed as her mother. They were married on November 9, 1882. Maud died in 1953 at the age of ninety-two, some thirty-four years after the death of her husband.

From the beginning, Baum was a remarkable father for the late nineteenth century. Maud punished; Baum comforted. Maud whipped with a hairbrush and sent the boys to bed without supper; Baum surreptitiously took food upstairs and invented stories to console the punished children.

Baum's personality was composed of a great many tender and nurturing characteristics. His first book, *Mother Goose in Prose*, was an outgrowth of the Mother Goose rhymes he told his children to amuse and comfort them. From the time his oldest child, Frank Joslyn, was born, Baum spent hours each day rocking and singing to the baby. It is a fact that he wanted a daughter and that he was prepared at one point to name a daughter Dorothy. It is also a fact that his books contain heroines, not heroes, and that in his second Oz book, *The Land of Oz*, Baum—who was always so careful not to frighten his readers with bloody enchantments—presented one of the most psychologically frightening of all enchantments: the book ends with the permanent transformation of a boy, Tip, into a girl, Princess Ozma.

Psychoanalyst Justin Call mused over the fact that "all the males in *The Wizard of Oz* are fractured, in some state of disrepair, incomplete in their anatomy." He wondered what association there was in Baum's head with the instances of so many of his brothers dying while his two sisters lived. Perhaps it was better "to be a living girl than a dead boy." Yet one older brother and one younger brother did live, as did Baum himself.

The birth of Frank Joslyn Baum on December 4, 1883, brought with it L. Frank Baum's retirement from the theater, although he continued to write plays (none of them was produced) throughout the 1880's. His father had deeded over to him the chain of little theaters. They were mismanaged by a bookkeeper and eventually lost to creditors. Their loss was not Maud Baum's fault: disturbed at the continually decreasing size of the weekly checks from the theaters, she kept begging Baum to investigate, but he was too busy writing a play to bother. The play, although commissioned, was never produced. About the time that the theaters were lost, all the scenery, props, and costumes for *The Maid of Arran* were burned when the town in which they were stored caught fire. So Baum became a salesman for Baum's Castorine, a petroleum lubricant manufactured by his older brother.

The next ten years were a series of disasters. In 1885, Baum's father was seriously injured when he was thrown out of a carriage. Most of his money was lost during his slow recovery, and Rose Lawn and the 160-acre farm had to be sold. The birth of Baum's second son in 1886 left Maud with peritonitis; she did not fully recover for two years. Eventually Baum's father and older brother died, leaving Frank Baum and his uncle the proprietors of Baum's Castorine. Having learned nothing from their experience with the careless bookkeeper, they made the mistake of leaving the office in the hands of a clerk who gambled away all the firm's money and then committed suicide.

Maud's two sisters and her brother lived in the Dakota Territory. She told her husband that she wanted to join them there. Baum hesitated; Maud insisted. They settled in Aberdeen, Dakota, in September 1888 and opened Baum's Bazaar. It was classically the wrong place at the wrong time. The Dakota Territory's boom was quickly turning into a depression, and Baum's Bazaar lasted less than a year and a half. Then Baum took over a weekly newspaper. But since there was no rain in Dakota, farmers had no crops to sell and advertisers no money to spend. The *Aberdeen Saturday Pioneer* was handed over to the sheriff slightly more than a year later.

Dakota had brought two more failures along with two more sons. In May 1891, Baum headed for Chicago and a brief job on one of the Chicago newspapers, the *Evening Post*. The need for more money drove him to become a department-store buyer and then a china-and-glassware traveling salesman. By 1895 he was doing well enough to move into a rented house equipped with gaslight and a bathroom.

Whenever Baum was back from the road, he would drop in at the Chicago Press Club. In 1896, he told one club member, Opie Read—a popular novelist of the day—that he had written a book, *Mother Goose in Prose*. Baum would never have written it if it had not been for the prodding and pushing of his mother-in-law. Matilda Gage was convinced that other children would enjoy Baum's stories and badgered her son-in-law until he put them on paper. Read introduced Baum to a young publisher, Chauncey Williams. Way and Williams accepted the manuscript and assigned a twenty-seven-year-old artist, Maxfield Parrish, who had never illustrated a book, to do the illustrations. *Mother Goose in Prose* consisted of twenty-two stories, including one about a chicken who laid one egg a day for twelve days and named the twelfth egg Humpty Dumpty, and one about a lonely girl named Mistress Mary who grew a garden while her father and brother were at sea. The book sold well enough to be reprinted several times, but it made little money for Baum.

About the same time, Baum began suffering from nosebleeds and chest pains. A Chicago heart specialist told him to quit his job as a traveling salesman. He wrote to his brother-in-law, asking for money to start a magazine but was refused. For some reason, Baum thought a magazine about window-trimming would be financially successful. His brother-in-law, well aware of Baum's various financial catastrophes, was understandably suspicious. For once, however, Baum was right. He managed to find the money, and *The Show Window,* "a journal of practical, up-to-date window trimming" for merchants and professional window-decorators, supported the Baums until *The Wizard of Oz* made that unnecessary.

At the Chicago Press Club, Baum then met William Wallace Denslow, another illustrator. He asked if Denslow would be interested in illustrating a picture book of poems for children. *Father Goose, His Book* was published by the George M. Hill Co. after Baum and Denslow agreed to pay the production costs. To everyone's surprise, it became the best-selling children's book of 1899. In 1900, twenty-six of the poems were set to music and published as *The Songs of Father Goose,* and that book also sold well.

Baum was now considered a major writer of children's books. In 1900, he also published two more books of verse, *The Army Alphabet* and *The Navy Alphabet,* and a book of fourteen saccharine short stories, *A New Wonderland.** In a letter to his brother Harry dated April 8, 1900, Baum wrote, "Harper Bros. sent a man here last week to try to make a contract for a book next year. Scribner's writes offering a cash advance for a manuscript. Appleton's, Lothrop's and the Century have asked for a book—no matter what it is."

All this interest in Baum on the part of book publishers was before *The Wonderful Wizard of Oz,* which was scheduled for publication on May 15, 1900†— Baum's forty-fourth birthday. (Baum often linked his creations with his birthdays: he began printing his amateur paper on his fifteenth birthday and opened *The Maid of Arran* at the Grand Opera House in Syracuse on his twenty-sixth birthday.)

Baum had started to write down his full-length fairy tale, "The Emerald City," soon after the publication of *Mother Goose in Prose.* In the fall of 1899, he and Denslow had taken sample chapters and drawings to the George M. Hill Co. Hill agreed to publish the book, but not under the title "The Emerald City"—publishers had a superstition that any book with a jewel in the title would be a failure. The book then progressively became "From Kansas to Fairyland," "The Fairyland of Oz," and "The Land of Oz." It wasn't until March 1900 that the title *The Wonderful Wizard of Oz* was decided upon.

Baum had published his first book when he was forty-one years old. During the last nineteen years of his life, he wrote and published sixty-two books.‡ Aside from the thirteen other Oz books, his fantasies included *Dot and Tot in Merryland, The Master Key: An Electrical Fairy Tale, The Enchanted Island of Yew, Queen Zixi of Ix, John Dough and the Cherub, Sky Island, The Sea Fairies,* and

---

* *A New Wonderland* was later changed slightly and republished as *The Surprising Adventures of the Magical Monarch of Mo and His People.*

† Publication was delayed, and the official publication date turned out to be August 1, 1900.

‡ Between the publication of *The Wonderful Wizard of Oz* in 1900 and his death in 1919, Baum actually published eighty-two books. However, many of those were rearranged or re-edited versions of earlier works, books of songs, privately printed books, and plays.

The Life and Adventures of Santa Claus. He also wrote, under the name Floyd Akers, the Boy Fortune Hunters series; under the name Edith van Dyne, the Aunt Jane's Nieces series and the Mary Louise series. He wrote under the names Laura Bancroft for three books, John Estes Cooke for one, Capt. Hugh Fitzgerald for two.

The Aunt Jane's Nieces books—a series of novels—were almost as popular and sold almost as well as the Oz series. What forever puzzled Baum was his inability to write other fantasies which would elicit that magic rapport. *The Master Key*, a kind of science-fiction fairy tale, was successful in 1901; *Dot and Tot in Merryland*, published the same year, was not. The two fantasies that Baum considered his best, *The Sea Fairies* (1911) and *Sky Island* (1912), had disappointing sales. The failure of his other fantasies forced Baum to continue writing Oz books, although he probably had no intention originally of writing a series. He tried to end the series in 1910 with the sixth book, *The Emerald City of Oz*, by announcing that Oz was now cut off from the world by a Barrier of Invisibility. But Baum went back to Oz in 1913 after the failure of *The Sea Fairies* and *Sky Island*.

The Wizard of Oz was kept off most public library shelves until the 1960's because librarians considered it hackwork. When Cornelia Meigs edited a 624-page *Critical History of Children's Literature* for Macmillan in 1953, there was not a single mention of Baum in the book. *The Wizard of Oz* does appear in the fourth edition of May Hill Arbuthnot's *Children and Books*, revised by Zena Sutherland and published in 1972— but it does not appear in the first three editions, and in the 1972 edition it is simply listed among "Books That Stir Controversy." Sutherland adds that "many authorities in the field of children's literature feel that the style is flat and dull."

Sutherland's "many authorities" rarely include the writers of children's literature. In an article published in *The New Republic* on December 12, 1934, James Thurber lavishly praised *The Wizard of Oz* and *The Land of Oz* and then dismissed the other books in the series. "They lack the quick movement, the fresh suspense, the amusing dialogue and the really funny invention of the first ones. . . . Mr. Baum himself said that he kept putting in things that children wrote and asked him to put in. He brought back the Wizard of Oz because the children pleaded and he rewrote the Scarecrow and the Woodman almost to death because the children wanted them. The children should have been told to hush up and go back to the real Wizard and the real Scarecrow and the real Woodman." Friends of the book—besides Thurber, including literary critics and college professors— have tried to explain the almost unanimous hostility of librarians toward it. One explanation centers on the fact that, as Thurber noted, many books in the series were, at best, uninspired in both plot and character. Other explanations are that the book is written in too simple a style to be considered literature, and that its inferior binding didn't stand up to hard use. Psychoanalyst Justin Call probably came closer to the mark. "The thinking processes in the book are similar to the thinking of a child," said Call, a member of the International Wizard of Oz Club.

"There is a great deal of primary process thinking—thinking dominated by wishes, fears, and visual imagery; magical thinking with no respect for time, or causality, or logic."

After the success of *The Wonderful Wizard of Oz* and the musical play he made from the book in 1902, it seemed that Baum would never have to worry about money again—which probably would have been the case if he had not been Frank Baum. He turned his second book, *The Marvelous Land of Oz*, into a musical play, *The Woggle Bug*, which was a failure. Baum literally put a children's book on the stage, and adult audiences refused to pay to see it. Then, in 1906, Baum got the idea of advertising his books by touring the country with hand-colored movies and picture slides to give a lecture he called "a fairylogue" about Oz. He was gifted at public speaking and was loved by audiences and critics. Several papers compared him to Mark Twain. Despite the popularity of the show, Baum lost all the money he had borrowed to put it together: he simply hadn't realized that the expense of mounting it—including the cost of moving an orchestra, a screen, and a projector from city to city—would make profits impossible.

On June 3, 1911, Baum filed for bankruptcy. During the bankruptcy proceedings, all of the royalties from Baum's Oz books were assigned to a trustee so his debts could be paid.

He was living at the time in Hollywood, having moved there in 1910. He and Maud had built a house—with money Maud had inherited from her mother—which they called Ozcot. Despite his financial problems, Baum was his usual optimistic self. He grew prize dahlias and chrysanthemums and won twenty-one cups in flower shows. He fed the several hundred birds in his aviary at Ozcot and competed with his sons on Ozcot's archery range. He played golf at a nearby public park, always dressed in the height of fashion.

The financial squeeze ended with the minor success of a musical he wrote, *The Tik-Tok Man of Oz*. As always, not content to leave well enough alone, Baum decided to make movies of his Oz books. In 1914, he founded the Oz Film Manufacturing Company. The Oz Company's films weren't bad, but the difficulties of distributing films entangled him in still another financial web. The Oz Film Company closed down, and the studio it had built was sold to Universal.

Baum's health began to fail in 1917. Despite painful gall-bladder attacks, he refused to permit an operation until the pain became unbearable in December of that year. The surgery seems to have caused more strain on his heart, and he spent most of the rest of his life in bed, still writing and still optimistic. On May 6, 1919, he died. (After his death, children refused to allow the Oz books to come to an end. Maud Baum entered into an agreement with a young woman, Ruth Plumly Thompson, to continue the series. She wrote one Oz book a year for the next nineteen years.)

Baum's Oz was surrounded by the Deadly Desert on the west, the Great Sandy Waste on the south, the Impassable Desert on the north, and the Shifting Sands on the east. After twenty-four hours in a coma, Baum is reported to have spoken once on the morning of May 6. He did not open his eyes, but a minute before he died he said quite distinctly, "Now we can cross the Shifting Sands."

A possible epitaph. But there is a better one. In the copy of *Mother Goose in Prose* that he gave to his sister Mary Louise, he wrote the following inscription:

> When I was young I longed to write a great novel that should win me fame. Now that I am getting old my first book is written to amuse children. For, aside from my evident inability to do anything "great," I have learned to regard fame as a will-o-the-wisp which, when caught, is not worth the possession; but to please a child is a sweet and lovely thing that warms one's heart and brings its own reward. . . .

Metro-Goldwyn-Mayer Presents
A Victor Fleming Production

THE WIZARD OF OZ

THE CAST

Dorothy	Judy Garland
Professor Marvel	Frank Morgan
Hunk	Ray Bolger
Zeke	Bert Lahr
Hickory	Jack Haley
Glinda	Billie Burke
Miss Gulch	Margaret Hamilton
Uncle Henry	Charley Grapewin
*Nikko	Pat Walshe
Auntie Em	Clara Blandick
Toto	Toto

and The Munchkins

Directed by Victor Fleming
Produced by Mervyn LeRoy
Screenplay by
Noel Langley, Florence Ryerson and Edgar Allan Woolf
Adaptation by Noel Langley
From the book by L. Frank Baum
Musical Adaptation by Herbert Stothart
The Lyrics: E. Y. Harburg
The Music: Harold Arlen
Associate Conductor: George Stoll
Orchestral and Vocal Arrangements:
George Bassman, Murray Cutter, Paul Marquardt and Ken Darby
Musical Numbers Staged by Bobby Connolly
Photographed in Technicolor by Harold Rosson, A.S.C.
Associate: Allen Davey, A.S.C.
Technicolor Color Director: Natalie Kalmus
Associate: Henri Jaffa
Recording Director: Douglas Shearer
Art Director: Cedric Gibbons
Associate: William A. Horning
Set Decorations by Edwin B. Willis
Special Effects by Arnold Gillespie
Costumes by Adrian
Character Makeups Created by Jack Dawn
Film Editor: Blanche Sewell

Running Time: 100 minutes

* *The head Winged Monkey.*

1. Most of the research for this book came through interviews with primary sources, men and women who worked on *The Wizard of Oz* or in the major studio system during the 1930's and 1940's. Also examined was all of the written material pertaining to *The Wizard of Oz* that still remains at Technicolor and at MGM and in the Arthur Freed and Roger Edens collections at the University of Southern California Library. Information about participants in the film who have since died was most often acquired from their survivors; and the quotations from Richard Thorpe came from oral history material at the American Film Institute. However, in addition to these primary sources, the following books were the most helpful of those consulted, either in giving an overview of the period or in authenticating details.

BEHLMER, RUDY. *Memo From David O. Selznick* (New York: Viking, 1972).

BURKE, BILLIE. *With a Feather on My Nose* (New York: Appleton-Century-Crofts, 1949).

CAPRA, FRANK. *The Name Above the Title* (New York: Macmillan, 1971).

CROWTHER, BOSLEY. *Hollywood Rajah* (New York: Holt, Rinehart & Winston, 1960).

———. *The Lion's Share* (New York: E. P. Dutton, 1957).

DARDIS, TOM. *Some Time in the Sun* (New York: Charles Scribner's Sons, 1976).

EAMES, JOHN D. *The MGM Story* (New York: Crown, 1975).

FIELDS, W. C. *W. C. Fields by Himself* (Englewood Cliffs, N.J.: Prentice-Hall, 1973).

FINCH, CHRISTOPHER. *Rainbow* (New York: Grosset & Dunlap, 1975).

FLAMINI, ROLAND. *Scarlett, Rhett, and a Cast of Thousands* (New York: Macmillan, 1975).

FORDIN, HUGH. *The World of Entertainment* (Garden City, N.Y.: Doubleday, 1975).

FRANK, GEROLD. *Judy* (New York: Harper & Row, 1975).

GRADY, BILLY. *The Irish Peacock* (New Rochelle: Arlington House, 1972).

HALLIWELL, LESLIE. *The Filmgoer's Companion* (New York: Hill & Wang, 4th ed., 1974).

JABLONSKI, EDWARD. *Happy With the Blues* (Garden City, N.Y.: Doubleday, 1961).

JACOBS, LEWIS. *The Rise of the American Film* (New York: Harcourt, Brace, 1939).

KAEL, PAULINE. *The Citizen Kane Book* (Boston: Little, Brown, 1971).

KNIGHT, ARTHUR. *The Liveliest Art* (New York: Macmillan, 1957).

LAHR, JOHN. *Notes on a Cowardly Lion* (New York: Alfred A. Knopf, 1969).

LAMBERT, GAVIN. *GWTW* (Boston: Little, Brown, 1973).

LATHAM, AARON. *Crazy Sundays: Scott Fitzgerald in Hollywood* (New York: Viking, 1971).

LEROY, MERVYN. *Mervyn LeRoy: Take One* (New York: Hawthorn, 1974).

MARION, FRANCES. *Off With Their Heads* (New York: Macmillan, 1972).

MARX, SAM. *Mayer and Thalberg* (New York: Random House, 1975).

MILNE, TOM. *Rouben Mamoulian* (Bloomington: Indiana University Press, 1969).

MINNELLI, VINCENTE. *I Remember It Well* (Garden City, N.Y.: Doubleday, 1974).

POWDERMAKER, HORTENSE. *Hollywood the Dream Factory* (Boston: Little, Brown, 1950).

ROSTEN, LEO C. *Hollywood the Movie Colony* (New York: Harcourt, Brace, 1941).

SARRIS, ANDREW. *The American Cinema* (New York: E. P. Dutton, 1968).

SKLAR, ROBERT. *Movie-made America* (New York: Random House, 1975).

TAYLOR, JOHN RUSSELL. *The Hollywood Musical* (New York: McGraw-Hill, 1971).

THOMAS, BOB. *King Cohn* (New York: G. P. Putnam's Sons, 1967).

————. *Thalberg* (Garden City, N.Y.: Doubleday, 1969).

THOMSON, DAVID. *A Biographical Dictionary of Film* (New York: William Morrow, 1976).

VIDOR, KING. *A Tree Is a Tree* (London: Longmans, Green, 1954).

WRIGHT, BASIL. *The Long View* (New York: Alfred A. Knopf, 1974).

2. The task of checking periodicals was made easier by John Fricke's "A Checklist of the Major Material on the MGM Wizard of Oz Film," printed in the Autumn 1969 edition of the *Baum Bugle*, published by the International Wizard of Oz Club. Mr. Fricke's checklist includes a description of most articles published about the film in major periodicals from 1939 to 1966.

Among the periodicals consulted were *Commonweal, Cosmopolitan, Daily Variety, Films in Review, Life, McCalls, MGM Studio News, The New Republic, Newsweek, The New Yorker, The New York Times, Photoplay, Show,* and *Time.*

3. The author acknowledges the help of Fred Meyer, Warren Hollister, Peter Hanff, and Rob MacVeigh for supplying various facts about L. Frank Baum and his work. The two most valuable written sources on Baum are *To Please a Child* by Frank Joslyn Baum and Russell P. MacFall (Chicago: Reilly & Lee, 1961) and *The Annotated Wizard of Oz* by Michael Patrick Hearn (New York: Clarkson N. Potter, 1973).

And the most valuable reference work of all was *The Wonderful Wizard of Oz* (Chicago: George M. Hill, 1900).

CHAPTER 7   THE MUNCHKINS

A list of 122 of the 124 little people who played Munchkins has been compiled from MGM daily time reports and by Steve Cox, who has been researching a book, *The Munchkins Remember*, to be published by E. P. Dutton.

The performers were:

Gladys M. Allison, John Ballas, Franz Balluck, Josefine Balluck, John T. Bambury, Charles Becker, Freda Besky, Yvonne Moray Bistany, Henry Boers, Theodore Boers, Christie Buresh, Eduard Buresh, Lida Buresh, Mickey Carroll, Colonel Caspar, Nona Cooper, Thomas J. Cottonaro, Elizabeth Coulter, Frank H. Cucksey, Billy Curtis, Eugene S. David Jr., Eulie H. David, Ethel W. Denis, Prince Denis, Hazel I. Derthick, Major Doyle, Carl M. Erickson, Jannette Fern, Addie E. Frank, Thaisa L. Gardner, Jakob Gerlich, Bill Giblin, Jack Glicken, Carolyn E. Granger, Joseph Herbst, Jakob Hofbauer, Major Mite (C. C. Howerton), Helen M. Hoy, Marguerite A. Hoy, James R. Hulse, Lord Roberts (Kanter), Charles Kelley, Jessie E. Kelley, Frank Kikel, Bernhard Klima, Emma Koestner, Mitzi Koestner, Willi Koestner, Carl Kosiczky, Adam Edwin Kozicki, Joseph J. Koziel, Dolly Kramer, Emil Kranzler, Nita Krebs, Jeane LaBarbera, Hilda Lange, John Leal, Ann Rice Leslie, Idaho Lewis (L. A. Croft), Charles Ludwig, Carlos Manzo, Howard Marco, Jerry Maren (Gerard Marenghi), Bela Matina, Lajos Matina, Matthew Matina, Walter M. B. Miller, George Minister, Harry Monty, Olga C. Nardone, Nels Nelson, Margaret C. H. Nickloy, Franklin H. O'Baugh, William H. O'Docharty, Hildred C. Olson, Frank Packard, Nicholas Page, Leona Parks, Margaret Pellegrini, Johnny Pizo, Prince Leon (Polinsky), Lillian Porter, Meinhardt Raabe, Margaret Raia, Matthew Raia, Hazel Resmondo, Little Billy (Rhodes), Gertrude H. Rice, Hazel Rice, Friedrich Ritter, Ruth L. Robinson, Sandor Roka, Jimmie Rosen, Charles F. Royale, Helen J. Royale, Albert Ruddinger, Elly A. Schneider, Frieda Schneider, Hilda E. Schneider, Kurt Schneider, Elsie R. Schultz, Charles Silvern, Garland Slatten, Ruth E. Smith, Elmer Spangler, Pernell E. St. Aubin, Carl Stephan, Alta M. Stevens, George Suchsie, Charlotte V. Sullivan, Clarence Swensen, Betty Tanner (Titus), Arnold Vierling, Gus Wayne, Victor Wetter, Grace G. Williams, Harvey B. Williams, Margaret Williams, John Winters (Maroldo), Marie Winters (Maroldo), Gladys V. Wolff, Murray Wood.

CHAPTER 8   "BELOW THE LINE"

More than one person has had a fetish about the ruby slippers. A costumer named Kent Warner, who died from AIDS in 1984, almost certainly stole several pairs when he was helping prepare for the MGM auction in 1970. Warner's involvement with the red shoes is detailed in a *Los Angeles Times* article by Rhys Thomas, published March 13, 1988. In the same article, Thomas raises the question of whether some of the shoes, which were manufactured by the Innes Shoe Company, were built into ruby slippers at Western Costume Company, Hollywood's biggest supplier of period clothes. Thomas, who is writing a book on the red shoes to be published by Tale Weaver Publishing, is sure that the red leather bows studded with rhinestones were constructed in MGM's leather department.

No records remain at either Western Costume or MGM, except in the memories of the people who worked there. Western Costume employees credit the decorating of the shoes to a man named Joe Napoli. MGM employees remember watching the sequins being sewn on by the ladies in Mrs. Cluett's Beading Department. (p. 239)

Roger Mayer, who is now president of Turner Entertainment, was assistant and then head studio manager of MGM from 1961 to 1986. He feels that it is unlikely that the studio would have farmed out the making of the shoes because "MGM had employees who did that kind of work."

CHAPTER 11   AFTER *OZ*

Interest in *Oz* shows no sign of abating. Dolls, beach towels, porcelain bells, Valentine cards, jewelry boxes, and baby carriages are among the hundreds of products being turned out by Turner's twenty-eight licensees. A Bradford commemorative plate of Judy Garland as Dorothy, which was sold by the tens of thousands for $16.95 in 1977, now sells for more than $200 to collectors. Jack-in-the-boxes of the Lion and Tin Woodman retail for over $100. The Yellow Brick Road in Chesterton, Indiana, is one of a number of stores devoted to the MGM movie.

A stage show based on the script and music of the movie will tour arenas in sixty-nine American and Canadian cities in 1989 and 1990. The $5 million show is sponsored by Ralston Purina's Purina dog chow and Procter & Gamble's Downy fabric softener, which put up $2.5 million each.

APPENDIX A.   THE AUCTION OF THE RUBY SLIPPERS

By 1988, the prices paid for Hollywood memorabilia had escalated almost unimaginably. The black wool Witch's hat, which sold for $450 at the MGM auction in 1970, was auctioned by Sotheby's in December 1988, for $33,000. The pair of ruby slippers that Roberta Bauman won in a contest in 1939 sold for $165,000 at Christie's East in June 1988. It is said to be the highest price ever paid for a piece of movie memorabilia.

IN MEMORIAM

A. Arnold (Buddy) Gillespie, May 3, 1978

Jack Haley, June 7, 1979 (In what may have been his last interview, I talked with Haley about the aftereffects of *Oz*. "I get more mail for the picture than I did when it was originally shown. And I've been retired for years," he said. Asked whether it was satisfying, he shook his head. "When you get my age and you're going to die pretty soon, I mean, what the hell is the satisfaction?")

Mary Ann Nyberg, September 19, 1979

E. Y. Harburg, March 5, 1981 (Harburg died of a massive heart attack while driving to a story conference for a film version of Robert Louis Stevenson's *Treasure Island*. He was eighty-four years old.)

Harry Warren, September 22, 1981

King Vidor, November 1, 1982

Margaret Hamilton, May 16, 1985 (The gentle witch died at the age of eighty-two in a Connecticut nursing home, apparently of a heart attack.)

Ray Bolger, January 15, 1987 (He died of cancer five days after his eighty-third birthday.)

Mervyn LeRoy (The last of the major participants in the 1939 movie, LeRoy died of Alzheimer's disease at his Beverly Hills home on September 3, 1987. He was eighty-six years old.)